VALE:

THE ILLUMINATI AND ITS PLANS FOR WORLD CONQUEST

VALE:

THE ILLUMINATI AND ITS PLANS FOR WORLD CONQUEST

By: Dr. A. H. Krieg

USA	$ 19.95	USA shipping pre paid
Canadian	$ 25.95	S&H Can $ 2.00
England Pounds St.	£ 20.00	FOB London
Euro	¤ 16.00	FOB London

ISBN # 0-9748502-3-3

Library of Congress Catalogue Card Number # 2004114577

a2zPublications

Printed in the United States of America, 2004

First printing 2005.

For information relating to permission to quote or other questions contact:

A2zPublications

Sr 70 E, #143

Bradenton, FL 34202 USA

www.a2zPublications.com

www.kreigbooks.com

941-322-2739 • Fax 941-758-7447

"Better Old History than New Lies"

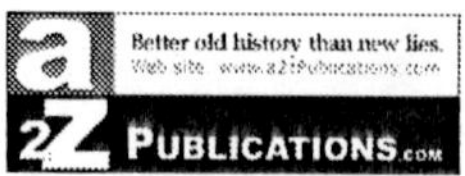

OTHER BOOKS BY
A. H. KRIEG:

Our Political Systems, Elderberry Press, 2004.

Published Articles and Essays, '92-'03, A2zPublications

July 4th, 2016: The Last Independence Day*, Hallberg Pub.2000

The Satori and the New Mandarins*, Hallberg Pub., 1997(a)

Marketing your Products through Distribution Channels,
Widder Corp., 1988

Plate Forming Machines, FMA, 1977 (a)

Distributor Marketing, Widder Corp.,1975 (a)

The Problems with Welding Fumes and How to Solve them,
Widder Corp., 1974 (a)

(a) Out of Print

This book was written, printed and bound in the United States of America.

*Illegitimus Non Tatum Carborundum**

–The Krieg Family Motto

"If we can defeat
or drive the armies
of the enemy from the field, we shall have peace.
All our efforts and energies
should be devoted to
that object."

–Robert E. Lee,
Commander, West Point, hero of the Mexican war.
Commander, CSA armies, to Jefferson Davis, Pres. CSA

* Don't let the bastards wear you down.

Dedicated to all my faithful readers,

and

my daughters,

Ewona and Cheryl.

There are those who honestly consider that justice is an option in the 21st century. This belief is delusional. Those in politics and those in justice are the lackeys of persons who provide for their continuance in office. Being beholden to them, they do their bidding, lest they lose their gracious gratuitous lifestyle. They are the mandarins who are indebted to their masters, the Satori.

Anyone who, in the 21st century, assumes that their elected and appointed government officials consider the general welfare, and individual rights of the electorate, as a responsibility, makes a grave error.

It is a fact that, under the present system of governance of the so-called "free world" no ethical, fair, or citizen-friendly outcome is likely.

If the assumption is made that the free press will be the watchdog of our disappearing freedoms – think again. The mainstream media is in the very same pockets.

I tell you the truth, and point out to you that I have nothing to gain from falsehood, but only endanger myself in exposing the secret truth. In our society those who control the currency dictate all functions of governance. They are the Illuminati; their process is called Illuminism. It was the driving force behind the French and Russian revolutions, as well as WW I, WW II, and both Gulf Wars.

– A.H. Krieg

TABLE OF CONTENTS

Dr. A. H. Krieg

PREFACE

Any criticism of Zionism invariably results in accusations of Nazi conspiracy, and worse. This preface is written to prevent that possibility.

THE outrageous cry of "anti-Semitism!" can be heard ema nating from many sources against anyone who for any reason ever makes any statement in contradiction to Zionist dogma. Zionism is not a religion, nor is any true Jew a Zionists. As Rabbi Weiss, the head of the Neturei Karta[1], so aptly puts it, "Zionism is blatant racism and is against true Jewish values." Neturei Kata was founded long before the state of Israel, in the 1930s. They are worldwide organizations which have thousands adherents in Israel. They are one of a large and growing group of Jewish anti-Zionist organizations that are opposed to this secular socio-political movement that utilizes the religion of Judaism as a cover for the nationalistic expansion of the socialist theocracy that Israel has become.

Many evils are rooted in Zionism: the f≤licit drug Ecstasy is a product of Zionist preparation and distribution sited in Israel. The extortion of money from insurance companies, banks, nations, and virtually anyone demonstrating the means to feed this monster, is another Zionist product. Cultural Marxism or political correctness is a means of enforcement. All these hide behind; "Never Again", "six million" and other political slogans not based in reality. Jews, for the most part, are the beneficiaries of this, through the small distribution of financial gains made by Zionists; thus they keep their opinions to themselves.

A clear definition of Zionism is: Zionism is a racist socio-political ideology that allows Jews from anywhere to go to Palestine/Israel to claim superior rights in law and equity at the cost of the indigenous population.[2] Furthermore, it allows all Jews to share in the spoils of extortion, as exerted by the World Jewish Congress and other Zionist organizations – and to share in billions upon billions of foreign aid extorted from nations, individuals and corporations worldwide.

This text will clearly show that Zionism, Illuminism and Communism have so much in common that they may be considered one and the same. All of the 20th century illustrates clearly that the philosophy developed by the Illuminist movement of Weisshaupt at the turn of the 18th century, became the prominent Zionist and Communist political philosophy of the 20th century.

Zionists as a group view Israel as their homeland, and in America or Europe see the nation in which they live as a cash cow to be milked by them. Their plan is a social and political hegemony over the societies in which they happen to reside. If you disagree, consider the Rosenberg's, Pollard, Gold, Greenglass, Bloch, Perle, Bronfman, Bohm, David, or any of the hundreds of other Zionist spies that double-crossed America and Britain in the 20th century to aid the Soviet Communist menace or for Israel to profit. Zionists are extreme chauvinists who believe in the absolute superiority of Jews over any other creature of nature; they express this in their dogma "We are the People Chosen by God."

One way this hegemony is expressed is to marginalize Christian and Muslim religious observance. Christmas is the birthday of Jesus, a Christian holy day, and has been supplanted by a minor and unimportant Hanukkah that was then simply changed into "The Holidays." Hanukkah is the celebration of a bloody massacre in 165 BC when Jews killed the Greek King, Antiochus IV, his family, and that of his prime minister and his ten sons. For Christians, Easter is the holiest day; while Easter holidays have been changed to spring break, the Jews celebrate Passover – the spirit passing over every Jew' house and killing the first-born of every non-Jew's family. Morbid! Or, better, sick! The Holocaust, which may now be considered a Zionist, trade-marked word, is relentlessly advertised, fictionalized and expanded, in order to justify the continued extortion of funds from Christians in support of Zionist goals. This includes such phony items as Holocaust Museums, usually in the midst of Christian communities and preferably across the street from a church. The one in Miami has listed the names of those lost; 26,000 names is the most they could come up with, 5,974,000 short of their six million number. In any event, with today's technology it would be simple to come up with a list of the claimed six million people, is it possible that this omission is due to the unlikelihood of coming up with even an eighth of that number of names?

One of the major supporting tenets of the thesis of this book is that the entire history of revolution, beginning with the French revolution and the Soviet era with the Russian revolution, was Zionist in nature, and that Karl Marx, the premier Zionist theoretician of the Communist philosophy, had in fact plagiarized his entire thesis from Professor Weisshaupt, who developed it in the 1700s as the primary philosophy of the Illuminist movement.

One last point. The entire neo-con conspiracy[3] is centered in Zionist control. Over 85% of the shakers and movers in the formulation of policy in Washington and London are Zionists. The war against terrorism has little to do with terror and a lot to do with establishing Israeli hegemony over the entire Middle East, using Christian blood in the form of British and American troops to attain it. Terrorism in the first place is because of our convoluted one-sided policies relating to the Middle East, and due to the 34-year illegal military occupation of Palestine[4], the continual humiliation of all Christian and Muslim Arabs, the building of over 250 kibbutzim[5] on stolen lands, the bulldozing of homes, the killing of rock-throwing boys, building a wall on other people's land, the willful destruction of generational farmlands, the theft of water resources, the dynamiting of villages, and the Israeli state-sponsored terrorism of political assassinations.

WHO?

Most people grow old within a limited scope of ideas. None seem to realize that in 1775 we had a great tyrant George King of England who was 3000 miles removed, and ruled over 3000 colonists; today we have 3 million tyrants ruling from our nations capital. Prepare now to accept the social and political reality governing the world.

WHO are *they*? They are, and we understand this well, not independent in mind or morals. They are tied, as if by chain, to an economic, political, and social philosophy that runs counter to every precept of liberty and common sense. They have tied themselves blindly to an organization, and devote their entire lives to achieving that organization's nefarious aims. They have abdicated their own identity and personal morality for the sake of granted power, and thus have become molded by mammon in judgment as well as in their own personal morality. They have abdicated their responsibility to their fellow man in favor of personal privilege and the power that mammon can afford them. They are almost exclusively atheists; those that are not, are agnostics. These individuals are the exact opposite of the founding fathers of the American republic, and their organization is grounded in the same time as that of America's foundation.

They gather their ill-gotten spoils; they will kill for them if they feel it will advance their desired ends. Truth is nothing to them;

they gather facts up like harvesters, and dispense them in distorted ways through the media that they control. They catalog, abuse, omit, divide, add, subtract, neglect and torture truth, to make it fit their needs. All this they do, not for us, not for society, not for anything but the greed and for personal privilege.

Look now, if you are old enough, over the history of the twentieth century. See it as a whole picture, and reflect on that most violent century in man's recorded history. Was there a plan? Many say that all history is happen-stance. Rubbish, no thinking creature could possibly believe that! The fact that we, as humans, plan precludes happenstance. All thinking creatures, no matter how dumb, plan. Thus history represents a scheme by the monied elite, those of power, to implement their desires. If you are in an elite, what is it you want? Power; you already have wealth. Thus the entire history of the twentieth century was driven by a group of elitists, whose only ideal is more power for themselves, over the rest of society.

Look carefully, and you will surely see that a devilish intelligence has been hard at work to undermine the moral structures of our society. The eighteenth century saw the awakening of a moral God-fearing society based on economic freedom, self-reliance, and a spiritual understanding of a greater intellect, a God who allowed us free will. Can you deny that the major portion of the twentieth century was spent in an orchestrated effort to destroy this concept? Consider the worldwide change in what was in the previous century seen in terms of good and evil. Pornography, which was so aptly used in the French and Russian Revolutions, has been made acceptable as well as legal. The perversion of a learned practice, homosexuality, whose practitioners were called sodomites in the last century, have remade themselves and call themselves gay. Murder now practiced worldwide is called "a woman's right to choose." We have become the only monogamous species on the planet that murders our young. Euthanasia has been legalized in Holland, and will be in many EC nations, under the banner of a caring society. The right of self-determination and property ownership is under severe assault everywhere. Governments have killed more of their own citizens in an effort to have them "contribute" to the common good than were killed in all the wars of the century combined. In only the Russian revolution the Zionist-managed bureaucracy through various means killed and deported 66 million Christians to Siberia, while destroying over 900 Christian churches and monasteries. China, in their cultural revolution, accomplished the liquidation of well over 100 million human beings. We are plagued worldwide by man-made and man-improved viruses. In effort to bring all of us into their fold they have created, through junk science, an entire plethora of lies about our planet and its environment.

They have infiltrated our churches, they control our governments, they have taken over all of academia, they control the mainstream media totally; they indoctrinate our youth with lies. Under the banner of "do-gooders" they now control the entire socialist environmental movement. Education and media have been their forte. We have in a short hundred years deteriorated toward their planned feudalistic state called the New World Order.

We began the twentieth century with Individual Economic Liberty – that was our starting proposition. We then had foisted upon us Social Justice, under the guise of Equality. This was then expanded to the social-democrat process called Affirmative Action, which in fact is racial separation. We then rapidly declined to social liberation and the end of individuality through the process called

Group Action. This set up our society to be communized. In the church we moved toward Liberation Theology and the kibbutz, an anachronism for Communist social structure. Group rights have superseded individual rights; with this they are able to pit various groups of society against one another. This keeps us in constant social conflict, thus allowing them the opportunity to implement their agenda over us all.

Taking this further, at the end of the twentieth century we saw the rapid expansion of a new process in expansion of group action, which I call Victimization. In this process small groups of society claim that some other set or group has victimized them and thus they are entitled to mammoth compensation, even from third parties, or for supposed wrongs done to their long deceased great-grandparents. The latest of these claims have been made against actions that took place in the nineteenth and even the sixteenth centuries, victims of which died centuries ago.

All these acts are planned. I call the evil planners of all this Satori or Illuminists. This book is about the New World Order and what they have planned in the past, and plan in your future. Ignorance of the facts presented in this book will not protect you from their plans; neither will inaction. This is not a work of fiction; every item written about in this book was derived from research of private archives, libraries, government documents, UN documents, NATO documents, EU directives, trade treaties, and international agreements, as well as numerous interviews.

– A. H. Krieg 2004

INTRODUCTION

Revolution is a necessity, so as to renew the tree of liberty.

THIS is hardly the first time in history that the forces of evil have assaulted man's freedom. Should we be fright ened and cower in slothful abandon of the assault on our well-tested and hard-earned liberty, which our forefathers bequeathed to us? Or should we fight against the forces of malevolence, against the feudalistic tyranny planned by the Satori? Make no mistake; their plan is the elimination of nation states, the abrogation of independent action, the curtailment of freedom and property rights, the total destruction of free enterprise, the reduction of world population to below one billion, with all humanity employed in their mega-corporations. They seek an age in which all humans are but serfs to their business enterprises. It should surprise no one that we are driven by a storm of Mammon, by Satori interests with an overriding aim of power over all mankind. The action has been building for well over two centuries, and has in the last forty years accelerated, and thus exposed its plan to scrutiny. Though their numbers are not great, their wealth controls over eighty-eight percent of our world's resources. When we combine that with government-held property that they also control, not much is left to the rest of us. We despise these wicked men for the evil they represent and the plan they have implemented in an effort to bring about the world conquest that is to be the New World Order. Their forces are strong but lacking; their desire is power, but their god is greed. The moral vacuum in which they operate will lead to their own annihilation. In Europe, society has already succumbed to agnosticism. America, as the world leader in 2004, is not far behind.

Their two greatest allies are the *System* of political control, which they wield in all nations that have two-party systems, and the media, which they either own or control in totality. The media include publications, the written press, cinematography, TV, as well as radio. This unholy alliance is the result of diligent planning that began in 1776 in Bavaria, Germany, and has come to control world financial systems in the 21st century.

It is an historic fact that societies based on greed, money, and power, cannot endure. It is a fact that without economic freedom there is no political freedom, and without freedom society stagnates. The Dark Ages were a feudalistic society. Not until the Renaissance, and its resulting economic freedom, did Europe recover from that horrid time. The newly- planned feudalistic society is a duplicate to the one of the Dark Ages, the only difference being that lordship is based not on heredity but solely on wealth. A society without a moral anchor will in all cases come to a bad end. We are, as of the twenty-first century, a society that is convinced of our own absolute power, which has abandoned God, morality, and all ethics. In April 2001 the Dutch parliament voted to legalize euthanasia. Infanticide has become a well-accepted practice in the entire developed world. A birthrate in all of the industrialized nations brought on by radical feminism is so low that these nations are aggressively courting immigration of labor in order to maintain their social systems. Perversion in the form of pornography has, in the

United States, become the largest single legal business enterprise. Drug addiction and the usage of hallucinogenic drugs is a leading business enterprise. Abortion of children in all Christian nations has reached the level whereby we murder our offspring at a rate close to the birthrate. Homosexuality is touted as an "Alternative Lifestyle" rather than the perversion it is. Individuals are enthralled with a materialistic desire for more and more useless "stuff". Our children attend schools in which the emphasis is not on education and the learning of relevant history, government, language, mathematics, or the three Rs. No indeed; the most important subjects in today's school systems are sports, sex education, and self-gratification. The three Ss have replaced the three Rs.

All these things and many more are the direct result of Illuminism, a political philosophy designed to destroy our society and to bring about the rule of the New World Order. The "Thousand Points of Light" of which G. Bush spoke are not the lights of freedom; they are a representation of the number of Illuminists who will rule the world.

We cannot remain secure on our ramparts, for the engines of our destruction are at hand. This book is a warning. Now is our last chance to oppose them. For God and country, for freedom and liberty, for the right of religious freedom, for our children, we must begin active and violent opposition to the New World Order. Not so to do is a personal indictment of our character as human beings. Speak out now against their planned tyranny; hide not, for evil shall triumph unless good men speak out!

FOREWORD

The world civil war, such as we are engaged in now, places all the separated segments of our society against one another.
Out of this planned chaos the New World Order intends its establishment.
It is proposed to institute the feudalistic dictatorship of world business, run and managed by the Satori and administered by the UN bureaucracy.

THE entire world at the onset of the 21st century has been cleverly divided into conflicting and separated groups. Virtually every racial, social, ethnic, religious, and financial group, as well as many nations, has been pitted against another. To further their ends more quickly, they have through unrelenting legal and illegal immigration changed the social fabric of all societies. I say this with absolute conviction, for I have reviewed funding for scores of these groups, and find that the very multi-national interests that presently employ so many people around the world fund most of these actions. Through such organizations as the World Council of Churches, the Runnymede Trust in England, the Carnegie Trust, Rainbow Coalition, and Southern Poverty Law Center in America, and hundreds more, money is channeled to meet Satori goals. Often the managers of those very organizations are not even cognizant of the end goal, as they are more interested in maintaining their lavish lifestyles than checking any of their organization's supporters' ends. If the partition and immigration affected merely a small portion of the population, the coming conflict could possibly be avoided. Immigration of uneducated third-world masses into our societies has been accelerated at unprecedented, and possibly geometric proportions. In the American State of California, Anglos represented 75% of the population in 1960; in 2001 they are down to a mere 47%. There is already talk of the "Reconquista", the process of making California, along with most of America's Southwest, an Hispanic entity.

In most of the urban centers of industry in all economically developed nations, the indigenous white populations have been reduced to fewer than 50%. London now boasts many neighborhoods in which Anglos are a minority. To further establish their control in all walks of life, old and young, rich and poor, male and female, healthy and indigent, black and white, retired and working, have all been set against one another through the manipulation of law, voting procedure, and socialist benefit packages. This keeps everyone's mind off the ball as it were, thus allowing implementation of the Satori plan. Not only have societies been separated linguistically where the immigrants refuse to learn the local language, but also laws have been altered to make those societies multi-lingual. Sex has been used extensively, by providing the homosexuals with funds so as to expand their war against normal society. This meets two goals: population reduction, and the destruction of the moral and ethical basis upon which our society is founded. On the feminist side, the specious "Glass Ceiling" issue is a commonly used item. Part and parcel of the plan has been the very effective effort to outlaw firearms. All of the arguments against firearm ownership are specious. Such as, Mothers against Guns – ten times more children are killed by mothers than by guns. Physicians against Guns; statistically physicians represent a death rate through medical malpractice 5000% greater than deaths caused by firearms. In Britain and Australia, where private ownership of guns has been all but outlawed, every form of violent crime has increased dramatically from the day that the laws were made. The fact is common knowledge that the Satori are terrified of an armed populace, who might well react violently to having their rights suspended by lackey judges and legislatures.

No stone has been left unturned toward the destruction of the confederations, constitutional monarchies and republics; in fact, the efforts have been dramatically increased over the last two decades. This book will expose the evil plan of the Satori, along with their goals. The ultimate plan is for a world without nations, without boundaries, with a homogenized multi-cultural society that is uneducated. Education is in the midst of radical change. In America, a system called Goals 2000 was established for the sole purpose of bringing in Outcome Based Education (OBE,) Team, and other programs designed to produce uneducated students specializing in single-aptitude functions that serve the industrial combine as a docile, manageable labor pool. When you homogenize milk, cream no longer separates and no longer rises to the top; the same is true of education. If all students are forced to the lowest common denominator, the end product is mediocre.

The "dumbing down" of our children in those brain laundries we call schools and colleges are not only ongoing but also relentless. The *Washington Times* reported in Dec. 2000 that a school district removed the names of Jefferson and Madison from their history books because both men had been slave-owners. "Team" is the process so strongly endorsed by the AFT and NEA* and introduced through Goals 2000. In Team students are separated into groups of five, who then work together on all projects. The immediate consequence is that the brightest student does all the work, while the rest do and learn nothing. This allows higher grading (due to group grading) which in turn makes the teacher look better. Personal achievement is eliminated in favor of an insect mentality. Lest we forget, Einstein, Tessla, Fermi, Newton, Plato, Mann, Cervantes, and Goethe were not part of any team. This book will demonstrate the digression of America, as well as Britain, from a constitutionally ruled Anglo-Saxon dominated society of Empire and then to decline as a multi-cultural backwater. It will show how the standard of living in all Western nations is being degraded down into third-world status, and how that serves the interests of the Satori, Social Democrats/New Democrats, more correctly socialists' and Communists' dupes who implement Satori plans.

In the political arena new ideology was developed to foster change. This has been accomplished through such invented anachronisms as "Social Justice," "Shared Sacrifice," "Contributions," and the "Elimination of Difference," all of which have imbibed our collective conscience with the fallacies developed in the French revolution, and extensively used by the Nazis. The libertarian economist and philosopher Friedrich A. Hayek in his book *The Fatal Conceit* lists no less than 150 nouns, which have had the appendage "Social", adjoined to them.

Notice how the political left, always the Satori stooge, attempts to glorify the French Revolution, a feat that has demonstrated a moral decay of society of proportions rarely ever reached. Its moral commander was none other than the Marquis de Sade, whose excessive perversion landed him in prison the Bastille. The difference between the American and French revolutions is as the variation between good and evil.

While the American model functioned with a moral and ethical compass, the French was completely devoid of any such moral basis. All this was the beginning of communization, developed by Weisshaupt and plagiarized by Marx. Social Justice has nothing to do with justice and everything to do with the theft of something from one individual and giving it to another, by the state, so that the acting politician can gain political constituency, on behalf of his Satori master. All politicians are slaves to their vices, and more specifically to the masters who provide those means to them; thus they are kept in perpetual servitude to Satori interests. This we learn from that master of politics, Disraeli. In all these "Social" actions a third and fourth party are involved: the government through which the action is facilitated, and the Satori who sanction and control it. This in every instance increases the size, scope and actions of government to the detriment of liberty, property and personal freedom, making that government more interventionist.

The French Revolution was orchestrated by the Illuminati, that evil Bavarian secret order, which succeeded in taking over the majority of European continental Masonic and Rosicrucian Lodges in the mid-1700's. At its head was Adam Weisshaupt, a defunct Mason and Rosicrucian, schooled by the Society of Jesus, the Jesuits, whose canon law chair at the University of Ingolstadt was placed in Weisshaupt's hands at a very young age, when the Jesuits were purged from education in Bavaria. It was to be the launching platform for the beginning of the most evil and vile secret enterprise in human history. The French Revolution took its motto from the Masonic bodies, which had been appropriated by the Illuminati in 1789. *Egalité, Fraternité, Liberté,* which translates in English to Equality, Fraternity, Liberty, was the revolution's motto. The first word of that slogan has been mistranslated for decades. *Egalité* is the root word for our egalitarian; this word in meaning has nothing whatever to do with equality. Egalitarian in fact means the leveling of values; in France of the late 1700s guillotining anyone whose financial or intellectual accoutrements exceeded the norm, and then stealing their assets to be distributed to the mob accomplished this. The change today is that Weisshaupt's laws of universal taxation obviate the guillotine, because only two classes remain. One might surmise that we have come full circle, whereby the Illuminati now are the oppressors while all the rest of us are the serfs. The very thing that they had claimed as their cause collapsed in their revolution. In modern history Communists simply disenfranchise their opponents financially and socially through confiscatory taxation and the implementation of law. The fact that the Satori has taken over the Illuminati organizational structure and even their initiation rites is 20th century history, and will be covered later. Suffice it to say in this foreword that the initiation rites for Skull and Bones, a.k.a. 322, or The Order of Death, or Bones, are totally identical to those rites practiced by the Illuminati a century ago. Not only are initiation practices identical, but also, all new members are called vandals prior to attachment, and all are given a new name. In the case of Weisshaupt, it was Spartacus. Other Ivy League college-senior organizations, like Scroll and Key, follow an identical pattern, which is then again reflected in some German, French, and English college and university fraternities. In my first book on this topic, *The Satori and the New Mandarins*, more detailed information on secret and semi-secret organizations, along with their memberships, may be found. The subject of this work is not the individuals as participants, but rather their philosophic, social and political direction. In other words, I will outline what their plans are, what they hope to achieve and how it will affect you and your children.

Social Justice is the egalitarian process by which government is interposed among citizens to level out individual wealth, and through the same means between nations, and geographic regions, by force if necessary. This more than proves the Communist nature of the action. Consider graduated income taxes. Think about free trade the anachronism that has lead to massive unemployment in all Western industrialized nations. Satori dupes inform us that it is only fair that a person of greater income should pay a higher percentage of taxes. If I earn $1,000 and my tax is 10%, I pay $100 in tax, and if you earn $100,000 you pay $10,000 or 100 times as much. The argument that the percentage should change as income rises is not only specious but comes directly from Karl Marx's *Communist Manifesto*, plagiarized by him from Weisshaupt, and published in 1848 in German in London, Point # 2, page 25: a heavy progressive or graduated income tax is advocated. Thus success, hard work, and achievement are punished, while inaction, loafing, and slothfulness are rewarded, with the state acting as the dispenser of all stolen goods and graces through taxation. The Satori, however, are excused from all these acts because they have created legal loopholes whereby they are exempted from taxation, while their bureaucratic functionaries remain rewarded through state largess in the form of entitlements, pensions, health-care benefits, and perks which are also excused from the normal tax structure.

Consider for example the remuneration paid U.S. representatives and senators. In just benefits they pay $340.00 per year for total healthcare for themselves and their families, including children to age 25. They obtain a fully funded pension of over $150,000 per year at age 62 after serving one term in office. The list of perks is so extensive that it would take an entire book just to list the available services and freebies. Their pay is about $160,000, but they have no expenses as the taxpayers fund all. Their offices, helpers, travel, haircuts, employees, and telephone bill – we play for everything.

Social Justice is the reason that the American standard of living has declined for decades. There is no question about this; consider the following facts. In 1950 a good automobile cost $3,500. and average income was around $9,000. A modest but reasonable house cost $15,000. Thus average annual income in 1950 would allow the purchase of 2.57 cars or a house every 1.66 years. This was easily accomplished with the father working and the mother as the housewife. Today the equation is radically different, in no small part because of the drastic increase of government spending, and the ensuing increases in government taxes, fees, licenses, tolls, etc. The average American family of four's cost of government has now risen to a national average of 49.20% of total income. In fact for six months American families toil to support their bloated government and its employed mandarins. For three of those months you toil to pay the interest on government borrowing paid to the Satori bankers. In 2001 almost all married women are forced to work, as the income of one family member no longer suffices to keep a roof over their heads. Feminists, surely among the most vocal Satori stooges, universally applaud this as beneficial to women: children, you see, no longer count, but feminist self-esteem does. The average national income in 2001 is $23,000: this equates to one fifth of what we pay our elected officials. Today a reasonable partially prefabricated home costs $120,000. It takes 5.21 years of income to pay for that house. A reasonable automobile costs $20,000, or one year's wages. This is the only way by which actual economic circumstance can be expressed; furthermore, if we go back to the 1930s the equation becomes downright diabolical.

Besides Social Justice, how has America's standard of living been so drastically decreased, and to what ends? Why are the rich getting richer and the rest of the population poorer? Obviously there is no one single answer in what is an orchestrated and planned effort. We can, however, easily locate the primary culprit of our financial decline. Ever since the mercantilism of over a hundred years ago, and the rise of the middle class, elites have wanted this class eliminated. The middle class represents a group of citizens that cannot be directly controlled by those in power.

Why? The middle class represents independently minded people not directly controlled by secondary forces. The poor are controlled through government programs; the rich predictably are interested only in protecting their wealth and power, and the middle class is a wild card, which since its inception has been outside the direct control of the Satori. The Satori had to find a means through which the middle class could be eliminated, and brought under their control. Bear in mind that this struggle is not new but has been on going for 200 years.

The presently popular slogan "Free Trade," which in fact is not new, is at the forefront of the economic destruction of the middle classes. Free trade is the Trojan horse that is devastating the middle class worldwide. The first recorded attempt at this was in Britain in 1908 to 1913 and proved successful in lowering the average wage of Englishmen by about 25%, and was in no small part responsible for the turmoil that brought on the First World War in 1914. First and foremost, you must understand that free trade is not in fact free trade at all but is instead government-controlled trade. If you now understand that the government acts and behaves at the behest of large business you will begin to understand how and why this "Free Trade" Trojan horse is being foisted upon us. Think of the dramatic changes brought on by this one single factor. What happened to your local grocery store, haberdashery, five and dime, drug store, gas station, appliance store, and all the rest that were owned and managed by one of your middle-class neighbors 30 years ago? All are gone, along with the American, British, and Canadian goods that they sold to you and your family. What took their place? Kmart, Ace Hardware, Wal-Mart, T.J. Maxx, Burlington Coat Factory, Marshals, Exxon, Eckert Drugs, all chains, all selling imports from the Pacific Rim, Middle East, and the Communist Peoples' Republic of China. All are multi-national corporations that simply purchase goods, which they import, from the lowest priced source, so as to maximize their corporate earnings. Are the prices lower? Yes, but less than ten percent. Are profits up? I should say so; Chinese goods and products sold in these multi-national stores earn these corporations huge profits. The most noticeable change has been the elimination of all family-based business in favor of multi-national based mega-corporations.

This then represents the first in a long series of steps taken to change society from a majority middle class, self-reliant one to a population dependent upon large business corporations and government for their employment and dependence. It has altered where we work, for whom we work, and what we purchase, as well as our entire social structure. An economic formula based on a series of popular slogans has replaced reason.

The concept of all of this is to force the elimination of independent middle-class business, i.e. small business, and force all of society into the multi-national mold.

The presently popular "progressive," "social democrat" and "new democrat" i.e. socialist/ communist theory represented by free trade, and supported by all major political parties in the developed world, consumes each nation's foreign policy. Let me clarify the hypothesis of the free-trade theory as presented to us: You as an individual will profit from free trade because goods will be less expensive, so you can afford more stuff, and foreigners that produce those goods will, by an increase in their standard of living, purchase more stuff from us. This is strongly supported by such consumerist demagogues as Ralph Nader, as well as the environmentalist, homosexual socialist alliance. It is factually wrong. The theory that government-controlled free trade will allow economies in the realm of production, and labor as well as consumption, to self-regulate an increase in the standard of living of all trading partners is just plain stupid. First, we are not trading on a level field. This is the crux of the free-trade fallacy. It is why the standard of living in the industrialized world has been declining for decades.

Consider now one of the premier chariots of the free trade movement, NAFTA. This economic disaster for Canada and the United States has three and only three beneficiaries; Mexico, multi-national business, and government agencies that manage it – they are its only beneficiaries. Prior to its implementation, America had a trade surplus of $5.6 billion with Mexico annually. Since the illegal implementation by executive order[6] (Clinton) of this agreement the following facts present themselves:

- America's trade surplus with Mexico has disappeared. We now have an average annual trade deficit with Mexico of 36 billion.
- American international corporations are investing over $2 billion annually building new plants in Mexico rather than in America.

- All USDC[7] reported statistics on NAFTA are falsification.
- All Maquiladoro exported component parts shipped to Mexico for re-importation to America are counted as exports; when re-imported they are not counted at all.
- All third-nation imports to Mexico (up to 40% of Maquiladoro assemblies) are not statistically included in any USDC reports.
- America has lost 3 million direct manufacturing jobs to Mexico.
- America has lost 4 million indirect manufacturing jobs due to Mexican plant expansions rather than American expansions by American, European and Asian multi-nationals.
- Total job losses attributable to NAFTA in the United States alone are over 7 million.
- In 2001, the trade deficit with Mexico has risen to over $40 billion. (USDC statistic.)
- Total trade losses as of March 2003 between America and Mexico due to NAFTA alone are $338 billion. This is without Maquiladoro production or re-importation statistics.

Consider now that service sector jobs on average result in pay scales 40% lower than in the manufacturing sector, and you begin to understand how free trade reduces your standard of living.

We are informed that NAFTA is to be expanded into FTAA[8], which is to comprise 34 nations of Latin America and the Caribbean Basin. Should this disastrous act be implemented, by giving the American president "fast track" trade negotiation authority, the Satori plan would be all but a fact. Consider that Mexico is one of the wealthier nations of the region, and that the average manufacturing blue collar wage there is, as of 2004, $1.47 per hour, without any benefits, pension, social security, labor unions, workman's compensation, nor any of the alphabet-soup of government regulatory agencies riding herd over our domestic producers.

Haiti, in this plan, represents the lowest, with an annual average income of under $400 per person.

Britain went through a general parliamentary election in May 2001. Only three issues were on the table for discussion: health care, crime and education. Politicians and their controlled media studiously avoided the European Union, trade, legal and illegal immigration, hoof and mouth disease, or any important issue for that matter. In an interview on the 11th May *Breakfast with David Frost*, Tony Blair evaded or sidestepped virtually every issue. Q: "Will 'New Labor' (old socialists) increase taxes?" A: "You will have to wait for the party manifesto to come out." Q: "Will 'New Labor' push to join the Euro?" A: "We have not reached a consensus on that issue." And I have a bridge for sale in Brooklyn! Britain's trade situation is beginning to look more like America's every day. The hoof and mouth disaster is being handled in such a stupid manner, that it must be with an ulterior motive. Crime is rampant, carried out by illegal and legal immigrants: not one party is addressing the cause – instead they propose hiring more police and prosecutors, and building more prisons. The solution to the poor showing in education is identical to that in America; hire more teachers, pay them more, and build more schools. In health care the debate is about the length of the list of citizens awaiting medical services. Is it 380,000 or 300,000; do you have to wait six months or a year? The real issue is, why is there a waiting list to begin with? So we see a re-run of the 1998 American election, right down to the statisticians and pollsters imported from America by the socialists. Sorry, New Labor. America's 2004 election between Bush and Kerry (Kohn) produced exactly the same sort of rubbish. I do not recall one issue of importance being addressed by either candidate.

Demographics, as reported in the 2000 American presidential elections along with Gore's scandalous attempt to steal the election, demonstrate some astounding information. First, Bush won the popular vote nationally by over 1.9 million votes. Second, by the latest counts in Florida, as carried out by the *Miami Herald* and the *Tampa Tribune*, Bush won the state of Florida under even Gore's mandated and lopsided counting method. Bush won even if only Dade, Hillsborough, and Broward counties were re-counted. National demographics and exit polls furthermore go to reinforce my previous statements about the divisions between all of us. The first and most noticeable factor is a map of America that colored in all counties that voted Democrat, letting Republican counties remain white. What shocked me was that the Democrats won less than 20% of the geographic land mass. The Democrats carried almost all the urban centers. On the West coast, all but seven counties bordering the Pacific Ocean, and on the East coast, all but twenty-five counties on the Atlantic voted Democrat. On the West coast of Florida they lost all but four counties. The 04 election proved to be similar, but with Bush wining even greater than in 2000.

In the rest of America they predictably lost all of Alaska and won all of Hawaii, along with all the major cities. They lost every rural county in America. Perhaps there is more truth to Pavlov's comment that when animals are too closely quartered they become irrational and aggressive; that does explain the high crime rates and socialist voting practices of urban dwellers. The exit polling listed below opens your eyes to what is transpiring in America.

<u>Demographic exit polling, U.S. presidential election, 2000.</u>

	Republicans	Democrats
Education:		
College	51%	45%
Did not finish HS	39%	59%
Income:		
50K – 75K	51%	46%
Over 200K	39%	56%
Stockholders:	51%	46%
Married w. Children	56%	
Unmarried		57%
Heterosexual	98%	
Homosexual		96%
Gun owners	61%	
Gun grabbers		62%
Pro-Life	74%	
Pro-choice		84%
Religious	57%	
Agnostic		61%

As the reader has surely surmised, I am neither a Republican nor a Democrat. This demographic, however, does point out that in support by population there is a decided difference between these two factions. The sad fact is that in the leadership there is not only no difference, but politicians of both parties in America, Canada, and Britain are beholden to the System, not to the people they supposedly represent. Reviewing the above statistics, it is small wonder that the primary drive of the Satori-guided political left is the dumbing down of the populous, and the utter elimination of any worthwhile educational pursuits. Obviously, from their perspective, the dumber you are the more likely you are to support their outrageous goals. This is a clear indication that when you pack enough people together in a tight enough space they relinquish reason and civility, common sense and self-reliance, in favor of state control. Pavlov was right! To further the statistics and prove my point that all collectivist thought emanates from urban regions, follow the expansion of data.

U.S. Presidential election 2000

Total number of voters: under 50% of population	
Population of counties won by Democrats:	127M
Population of counties won by Republicans:	143M
Square miles won by Democrats:	59,000
Square miles won by Republicans:	2,427,000
States won by Democrats:	19
States won by Republicans:	29
Average murder rate per 100,000:	
Democrat-won area	13.2
Republican-won area	2.1

American elections are entirely controlled by the two principal political parties. The process begins long before the primaries. Mexico, as a matter of fact, as of the year 2004, has a more open electoral process than does America.[9] Access to the American presidential debates is tightly controlled by the Presidential Debate Commission, which is staffed by three Republicans and three Democrats.

In America elections are purchased. In the 2004 Iowa caucuses, Kerry (Kohn) purchased the vote by infusing $6 million in cash. The New Hampshire primary, the nation's first true test, demonstrates the clever NH way of bringing mammon into the state. NH voters are listed on the town lists as Republican, Democrat or independent. In primaries they can switch parties by simply telling the registrar they want to switch. Thus if there is no Republican primary candidate, many Republicans will vote in the Democrat primary, along with independents, all of whom will have switched party affiliation for the sole purpose of voting in the primary.

Large corporations privately fund all the debates. Thus in order for any large multi-national to have guaranteed access to the future president it must fund the Debate Commission and each of the two political parties. Through this process all third party candidates are eliminated, the system wins, the two major parties win, and the people lose because the issues debated and spoken of in the pre-election cycle do not reflect the peoples wishes, needs or best interests. In the 2000 presidential debates as well as the following campaign, the following ten issues were completely omitted:

- Why does America have the largest prison population in the world?
- Should the PRC continue to retain most favored nation trade status?
- Should we, due to of our poor experience to date, continue with NAFTA?
- Should we expand NAFTA into FTAA?

- Why do we continue to uphold arms treaties with the Soviet Union, a nation that no longer exist?
- Why are we told there is a massive surplus when the General Fund owes various agencies over $34 trillion it holds in IOUs?
- Why is America now the world's largest debtor nation?
- Why have the candidates from the Reform, Libertarian, Natural Law, and Green parties been blocked from this forum, particularly in view of the fact that three of those parties had obtained ballot access in almost all 50 states?
- Why do we continue to loan billions upon billions of dollars to Russia, which funds are collectively stolen and deposited in western banks?
- Why do counties and states with gun carry permits have crime levels 60 to 80% lower than those without?

Needless to say, I could come up with several hundred questions whose answers would interest most of us, but that would be pointless.

The issue of race has been particularly evil, in Europe as well as in the Americas. Unfortunately, there have grown up in our midst a bunch of revolting racial hucksters who do a great deal more than just make a living off this issue. These people in England and America will not be satisfied until Caucasians are a minority's in their own nations. There is little purpose in listing the names of these predators on Western Culture and society, we all know exactly who they are. Personal incomes of many of these individuals exceed $ 200,000 per year, testifying to the fact that causing misery is a very profitable business.

All these people are despicable; they are a cyst on society, parasites who for their own and their constituency's enrichment work for the Satori interests. Not one of them can be shown to have influenced racial harmony in any community; to the contrary in every single instance they make things worse. There are others – they grow like mushrooms they're all in it for mammon.

Nations exist because of the bond between the families that makes up their citizenry, and the bond that exists within racial groups. The most expedient method for the destruction of nations is the rupture of that bond. The best way of accomplishing that goal is through unrelenting legal and illegal immigration, radical disharmony, and wars of expansion. America, Britain, and Canada presently have military operations in over 100 nations. Russia is no different; only their client states are not the same as those of the West.

That we are currently in the midst of a *Kulturkrieg* that is being waged by the Satori against Western Civilization is an unfortunate fact. Their attack is centered upon the foundations of our society, our religion, and our moral basis, our ethical understanding of the relationships between our Maker and us, and between ourselves. Every action taken by the Satori boils down to a systematic organized destruction of the tenets of Western society and culture. One of these attacks is based on the falsification of the history of the Germanic and English peoples, as well as those of our American forefathers, in an effort to separate our society from its past. Much of this is done in education, where in 1998 a popular student shout at the university of Berkley was; "Hey Hey, Ho Ho, Western Civ. has got to Go." The replacement of Western culture at the U. of Northern CA will no doubt be Aztec human sacrifice.

Black culture is now a subject commonly taught in many of our universities; my only comment is that not one black tribal group in all Africa progressed to the Iron Age, nor developed the use of the wheel, a written language or a numeric system and only one, the Benin, even attained the Bronze Age. What Culture is being studied? The proposed concept by some academicians that Beethoven, Bach, Goethe, and Vasquez are somehow paralleled in some African or South American culture is so ludicrous that I won't comment on it. Beauty, art, music and literature are defined by their intrinsic value to mankind, and their inherent aesthetic acceptance by all people, regardless of culture, not by some vague media or academic critic.

There are most assuredly values other than those brought forth in Western culture, but does not the fact that every single culture in the world tries to emulate ours prove that in the last 300 years our culture has come to the forefront of human achievement?

There will always be freedom.
It is impossible for rational nature to exist without it.
Should no freedom remain, no hope will exist.
Then the best reply would be the one given by Canius upon Caligula's charge of conspiracy against him:
"If I had known of it," he said, "you would not."

Freedom and social justice are economically as well as politically linked. Without economic freedom, political liberty is a mere mirage.

Our society worldwide in the twenty-first century is about the curtailment of economic and political freedom for the sole purpose of installing a cabal called The New World Order.

The goal of the N.W.O. is the enslavement of all mankind to an Illuminist feudalistic dictatorship run by multi-national corporations for their pleasure and benefit.
The vehicles for accomplishing these ends are: the UN, free trade, NATO, EU, NAFTA, FTAA, WTO, and GATT.
And all the international treaties and agreements controlled and instituted by the Satori.

PERSONAL EXPERIENCE

A SHORT BIOGRAPHIC SKETCH.

Illegitimus Non Tatum Carborundum
(Lat.) Don't let the bastards wear you down.
– The Krieg Family motto;

A PERSON is the sum of his learning, education and life experiences. More than that, he is the product of his par entage and culture and environment. It serves my purpose that you, as the reader, understand to some reasonable degree how I reached the beliefs and opinions that I express in my text, if for no other reason than to support my positions. I was born in 1938 in St.Gallen, Switzerland. My parents were married in September 1937, an historically tumultuous time.

My father, Vicktor Joseph Caspar Krieg, was a graduate textile engineer. My mother was brought up through finishing school, a common practice in upper middle class families. She was multilingual, speaking French, Italian, English and German. She was brought up in St. Gallen. As was the custom at that time for girls, in rounding their education she went as a governess to foreign nations. Her first job was for a French family in Tunis, North Africa, which was a French colony at that time, where she saw to the education of three children. Her second job took her to the British Midlands, where she oversaw the management of a household. This was a normal occurrence in the late 19th and early 20th centuries for young ladies, so that they would become proficient in the language and the culture of other lands, and so round out their education.

My father was brought up in Ticino, the Italian part of Switzerland, and Schwyz, its heart. By the time he was 30 he was fluent in six languages; after the war he learned seven more. Not only was my father a gentleman in the true sense of the word, but he was also a genuine intellectual. He often told me stories about the great German inflation when he was at university in Germany. His father would send him 100 Swiss Francs in five-franc notes; he frequently went to the bank and exchanged five franks for a briefcase full of Marks. He told me of his friends – almost all of who were later killed in the war – coming into his room and asking if they could have a handful of money to go to the Gasthaus for a beer. I learned also of the estanza, almost the size of Switzerland, which he managed in Argentina for two years.

Prior to meeting my mother and going to Argentina he had lived in Spain, where he was involved in the civil war on the side of Franco. (Many people think that the Spanish civil war was between Fascists and Communists, when in fact it was between Spanish nationalists and international Communists.) He was, at the time he met my mother, the sales manager of AMAG, the Swiss Chrysler importer: Switzerland has always been a substantial consumer of American automobiles, as Switzerland does not have a car industry, and American autos were popular. It was a very good job, and my father was good at it. History, however, can be an evil taskmaster, and so it was to my father. In 1939 he was drafted into the Swiss army, to be followed within months by the fathers of all my relatives and friends. By the time I entered kindergarten at age six, Swiss society had become one of children and women. Virtually every male from 18 to 45 were in the army, while those from 45 to 60 were in the Home Guard. By 1944 my mother was in the civil defense and I, along with most children from Zurich, worked part time on a farm, where there was considerably more food than in the city. During the war, and for some time thereafter, my mother was my best friend, because my father was so often in service. We must have hiked every trail within 50 miles of Zurich, always packing lunch and returning by evening. No one had a car, except the military, and after the war they came back slowly.

We were poor but happy; I actually cannot remember ever getting a present from my parents until after the war, when my father traded a power tool for a bicycle. We made our own toys, parachutes, airplanes, bows and arrows, and tomahawks, all homemade by kids. I distinctly remember a few occurrences from my time in kindergarten. Shortly after I was enrolled this 2nd grader would stop me and thoroughly beat me up. When I told my wise mother, she explained to me that I was the man of the house and would have to deal with this problem on my terms and in my way. The next day I untied my shoelaces before reaching the place where I knew the bully waited for me; when he approached me I pulled off my shoe and hit him on the nose. I did not wait around but did notice a broken nose and blood; I never saw him again. I had learned a primary lesson of life – self-reliance, how to deal with bullies.

The second case, in retrospect, is very funny. One day my mother received a note saying that I had not been in kindergarten for two weeks, and the teacher hoped that I would be better soon. Mother also found six Francs in my room. Considering that this was one Franc more than my father got in the army, she was anxious to get to the bottom of it all. The next day, unbeknownst to me, she followed me as I left our little apartment. I went down the stairs and hid my schoolbooks in the lower hallway, and went to work. I had located a construction site and had made myself the official "gofer" for the laborers. They would write on a piece of paper what they wanted, usually beer, bread, cheese, etc. and gave me money and food coupons, and I went shopping for them. By the second week they even sent me into the city for parts, nails or whatever they required that was small enough for a little boy to carry. They gave me a tip for every service. Not only did I learn more on the construction site than in the kindergarten, I earned a reward, which was for 1943 better income than many Swiss soldiers. It was a great beginning lesson – entrepreneurship.

When I was in first grade, during Easter vacation my friends and I decided that we would go to see the Rhine fall at Schaffhausen on our bikes. Not only was this a longer trip than we had anticipated, but the best way to get there was to go through Germany. Everything went fine until we got to the border. The Swiss border guard asked us where we were going, we told him, he said, "Fine, go ahead." Then we came to the German crossing, where we were promptly saluted with "Heil Hitler," whereupon my friend Spiess sarcastically asked, "Who's Hitler?" Needless to say, this did not sit well with the German guard; Swiss in general were not popular with the Germans of that time, as they were the only Germanic nation who did not support them. We got a stern lecture about the Fuehrer, and were told not to stop until we returned to Swiss territory at Schaffhausen. We paid no heed, and took a break in a depressing German village. We got to Schaffhausen and the Rhine fall, and decided to go home via Switzerland, as we were not impressed by our German experience. At about three in the afternoon I had a flat tire and we were easily five hours from home, so we decided to split up: my friend Peter would stay with me while we repaired the tire, and the other two would go home and tell our parents that we would be home late. By six all our parents were frantic, and had the police, and who knows what other, organizing a search for us. At 9 PM two of the party returned, to the relief of all our parents; we got home at 10.30 PM and were so tired we could hardly move. This was yet another object lesson about being on time and carefully planning ahead.

This leads me to one of the points about my childhood experiences in wartime Switzerland. I had a number of friends, and believe it or not even a girlfriend, whose name was Freneli. What strikes me as profound was our social structure. Spiesse's father was a policeman in Zurich, Peter's father was in the Army, and all the other kids whose parents were not in the military had small businesses. One boy's father was a baker, another owned our local grocery store, one had a machine shop, and a fourth had a lumberyard. We had lots of Jews, gypsies, and other refugee kids in school, whose parents were not in military service, many of whom attended university. Some of their parents were required to work by the Swiss authorities; many spent the war in resort communities that had empty rooms due to the war, and because Switzerland was completely surrounded by the Axis. What I notice today is that independent entrepreneurship by individuals is rapidly disappearing in favor of working for some large corporation. This movement from private enterprise to employment with large corporations has been accelerating dramatically in the last 50 years. It is not for the betterment of society; quite to the contrary, it benefits none. In fact I am convinced that over the last 70 years small businesses have been disappearing while large ones were growing. It is my personal observation that this is not a good thing. I further think that this has to do with the general deterioration of liberty and freedom, as well as our decline in ethics and morals. There is a distinct relationship between economics, morality and liberty. I am convinced that large business imbues people with unhealthy social and economic attitudes, and a dependence on structures, not on self. That a population primarily employed by multi-national corporations breeds a society that destroys individuality, and self-reliance, creating people who are dependent on an outside structure, is a fact. It is more than plain that when I began in business there were very few contracts. When my company bought something or contracted for a service, the owners of the businesses shook hands and it was a done deal. After all, it was the word of the boss or his agent behind the commitment to live up to the agreements. This is certainly no longer the case today, and I can tell you that it is the result of a society that has become so litigious, self-centered, greedy, and materialistic that it is destroying itself. Since W.W. II the acceleration toward a society controlled by larger and larger corporations has become the primary motive force of change in the society of the Western world. Hand in glove with that trend, were the larger national entities such as typified by Soviet and Chinese hegemony, an act that is now reversing, but with the ascendance of America into that venue. I must add that except, for a stint in the U.S. Army and some seasonal work in college, I have never worked for anyone except my father or myself. If you have been self-employed for over forty years you develop an outlook that differs radically from the mainstream. It is this outlook that I want you to understand; Americas forefathers shared individualism, self-reliance, and independence, attributes that are hard to come by. Such persons, and I speak from experience, are not altogether easy to get along with: they tend to be stubborn and opinionated. It is my judgment that our national and international business consolidation debacle leads us down the slippery slope towards a world-wide feudalistic system run by the large multi-national corporations; I will say more on this later, as well as providing ample proof of it.

The war also had some bitter consequences for me personally; I was bombed twice, once by the U.S. Army Air Force who thought Zurich was Stuttgart. They only missed their target by a hundred miles (shades of *Catch 22*). My best friend was killed. It was a day on which my father was home on leave and he was reading me a story in bed; we were both dumped on the floor, but aside from some broken glass and a few scratches we were OK. Later, when I was hiking with my grandfather in the Ticino Alps, an Italian bomber targeted the Swiss federal radio station near Belinzona and hit us instead. The Italians were no more skilful than the Americans; the Swiss radio station on whose signal the Italian could have honed in was on another mountain. It was not bad, just some fragments in my knee, which my grandfather, an accomplished dentist, skillfully removed. Our great joy was watching a Swiss Messerschmidt shoot the Italian down. Natti, as I called my grandfather, was often my great companion and friend; I could never wait to visit him, and return to our hikes in the Alps.

The war was a hard time for us, especially for my parents. They were newly-weds, separated by the war, poor due to lack of income, with a child and not enough food. I can never fully forgive the Germans for what they did to us, nor the fact that my father died at a relatively young age because he had contracted rheumatic fever in the military, which was at least partially responsible for his early death. Nor can I forgive any of the Jews that lied about Switzerland and used their financial and political power to extort monies from the Swiss nation and Swiss business, which by percentage of population saved more Jews than any other country in the world, over 30,000. In fact, Switzerland had refugees and interns from Axis as well as Allied armies representing close to 30% of the total national population.

When we lived in Zurich, my mother and I would go hiking to one of the castles or up on Uetliberg, or into the Sihltahl. Often we would visit my aunt Berti, my uncle Kaspar's twin and my father's younger sister. Fredy, Berti's husband, was a staff officer also in the army; Kaspar was in intelligence. While there was absolutely no black market in Switzerland, through the war, if you had cash sometimes an opportunity of purchasing food from a farmer presented itself. The Fishers were very wealthy, and my aunt was, and remained until her death, the person most important in my life, next to my parents. It was Berti who produced my Christmas and birthday presents, from things her own son Robi no longer used. It was Berti who provided food when no one else could. And it was Doris, my cousin, who is older, who became my idol. At least until I was 16 I was convinced that Doris was the most beautiful woman in the world. When Doris became engaged I was visiting Zurich. I still don't know why her husband Lelio did not beat me up; I was insufferably jealous, and certainly a pain in the neck to both of them. I learned from my association with my cousin and aunt, and later after the war, with my uncle Fredi, that wealth was not everything but it sure as hell beats poverty.

My father was an extraordinary man. While we argued often when we were in business together, I attribute most of it to my youth and foolishness. He was fluent in 13 languages; his Spanish, Italian, and French were so good that natives of those nations always accepted him as a local. His Spanish was Castilian, his French, Genevaín, his Italian, Milanese. He learned English at age 41, while speaking with an accent his vocabulary was better than anyone I have ever met, and he could spell, something I have never mastered.

This brings us to another lesson. When we came to America in 1952, I began in the sixth grade, although in Switzerland I had only just entered the fifth. I did not speak one word of English except up, down, left, right, and yes and no. I found American school boring, teachers all female, disorganized bedlam, and that was fifty years ago. When I entered junior high my father wanted me to take German so that I would maintain knowledge of my native language. My teacher was Mrs. Allen; I honestly have no idea how she became a German teacher because her knowledge of the language was vacuous. She flunked me! Every time I used a word she did not know she told me it was wrong. I had never seen my father, who in my memory rarely if ever lost his temper, so angry; all my pleas that the teacher was incompetent went over the dam, he would not listen, but finally I convinced him that the school was valueless. He agreed to come to school with me and interview my teachers. In the presence of our principal he began to interview Mrs. Allen in German; she proved unable to meet the challenge. My father turned to the principal and suggested that Mrs. Allen should be retired, as she was obviously not capable of teaching a language she could not speak. Then came French, Spanish, mathematics, my father was dumbfounded. Off I went to Hatch prep. in Newport, a private prep. school. I forgot to mention that I took the senior college entrance exam in German and made four corrections on the NY State Regents exams, and had the highest score that year. The object lesson here was that American public school education is, and has been since the '50s more or less inferior – a fact borne out by my stint in New Hampshire on the Fall Mountain school board in the '90s. I did not fit in well at Hatch, a school infested with rich kids, and transferred to Pembroke in Suncook, NH, from which I graduated with honors in June 1957. Education is the primary target of the Satori; individuals uneducated in economics, government and history make easy objects for political control and manipulation.

Whenever I was not in school I worked in my father's business. He had, at the close of W.W. II, made a great deal with Scintilla SA of Soloturn, Switzerland. He was their world sales manager; after working there for some months he talked them into a five-year contract on a draw against a modest commission. They bit the bitter apple, and within two years his pay was the highest in the entire company. Considering that this, by the end of the war, included Robert Bosch of Stuttgart, it was quite a coup.

It was the first of many lessons my father taught me; if you are capable and self-reliant commission is always better than salary, and piecework is better than salary. When I was in college I got a job working for a stamp redemption center, trading stamps being very popular at that time. Stores and gas stations offered Green Stamps for most groceries, gasoline, furniture, etc. as an inducement to shop with them. I was hired to assemble products, and convinced the redemption manager to change my salary from hourly to commission based on piecework; I made more money and worked fewer hours than any other redemption center employee with the same job.

Greed is man's worst enemy. Greed was the reason that my father was forced into a situation which perhaps he wanted anyway. By 1950 the management at Bosch and Scintilla were angered by the size of the paychecks they were making out to my father. This was another object lesson that has stayed with me ever since. If you hire salesmen on commission, the more money they earn the more you make as the owner; so the management should be delighted to make out huge paychecks for commission agents or commission employees. In '49 my father had gone on the first scouting mission to check out the American market. While doing so he visited Black and Decker, which was at that time America's largest power tool manufacturer. My father, together with a man named Stoller, had invented an item manufactured by Scintilla, which was selling like hot cakes in Europe. It was called the Jigsaw. He went to B & D, and offered the product to them for the American and Canadian markets. They told him such a device had no future, as nobody would be interested in cutting out jigsaw puzzles. Interestingly, by 1960, just ten years later, the jigsaw was the second largest-selling power tool, after the 3/8-inch drill. The object lesson, borne out a thousand times since, is that large corporations are run by the accountants and lawyers who stay long enough to get to the top.

One of many cases that more than proves my point is when in 1987 I approached B & D, suggesting that I take over their entire new product development department and work independently on a royalty basis of new products developed, based on their sales force requests. They were at the time wasting over two million annually on unproductive R & D. Brother, was I naïve! The proposition was immediately opposed by their marketing people, who after all knew more than a bunch of their "stupid" salesmen actually involved with their customers and users. Next came the research department who in fact had hardly developed anything in years; to the best of my knowledge the only thing they had ever come up with was the trigger switch. Then came corporate attorneys who would be out of their jobs. I pointed to my track record; all alone I had produced more power tool patents in ten years than their entire company in its total lifespan. In addition, I had over twenty-five issued U.S. manufacturing patents in the field. Not only that, but I introduced scores of new power tools on the American market, including corrugated nibblers, weld preparation bevellers, slotting shears, pipe drills, automatic torque controllers, orbital pipe cutters and orbital pipe robots, rail-road rail saw, and RR rail cross drills, along with the first robotic arc welder, which we introduced at the American welding show in Cleveland. I was turned down.

My very first patent came about when I watched my mother struggling with a jar top lid. She simply lacked the strength to twist it open. I gave the matter some thought and came up with a different top that could be punched out on the same lid-forming dies but had ears that stuck out on top, which allowed a butter knife or a fork to be used as a leverage tool. (Pat. # 4,078,689, 1978) I attempted to sell it to General Foods. Never got past their patent attorneys, who did everything in their power to prevent me speaking with or contacting anyone in sales or marketing. Corporate policy was that it had to pass legal before anyone could even see it. The CEO of GF was a lawyer at that time. After six months I gave up.

My father's exclusive contract with Scintilla management for the American market was the product of Scintilla's management's desire to stop paying those huge commissions to him. By contract Scintilla would make my father their exclusive agent for the American market of all their products until he died, and would give him a revolving 180-day merchandise credit of SFr. 100,000. Our family sold everything that we could not pack into two huge crates and immigrated to the United States. Five years later we were all made citizens. The judge who swore us, and several dozen other people, in pointed out how pleased he was to have three Swiss in the group, especially pointing out my parents. The fact that Messer Peret' was our family *consilatore* may well have had something to do with it. He was a Swiss-American lawyer from Lausanne who was advisor to the DNC on international law. Another object lesson; good friends are worth more than money.

In my life I have been a salesman, manufacturer, importer and exporter, engineer, designer, inventor, and author. If there were one lesson I would impart to you it would be that in relationships of business the small guy always, always gets screwed. It is not ability or knowledge that is power in business, it is size and money. Much the same is true of governments. Before I began to manufacture, I spent years importing machinery from European companies. In every single case, when I became successful in sales and distribution of some manufacturer's product, I was dumped and they opened their own shop. Fein is the oldest power tool manufacturer in the world: I took their American sales from zero to an annual volume of over $3 million. Trumpf from zero to over $3 million, Ackerman U. Schmidt, zero to $400K, Irle from zero to 3 million – all together about 10 companies, German, Swiss, Italian, Swedish: every one of them with two exceptions dumped me after I had built up their sales, upon expiration of contract. They did almost all get their just rewards: not one of them was successful on their own except Trumpf, and they were the worst of the lot. Their owner, Leibinger, is a devious scoundrel. That was certainly not the case with Mr. Trumpf, who was the firm's deceased founder. It was also not the case of Dr. Hans Fein, with whom I made the Fein distribution agreement. In both cases, when the originator died the inept heirs took over.

When I finished high school the matter of college was brought up. Now I must tell you that I was no scholar; I hated education, it was a bore. The fact that I have dyslexia, which presents a considerable challenge, particularly when taking exams, has not been much help either. My mother wanted me to have some religious education, and prevailed on me and my father that I should go to Elmhurst, a Lutheran college. The only professor with whom I had a good *rapport* was my German professor. The college allowed me to take fourth-year German literature which included Goethe, Heine and Mann, and we had only 6 students in the class – it was a great class. In European history I had for a professor a fool who was of the opinion that the study of history was the memorization of dates. At the end of every two-week period he would list about 40 dates and we had to indicate what took place on that date. I started a student protest, unheard of at that time, and succeeded in getting over 80% of the students to drop the class. In Philosophy I was stuck with a Lutheran theologian who gave everyone not in agreement with his ideas a C. Needless to say I, as one of his most dynamic critics, got a C-. I had to get out of there, and was accepted by several schools. Elmhurst College, however, did not notify my draft board that I was transferring; they said I had quit. So I was drafted into the U.S. Army before I could do anything. In all honesty, in accordance with the Swiss-American friendship treaty I could have gone into the Swiss army, but I lived in America, so what would have been the point of that?

The U.S. Army taught me that in the military rank is not necessarily evidence of intellect; that is true at least up to major. Having then learned FUBAR and FTA, I was well established for my military non-career. I was drafted into Ft. Dix, NJ, where I learned not to ever volunteer for anything. On my second day the sergeant asked who could type; when I indicated that I could I wound up on KP for three days. First, as all do, I went to the infantry school that is called basic training at Fort Hood, Texas. It was not at all like the wimpy feminized army of today. Women in the infantry are way beyond stupid – suicidal is more relevant to it. Then to advanced lineman and communications school at Fort Ord, California. I was then asked to go to officers' school, but when I asked what that entailed, and was told another year in the army, I respectfully declined the offer. I was eventually posted to Flack Kaserne in Kitzingen

A/M in Bavaria. The first time I was allowed off base, about two weeks after my arrival, (we could not go in civilian clothing until our third month); I went to a bar and sat in a booth. Behind me were three sergeants and their hookers. The women, speaking German fluently, thought that no one could understand them; my education began. Sometimes it was difficult not to burst out laughing. After some time I made friends with the women, who appreciated the only GI who was not trying to hustle them. I eventually learned that almost all of them had been forced into prostitution by the East German security service, which held their parents or siblings as hostages. Now, once a month we had an alert drill, which was a serious pain in the posterior. I was in a nuclear artillery unit; we had to move our entire over-400 vehicles, two Honest John batteries and four 210mm (8 in) howitzer (not self-propelled) batteries to some map location, which we then changed every 48 hours. Not so terrible in summer, but a horrible nightmare in winter. The girls proved to be a big help. It seems that among other things they also serviced some staff officers, from whom they learned the dates and times of the alerts. From then on forward I never participated in another alert, as I was always off on a three-day pass. Lesson: it is whom you know, not what you know, in large organizations.

When I had been in Bavaria for about five months I received a distressing telephone call from my mother; my father had had a heart attack and was to have by-pass surgery. I was immediately granted emergency leave and went directly to Roosevelt Hospital in NYC where my father had had his operation. After a few days, when he felt a bit better, he asked me to go out and get some wine, Scotch, and a decent meal, as the hospital food was not to his liking. When I returned, as we were having a Scotch and water, his nurse came in and had a fit. I remember his surgeon, Dr. Ford, who was called and promptly came to the room; he told the nurse to take a powder and had a Scotch with us. My father asked if he could smoke, to which Dr. Ford asked how long had he been smoking; my father retorted 53 years, Dr. Ford said, why not, the damage is already done. These were great lessons; hospital food was awful, a fact repeatedly reaffirmed throughout my life. Alcohol, contrary to Baptist and Puritan belief, is good for you in moderation; common sense can be a greater asset than education. When I finally went back to Germany, now my third crossing on one of those army garbage scows called troop transports, I almost immediately applied for a teaching position, which was granted. I taught German, math, and history to officers and non-commissioned officers. My commanding officer was Major Sims, an all-around great guy patiently awaiting his advance to the next ranking. I was officially TDY and was paid an additional $3.50 per hour for all my teaching duties. My company commander was an over-the-hill captain of 48 who was given the rank so that he could retire on a reasonable pension. Capt. Kiley was without doubt the worst leader and officer I have met in my entire life. When payday came around and I had the highest salary in our company he would get livid. At one point he reduced my rank from PFC to Private, only to have my major countermand his order. All my classes were taught in civilian clothes, as it would not do to have a PFC teaching ranking personnel. One caveat; my students in German had the highest test scores in the 7th Army. This was attributable to my throwing out the army's German language book and instead teaching my students how to order food in the local Gasthaus, how to pick up a Fraulein, along with scores of useful things like asking for directions. What I did was to motivate my students to learn on their own; in three months every one of them could get by on the local economy.

During this time the U.S. Army had decided to sell some of their miss-designed APCs (Armored Personnel Carriers) to allied armies in Europe. I had already had considerable experience with Dutch, German, and French military, and thus Major Sims, who had been placed in charge of this effort, made me his ground commander at Harvey Barracks. These APCs were lousy; we called them Zippos because if they were hit by enemy fire they had the unpleasant reaction to have their fuel tanks (gasoline) ignite. To make matters worse, they were supposed to float to cross rivers, but invariably sank. The army staged quite a show at Harvey Barracks; four transport planes landed seconds apart and the APCs came out, four from each plane, in formation across the airport, and to our command center. I made announcements over a PA system of what was occurring in German and English. I scuttled the entire effort. A German general (whom I was to meet again later in Stuttgart at a social gathering) asked me what I thought of the APCs. I indicated that he might ask to see a river crossing at the Main river close by, which he did. Two APC's went down; the army did not sell one of them. My term in the army was getting short, but I was extended at the convenience of the army during the Berlin crisis because they said they could not locate anyone to replace me. When I finally came home, I was devastated by my father's poor health, and went immediately to work in his company, Victor J. Krieg Inc.

My business education finally began. In order I learned shipping, bookkeeping, inventory control, repair, mechanics, machining, marketing, correspondence in two languages, sales, and management; in four years I took over the day-to-day operations of the business. About this time Scintilla withdrew their contract from my father, in violation of their agreement; we had been very successful for them, having become the largest machinery and power tool importer in America. Bosch, which was now the parent company, opened its own American Bosch Corp. that became the Scintilla importer. My father had an office manager named George Malencoff at that time that my father had hired straight out of NYU, double-crossed us in the most underhanded way imaginable. He had accumulated $45,000 in pension benefits, as well as a large amount in profit sharing; my father even gave him a severance bonus of several thousand dollars. Malencoff, unbeknownst to us, had made a deal with the German Bosch Company to become their power tool manager, and to bring with him our customer lists, accounts receivable lists and accounts payable lists.

We decided to start a new company with a short and easy name; my father said he liked Widder, which was his astrological sign in German. So we named the new child Widder Corp. We had by that time already amassed Mamaroneck Dept. Plaza Corp., Rovic Manufacturing Inc., Nugget Realty Corp., and Victor J. Krieg, Inc. all of which I managed. We had had some contact with other manufacturers; among these was C. & E. Fein of Stuttgart, the oldest power tool and machinery manufacturer in the world. I met the principal, Dr. Hans Fein, and we made an exclusive sales agreement for America. Starting from no sales in America, we began to build the business. In due course we also picked up Trumpf, having also made an agreement for all their power tools with Mr. Trumpf. It was about this time that my father retired. Second-generation management is not always what first was, and this was certainly the case with both Fein and Trumpf.

Gradually I began to subcontract self-designed components and power tool accessories. This expanded, and I purchased a small manufacturing company, and then another, eventually building a manufacturing plant in Naugatuck, CT. I did the architecture, plant layout, and office all myself, and had a local tilt-slab contractor build the plant. My general manager was Leo Frajacomo, not only a friend with whom I am still well acquainted, but also an excellent, capable and loyal co-worker. By this time our sales had attained about $3.5 million, so we expanded with a second plant at San Leandro, California, and offices in Randburg, South Africa, and in the English Midlands. We also had a wholly owned subsidiary, Panox Trading in Zurich, Switzerland. We manufactured, imported some but not much, exported a lot, business was good.

At about this time I succeeded in becoming a manufacturing engineer certified by the Society of Manufacturing Engineers, sometime later getting a Cultural Doctorate in Manufacturing Science. It is, in my opinion, all just window dressing, for some unknown reason the world is enthralled with school learning degrees and PhDs. Along with my award for the best fuel-gas cutting invention, the NATTCO award for the best welding developments in 1983, the Advertising Effectiveness Award in 1981, and numerous others, are much more impressive than any college degree. It's all for nothing, I know professors who wear loafers because they are incapable of tying their shoelaces. I know men and women with more degrees than you can count who support preposterous socialist/Communist political social and economic theories, which have never worked and will never work. Education is important but does not make you smart, and professors who have never worked in the private sector should not be allowed to teach. I always recall the real success stories in college, most often, the A students are failures in life while the C students are the real movers and shakers. There is an old saying "If you can't make it in the private sector, teach or work for government" – nothing could be truer.

My father died. This was not only a personal disaster, but a business one as well. Unacquainted with American death duties, my father had retained the bulk of Widder stock. Widder was the sole surviving company into which we had merged all our other firms. The IRS visited me and advised that they wanted $140,000 in taxes. Why you would be forced to pay taxes on earned income on which you had already been taxed with an illegal graduated income tax, a Social Security tax, and a state income tax completely escapes my understanding. Nevertheless the case was made, I was stuck. My mother inherited the cash and the house I inherited the business. Eventually I prevailed on the IRS, pointing out that if I had to liquidate Widder 60 people would be put out of work, they agreed to a ten-year payout plan at 2% over prime. Then some time later America elected a true moron, Jimmy Carter, under whose awful leadership interest rates rose to 20+%. I lacked the funds to pay down the principal, and Uncle Sam collected well over $300,000 from me in estate taxes. It prevented R & D, it stymied growth, and it eventually destroyed my business, allowed foreign competitors to dominate my previous market, un-employed sixty Americans, all for the greed of socialists whose interest was in the re-distribution of my assets to worthless-loafer political constituents of my elected representatives. A large percentage of my American-made business went to foreign interests, so everyone lost; I lost, my employees lost, the country lost.

If you think that I am bitter about government, you have no idea. I find civil servants uncivil, stupid, lazy, and in most cases ignorant. In the late '70s my company had some major U.S. Navy contracts. From one day to the next they began purchasing our German competitor's product. Now our product not only had a patented feature, which the German product did not have, but had been tested by the Navy in their TPR (Tool Performance Report) program and come out with the highest praise. Nevertheless, the Navy began purchasing our foreign competitor's product, at a higher price. The Department of the Navy informed us that, according to new NATO directives, they would be purchasing much of their equipment from NATO member states, and that by their arrangement we could also sell to all NATO navies. Stupid us, we tried. The French, Dutch, and Belgian naval purchase offices did not let us in their office buildings, while the Germans were polite but informed us that if a similar product were made in Germany they were required by law to purchase it.

In the meantime Widder had grown to a small international; we had two plant locations in Naugatuck, CT., and San Leandro, CA., offices and a warehouse in the English Midlands, Randburg, South Africa, and a subsidiary, Panox Trading, in Zurich, Switzerland.

I came to an astounding conclusion at the end of 1984. My name was on the loan papers, my capital was at risk, Widder had a substantial payroll, and several employees made more than I did. When I analyzed our corporate annual report, together with my accountant, Larry Dix, we concluded that my employees, the banks, and the government were earning the lion's share of corporate profits, certainly more than I made. The estate taxes from my father's estate had finally been paid off, but it had crippled the business. If I liquidated the business I could make more sitting on my duff than working 15 hours a day, about 90 hours a week. In 1986, with much regret, I liquidated Widder. In the process of liquidation I had an astounding lesson in the state of national moral decay.

American governance, that had such a great start, has turned into a wasteful empire whose only interests lie in re-election and continuation of employment of an ever-increasing mélange of hapless mandarins. They have little interest in our nation, business, or individual citizens, whom they generally treat with contempt. When I hear the arrogance with which people like Schumer (S., NY) and Clinton (S., NY) – that is right; they are not Democrats, they are socialists – respond to questions from the – also socialist – media I get livid. When I have to deal with some federal agency and I am run around, lied to, sidetracked, misinformed, stonewalled, and my time wasted I am angry. No wonder most federal offices post signs saying that you cannot carry a gun on their premises; they have good reason to be afraid.

In 1986, when I was regretfully forced to liquidate Widder Corp., I wanted to apologize to all my fine employees for having failed them. There was simply no option left. It was either liquidate the company and respectably pay my debts, or go bankrupt and screw my suppliers; something I could not honorably do.

In auctioning off our machine tools, I was able to get about 60 cents on the dollar of value; it was so heartbreaking that I could not stay in the plant during the auction – a full 20% of our machine tools had been built and designed by us for special applications.

As I found out, much to my surprise, not everyone is as honest as I am. When I closed my doors I had about $580,000 in open accounts due to Widder. Much of this was from customers with whom I had done business for over 30 years. I was able to collect about $280,000 of that money; the balance of my customers told me, "Sue us," or worse. I remember one in New Rochelle, NY; I had been selling the company run by the father for 33 years; the son who had taken over the business simply said "explicative-deleted you!" I was so angered that I went to his store, opened his cash register, took out the money, all $537 of it, gave him a receipt and walked out.

I learned a great deal about the character of this new age, the latter half of the 20th century. All of it has become worse. When I started in business we had virtually no contracts, it was the shake of a hand and a man's word, which was more binding than any contract. Today, with our immoral and unethical society, contracts and patents have become worthless. The new prime business directive is, screw him first before he gets you! Sad!

Patents are of particular interest for a number of reasons. Independent inventors, not teams or corporations, developed most patents. All patents are individual efforts. My first patent cost about $500: after that I wrote my own for a time, and just paid the filing fee of $300. The law-shark business, however, could not abide that the process allowed individuals patent-filing ability without hiring a lawyer. Eventually the process of filing patent applications was so complicated, legalesed, convoluted and expensed by the Patent Office that you were required to hire a patent attorney. The cost was driven form $300 in 1977 to well over $3,000 in 1990, a ten-fold increase in just 13 years, which benefited no one except lawyers and government. That, however, is not the worst part. I have completely stopped patent applications; they are factually worthless under current law and jurisprudence. If you produce a good idea, (delayed windshield wipers for cars, for example) large corporations will simply violate your patent at will, you can then sue them. It took the aforementioned idea's inventor 14 years to collect. Most don't have the funds for such expensive legal actions, and reap nothing from their effort.

The worst part in present filing is Patent Office employees, most of whom lack the ability, intelligence, or education even to understand most of what they review. Equally bad, however, has been the internationalization of the process. In an invention that I made at the request of a German firm, they requested preliminary drawings before going ahead with the patent process. I sent them the drawings and applied. They, however, applied in Germany, whose government is quicker, and were granted a preliminary application pre-dating mine. Litigation would have cost more than the value of the patent, because under German law you have to sue in a German court.

After I had liquidated Widder, I began a consulting business. I hired one of my best employees at the time of dissolution, Dora Miller, who worked for me for a number of years. Without Dora I could not have started the business; it is a fact that every executive needs an organized intelligent secretary, and Dora was certainly that. Here is some good advice; the CEO's secretary has more power and access in a corporation than the VP, and that is a fact. I ran Widder for 35 years and had a number of secretaries; I always counted on them more than I did anyone else. I was never disappointed by any of my female employees, but can't say the same for the men. I can also say that if you trust people, are fair, and challenge them, most of them will do their very best.

Eventually I moved back to New Hampshire, and did some consulting, plant liquidations, and expert-witness work. In 1995 I wrote my first non-technical book, *Opinions of an Immigrant*. It was never published, and then came *The Satori and the New Mandarins,* published in 1997, and *July 4th 2016: The Last Independence Day* in 2000, *Published Articles and Essays 1992-2003*, in 2003, and *Our Political Systems* in 2004.

CURRICULUM VITA

2004

DR. ADRIAN H. KRIEG, CFMGE

Personal

Born in St. Gallen, Switzerland in 1938

Is a dual national, fluent in German and English.

Resides in Bradenton, FL, USA

Education:

HS Pembroke (Suncook, NH) class valedictorian.

Elmhurst College, University of Mexico (San Miguel de Allende campus), various courses at CCU.

SME (Society of Manufacturing Engineers) certified Manufacturing Eng. (CfMgE)

U.S. Army Message center, bi-lingual communications, served with nuclear artillery in Germany, top-secret clearance.

World University Cultural doctorate in Manufacturing Science.

Special:

AWS (American Welding Society) Speakers Bureau 1985-98. SME Speakers Bureau 1979-86, Silver Certificate. Vice Chair AWS/

ANSI Committee on fumes and gases & ventilation, 1982 until disbanded. Wrote ANSI-OSHA standard for welding safety. Recipient of the AWS NATTCO award for best welding product (invention) of 1983. SME Science in Engineering Award. AWS, SME, ASM, consultant's directory. Thomas award for best advertisement, 1983. Académie Européenne des Sciences, des Arts et des lettres, 1989. Eli Whitney Entrepreneur of the Year recognition award. Rolex Award recognition, 1987. CT/RI District Export Council first appointed by Sec. of Commerce Malcolm Baldridge (Reagan) and then by every Sec. of Commerce ending with Ron Brown (Clinton) resigned under R. Brown due to politicization of DEC. Elected to Fall Mountain Regional School Board, NH.

Past memberships:

American Nuclear Society (ANS) Ret. 1997
American Welding Society (AWS) Ret. 1999
American Society for Metals (ASM) Ret. 1998
Society of Manufacturing Engineers (SME)
Certified life
Society of Pipe Engineers and Designers (SPED)
Ret. 1997
Nuclear Suppliers Association (NSA) Ret. 1997
American Arbitration Society (AAS) Ret. 1987
World Affairs Council Ret. 1990
Ct/RI World Trade Association Ret. 1993
Other memberships of retirement are:
World Affairs Council, N.Y.
Academia of Science.
U.S. Department of Commerce:

Ct/RI District Export Council, Co-Chair, Strike Force for Fair Trade, legislative committee, finance committee. Service in the CT/RI DEC exceeds ten years. (Advisor to US Dept. of Commerce)

Published:

Technical books:

Plate Bending Machines;Fabricating Machinery Association 1974

The Problems with Welding Fumes and how to Solve them. Widder Corp. 1976

Marketing your Products through distribution Channels. Self-Pub. 1981

Distributor Marketing Widder Corp. 1970

Structural Steel Cutting Section of— *American Machinist* Reference Book 1971

Plate Section Data Book FMA 1980

Articles:

Published in: New Equipment Digest, The Welding Journal, Welding Design and Fabrication, IMPO, The Welding Engineer, Manufacturing Engineer, Metal Building Review, Contractors Electrical Equipment, The Tool and Manufacturing Engineer, Industrial Safety, The Fabricator, Grinding and Finishing, Maintenance Engineer, Current Concerns, The Idaho Observer, The Nationalist Times, and many others.

Interviews:

Dr. Krieg has been the guest on over 250 radio and TV shows and has been interviewed by: The Wall Street Journal, The Hartford Courant, The Waterbury Republican, The Nationalist Times and many others.

Other published works:

(20th century history)

The Satori and the New Mandarins

Hallberg Publishing 1997

July 4th 2016: the Last Independence Day

Hallberg Publishing 2000

Published Articles and Essays '92-'03

a2zPublications.com 2003

Our Political Systems

Elderberry Press 2004

Dr. Krieg is a contributing writer of The Nationalist Times, and is a frequent contribution columnist to: The Edgefield Journal, Media Bypass, The Nationalist Times, The Oregon Observer, *Schweizerzeit* (Switz.), Current Concerns (Switz.), The Free American, Culture Wars, The Portman Papers (UK), Taxing Times, The Jubilee, The Idaho Observer, and others.

U.S. Patents:

4,094,612	Tool Mounting Apparatus.
4,064,771	Automatic Torque Controller for Air Impact Wrenches.
3,845,655	Press Brake Loading and Unloading Device.
3,788,192	Metal Forming Tool.
3,787,970	Hydraulic Weld Preparation Beveling Tool.
4,192,487	Apparatus for Oxy-Fuel Cutting of Plate Steel.
4,216,945	Apparatus for the Automatic Cutting of Pipe.
4,143,862	Orbital pipe cutting robot.
4,317,280	Power Feed Apparatus for Remote Control of Power Tools.

4,218,459	Portable Power Metal Nibbling Tool.
4,294,013	Hacksaw Blade Quick Holding Device.
4,252,481	Cutting Tool for Grinder on Aluminum.
4,078,689	Jar Top Removal Device.
4,340,804	Welding Fume Extraction Nozzle.
4,788,027	Nuclear BWR Remote Controlled Underwater Stellite Ball Removal Device.
4,757,977	Universal Chain Guide for Orbital Pipe Cutters.
4,747,955	Nuclear BWR Remote Controlled Velocity Limiter Shear.
4,842,139	Dangerous Chemical Cylinder Containment Vessel.
4,873,902	Portable Power RR Rail Cold Saw.
5,055,236	Nuclear BWR Control Rod Reduction System.

Special Listings:

NASA/LBJ Space Ctr.	Advanced Projects Design Capability.
Naval Underwater Sea Systems Command Designer	(USN).
Ontario Hydro	Special designs.
British Nuclear Fuels (BFNL)	Robotic designs.
PP&L	Special designs, turbine shaft repairs.
Argone (Canada) Nat. Labs.	Special designer.
Lawrence Livermore Labs.	Special designer.
General Atomics	Special designer and builder.
Torrey Pines	Special Designer.
Brookhaven National Labs	Designer.
Alamogordo	Designer.
US Navy	Multiple Yards.

Commercial Contracts:

Combustion Engineering

Westinghouse R & D

Westinghouse, Hanford

Westinghouse Advanced Engineering

Proto Power Bisco Nuclear

Fairey Engineering (UK)

Union Carbide West Valley

Exxon Shell.

GAPCO TMI.

Torrey Pines.

Chem Nuclear.

Waste Chem.

NES.

Diametics

Bechtel.

General Atomics.

Nuclear.

Machine Tools designed but not patented:

- Hydraulic Lay Shaft Drill for Electric Generating Turbines
  (For Ontario Hydro.)
- Hydraulic 3-axis bore Plug and Flange Milling Machine
  (For PP&L.)
- BWR Nuclear Fuel Channel Cutting Device
  (numerous firms.)
- Neutron Window Cutter.

For Nuclear Fuel Pool work:

- Fuel Pool Light Stanchion Cutter.
- Remote Re-racking Sawing System.
- Fuel Pool Rack Cutter.
- Remote Profile Cutter.
- RR Rail cross drilling machine.
- Remote Light Stanchion Cutters.
- RR Rail Saw (Portable.)
- BWR Control Rod Crusher
  (For General Atomics.)

BWR Velocity Limiter Shear.

MSPT Rotor Bore Plug Drills.

BWR Stellite Ball Reducer.

Lay Shaft Drills.

BWR Poison Rod Reducer.

Robotic Assemblies.

Robotic Manipulation Arm
For BNFL (UK.)

Licensed Products:

Oxy-Fuel Pipe Cutters	Mathey.
Remote controlled power tools	High Precision Inc.
Welding Fume Nozzles	Fab-Tech Corp.
Saw Blades	Rule Industries.
Saw Blade Locking Device	High Precision Inc.
Remote Controlled Cylinder Actuator	United Gas Supply.
Portable Power Hacksaws	High Precision Inc.
Widdervac Fume Eliminators	Fab-Tech Corp.
Nibblers	Cal Tool Corp.

Trademarks licensed:

Widdervac Æ

Widder Æ

Versiflame Æ

Kriegblades Æ

Versiflame O_2 Æ

Business Experience:

Past CEO of: Widder Corp, Rovic Manufacturing Inc., Nugget Realty Corp., A. Krieg Consulting Inc., Consumable Trading Inc., Panox Trading Ltd. (Switzerland), Widder UK Ltd. (UK), Widder RSA Ltd. (RSA). Secretary of Victor J. Krieg Inc.

Was or is on the board of directors of: Widder Corp, Rovic Manufacturing Co., Nugget Realty Corp., Mamaroneck Depot Plaza Corp., Pannox Trading Corp. Colonial Bankcorp. Ct., World Trade Assoc., Fall Mountain Regional School Board, AWS Fume Committee, AWS Z-40-1 Safety committee, Vice Chairman of SME Chapter 216, Paul Riley Ltd. (UK), Permabond Europe Ltd (UK), Ct/RI District Export Council.

Web Sites:

www.kriegbooks.com &
www.a2zPublications.com

THE BEGINNING

ACT I

The tree of liberty must be refreshed from time to time with the blood of patriots and tyrants. It is its natural manure.

–Thomas Jefferson
Letter to W. S. Smith, 1787

Speech:
Apprehension seems to exist among the people of the Southern States that by the accention of a Republican administration their property and their peace and personal security are endangered. There has never been any reasonable cause for such apprehension. Indeed, the most ample evidence to the contrary has all the while existed and been open to their inspection. It is found in nearly all the published speeches of him who addresses you....

–Abraham Lincoln
First Inaugural Address,*March 4th. 1861.*

Illuminism

THE proof of Illuminism was the publication by the Bavarian government in 1785 of Jakob Lanz's secret documents after lighting killed him.* Lanz was an Illuminist with close ties to Adam Weisshaupt (Illuminist name, Spartacus) whose documents in 1785 confirmed the plan of the Illuminati to take over all possible Masonic and Rosicrucian Lodges, in Germany, France and Italy, and thereby develop the power to manipulate governments.

The conspiracy to rule over ones fellow men, contrary to present opinion, is not a new thing. Since the dawn of recorded history, when man became able to think and speak, groups of men have conspired to lord it over others of their species. I see little point in exhuming the historic tyrannies, which resulted from such acts in Babylon, Athens, or Rome. I am, however, convinced that our present state of affairs is directly linked to one evil organization, the Illuminati. This historically secret organization remains with us today, much spoken of in various direct and indirect secret and public associations. Unfortunately, the greatest mass of information on this group comes from poor research, and often from people who performed their research based on a predetermined social, religious, or political goal. I have but one goal, to warn the citizens of nations with republican governance exactly what are this New World Order's plans for you and your children.

The quotation at the beginning of this chapter was made in 1787; the reasonably assumed time of the formation of the Illuminati was 1776. Not long before that time, in 1773, Pope Clement XIV issued a Papal Bull in suppression of the Society of Jesus, more commonly known as the Jesuits. In view of the fact that Jesuits had been outlawed in numerous nations, including Switzerland, France, and Portugal, for their political and revolutionary acts, this was not altogether surprising. Readers should be aware that the Jesuits are a military order that's Commander General is often referred to as the "Black Pope." Jesuits have historically been involved in more than just one insurrection, or revolution, and are presently one of the

Roman Catholic orders that concern themselves with "liberation theology," the communization of Roman Catholicism. Jesuits have historically often been at cross-purposes with the Roman church as well as the Papacy. This remains true today: John XXIII often spoke out against this nefarious politicization of the Roman Catholic Church and its plans by the Jesuit order.

The Illuminati was the brainchild of an evil, brilliant, devious Bavarian professor by the name of Adam Weisshaupt, a native of Ingolstadt. Jesuits educated him from childhood until his mid-teens. Showing good aptitude, he was allowed to go to Gymnasium, which remains through today in the German-speaking world a precursor to university acceptance – something akin to prep school, except that acceptance is based solely on academic performance. At the time of the Papal order, Weisshaupt was already a professor at the university of Ingolstadt. This papal order proved to be the lucky charm for Weisshaupt, because a Jesuit had held the canon law chair at the university for almost one hundred years, and now had to be replaced by a non-Jesuit. Weisshaupt was given the chair as the head of the canon law department at the university. This was at that time not only a seat of considerable importance, but it also provided Weisshaupt a certain social position, which he would exploit to the best of his ability. Canon law was in many respects of greater importance than civil law in the 17th century.

Between 1773 and 1776 for a time of three years Weisshaupt first became a Rosicrucian – this was a very popular fraternity in the 1700s – and then a Mason, as were most American, English, German, and French gentry. Indeed many noblemen also had joined Masonic lodges. He joined a lodge in Muenchen in 1777. Weisshaupt, however, was uninterested in the equality, (meeting on the level) of the Masons, nor did he think much of the Rosicrucian's. What he wanted were two things; firstly, an education in organizational structure of a secret organization, and secondly access to membership lists and Lodge lists of the Masonic as well as the Rosicrucian orders. It is important that the reader understand that the American, Scottish, Irish and English lodges were never penetrated by the Illuminati, as were those of the Continent, and that not all those lodges were penetrated. Before in 1773 he had started a secret sect called the Order of Pervction or (perfectibility) but it failed.

Weisshaupt then began to experiment with some organizations of his own which eventually became the Illuminati. Beginning in 1779 this new organization, which was attracting both Protestant as well as Catholic lodges, due to the inclusion of some Protestant noblemen, began to grow rapidly: in 1779 he already had 54 members who succeeded in infiltrating many Masonic lodges, as well as enrolling scores of the intelligencia and nobles, by the end of that year the Illuminati had well over 800 adherents in Germany. In 1780 Weisshaupt sent the Marquis de Constanzo one of his Masonic converts to Northern Germany where he met with considerable success. Then he succeeded in converting Jonann J. C. Bode a very prominent Mason Grand Master to his cause, thereafter conversion of lodges became very common in Germany, France and Italy. By this time the Illuminati had over 2000 members in Germany, most of who were prominent and important people. Gradually lodge after lodge fell to the Illuminati. They had not only signed on much of the German nobility, but also almost the entire German and French "Enlightenment". The internal war between Illuminism and the Masonic lodges of strict observance reached a crescendo, and the entire Illuminati house of cards began to fall in the mid- 1780s. This, however, was not before the organization was successful in expanding into France, and accomplishing much the same there. So we see that at the outset of the French Revolution the vehicle for setting the entire thing in motion was well in place.

Weisshaupt, who had a Roman Catholic background, appreciated the value to that church of individual confession, and thought to find a way in which he could exploit this act in conjunction with what he had learned from the Rosicrucian's, and the Masons. His stroke of genius was the perversion of the initiation rights of the Masonic orders, while incorporating the misrepresented Roman Catholic confession into the ceremony. What Weisshaupt produced was a wicked initiation ceremony, which could thereafter be used by the select of the order to blackmail members into obeying orders of the leadership. The Yale secret fraternity most commonly referred to as Bones[10] today still uses this exact same ceremony.

The Illuminati initiation ceremony takes place in a darkened chamber without windows. Aside from a number of arcane and scary objects, the center of the chamber contains an open coffin, on a mantle close by are the skeleton remains of at least three humans. On the wall above the skeletal remains is a large pentagram, not exactly a Christian symbol. The initiate is led blindfolded into the chamber, whose door number is 322, and stripped of all clothing, the blindfold is removed and a red ribbon tied about his genitals. Bones (The Order) has the identical initiation ceremonies, which takes place at their New Haven Connecticut building called the tombs. Furthermore in both The Order as well as Illuminism uninitiated are called Vandals and upon attaining membership are given a new name, in the case of Weisshaupt it was Spartacus, his adjutant Knigge was Philo. Both The Order as well as Illuminists uses a different calendar by adding 322 years to the standard calendar.

Why use a different name and different calendar? It's really quite simple, if anyone happens to overhear a discussion between any two or more members they will be unable to understand the names or dates spoken of.

In the initiation he is laid into the coffin and the room is totally darkened. For many hours he is asked to tell his interviewers his most intimate secrets, all matters relating to his sexual experiences, any perversions ever witnessed. In the end the masters in most cases have more than enough information to blackmail the new member. The only thing that has changed over the years is that today the record is kept by electronic means, where in the past a secretary wrote it down.

First Success; the French Revolution

Communists and their cohorts of the political left have succeeded in glorifying the French revolution. They have done this as admirably as Germans of the 21st century have demonized the political right. In April of 2001 the German Bundestag is seriously debating the outlawing of all the politically right parties as they planned to seize them, along with the confiscation of their assets. Interestingly, no action against the left is contemplated, not so strange when you consider that the present German government is a coalition of the Communist, socialist, environmental and homosexual parties. Making an allowance for, however, that every violent act against the German government and people has been from the left, Red Army Faction, Bader Meinhoff Gang, etc., one does find it bizarre.

Let me be specific; in the latter half of the 20th century Communists, socialists, and the left succeeded in changing realistic political understanding. They did this of necessity, in order to distance themselves from the (socialist) Nazi movement. Liberalism, per example, was the economics of von Mises, Hayek, and the Austrian school of economics. Liberalism was stolen by the left as the title by which they would henceforth be identified. They then separated themselves from the Nazi movement, calling it a right-wing movement, while maintaining that Communism represented reformation from the left. This is an outright lie. The Nazi party was called *Die Nazional-sozialistische Deutsche Arbeiter Partei*, translated The National Socialist German Workers' party. The Soviet Russian Communist country was called the Union of Soviet Socialist Republics. The fact is that both the Nazi as well as the Soviet political movement was socialist from the ground up, and both were from the political left. The war between Russia and Germany was nothing but a disagreement between two branches of the socialist tree. Remember the treaty between Hitler and Stalin and their joint rape of Poland, the socialist atheists were dividing up the Catholic Poland between themselves. The war between these factions of the left has raged unceasingly from 1910 to today. The political right was never once involved in these disputes.

It is by these means that the present confusion of the political arena in regards to the French revolution has come to pass. The educational institutions of all Western nations and particularly the so-called "intelegencia," which are in fact non-intellectuals, have been in the hands of Communists and socialists since the 1920s. Through their actions of revising the historic reality, rewriting the history of the French Revolution, as it were, they have succeeded in glorifying one of man's vilest acts. Furthermore, they have attempted to link the French and American revolutions for the sole purpose of introducing the Communist concepts of Adam Weisshaupt, as plagiarized by Karl Marx, into 20th and 21st century mainstream thought. The masters of the Illuminati are no dummies; their efforts have in large part been remarkably successful. Their success is in no small part due to the changes they have succeeded in implementing in our social and economic lives, and the divisive manner in which they have structured the *Kulturkrieg* that has been raging for the last fifty years.

The difference between the French and American revolutions could not be greater if they had taken place in alternate universes. The French Revolution of 1789 was without question one of history's greatest debacles. The American Revolution, from the issuance of the Declaration of Independence to its culmination with the English monarch withdrawing from the field, took eleven years, from 1776 to 1787. The American Revolution was a military action between the armies of Britain and those of the Colonies. It was based on principle and had a basic underlying moral and ethical attitude. In France, the Revolution traveled the road from the decapitation of the King and the slaughter of hundreds of thousands to the crowning of a new emperor in eleven years, 1793-1804. There was no moral basis, there were no ethics, and the entire exercise was based on the elimination of any Frenchman who was educated, owned property, was of noble birth, or in some way annoyed the organizers of the slaughter. Consideration of the fact that France just at that time had produced such luminaries as Voltaire, Rousseau, Diderot, and Montesquieu makes these actions all the more appalling.

To understand clearly the structured organization of the French revolution it is necessary to return to the Illuminati and Adam Weishaupt. As previously stated, Marx copied his ten Communist rules from Weisshaupt. If we now look at those rules, the principle, which Communists and those of the political left have used as their modus operandi, will become clear.

- Weisshaupt's Illuminist principles to bring about the new state: (N.W.O.)
- Abolition of property ownership.
- Progressive taxation.
- Abolition of inheritance.
- Confiscation of property of all opposition members.
- Centralization of all banking.
- Centralization and control of all communications.
- Communization of farming and production of goods.
- Equalization of labor.
- Redistribution by force of the population.
- Centralized state education of all children.

These ten points appeared publicly for the first time in 1848 as *Manifest Der Komunistischen Partei* (Manifesto of the Communist Party) published in February 1848 in London, England, and dedicated to: *Proletariaer aller Laender Vereinigt Euch*; Workers of the World Unite. While the wording may be slightly altered there can be no doubt as to the origin of Marx's Manifesto as the original Illuminist document that he plagiarized.

- Consider now the aforementioned Illuminati principles in the context of the twenty-first century:
- Implementation through the implantation of envi-

ronmental law, the creation of national parks, the creation of national monuments.

- The 1913 illegally (not ratified by states) enacted FRS and IRS
- Ridiculously high death duties (estate taxes)
- Property confiscation by eminent domain, national parks, endangered species, environmental legislation, national monuments, and historic property.
- The 1913 enacted FRS (Federal Reservc System), an illegally instituted private banking monopoly.
- CBS, ABC, NBC, CNN, PBS, BBC, DW, CBC, and insider control of all mainstream media.
- The destruction of small farms by instituting laws and regulations favoring large farming corporations and through farm subsidies.
- Glass Ceiling, Equal Pay, Affirmative Action, Set-Asides, and Union Preference on government jobs.
- Uncontrolled immigration, multiculturalism.
- Public schools, Goals 2000, Outcome Based Education, Team, and schools controlled by teachers' labor unions.

The most ominous of all being the 1913-enacted XVIIth. Amendment, which changed America from a Constitutional Republic to a Democracy, by having Senators directly elected by the people instead of the legislative chambers of the several states. This altered the entire functioning of government, because senators were no longer insulated from public opinion, and thus now vote not on principle but on elect ability.

The most astounding fact of the original Communist manifesto is that it is printed in old German script, and the printer, Burghard in Liverpool, would have had to import the typeset especially from Germany. Since Marx was a German as was Weisshaupt and since the original Illuminist documents were all written in German one begins to understand this strange stream of events. We can now return to these positions, which without doubt were the underlying principles of all leftist revolutions and wars of the 20th century, whenever the need for clarification of cause becomes apparent. It is my contention that every war in the 20th century was an act brought to fruition by the Illuminati in order to advance their cause. To clarify my position on 20th century wars; all of them, every last one, were started and carried to fruition by the political left and, behind the scenes, organized and controlled by the Satori. These actions in opposition to established governance have caused the death of well over one billion human beings in just one century. This senseless slaughter is planned not only to continue but also to accelerate dramatically in the 21st century, and thus achieve one of the widely published goals of the N.W.O. – world population reduction to below one billion. Current organizations who have publicly postulated this are: The Club of Rome (Paris, France) The United Nations, (NY, NY) The Royal Institute For International Affairs (London, England) The Tavistock Institute, (UK) The Runnymede Trust, (UK), The Roundtable (UK) The Council on Foreign Relations, (NY, NY) The Trilateral Commission (NY, NY) and numerous documents by the Bilderbergers and various controlled environmental groups. Do not suffer the delusion that war is the only instrument of the Satori; no; indeed, all the four horsemen of the Apocalypse are all members of this fraternity.

As we now have some background into the thoughts of the left, which they so cleverly hide through their façade of lies and misinformation, we can examine their first great success. But first we must understand the planned outcome, the goal to which Satori aspire. Only by understanding what the planned outcome is are we able effectively to oppose it. Communism, and socialism, is an instrument, a tool to achieve a desired outcome. None of the widely published and touted political, religious, social, or economic theories, and postulations has anything to do with the planned outcome. They are only a means to an end. Tools, that is all. Weisshaupt and his Illuminist followers developed these outcome goals in the 18th. and 19th. centuries.

- The Goals of the New World Order
- The elimination of nation states.
- Centralized world monetary issuance and policy.
- The elimination of private property.
- Separation of the world into geographic regions managed by administrators.
- Total and absolute multi-culturalism through the elimination of ethnicity.
- The elimination of private ownership of any weapons.
- All land to be owned by the State and managed by multi-national corporations and the UN.
- The elimination of elections for individual candidates in favor of having people vote for a political party which then appoints officials.
- The administration of all law and governance by appointed officials.

- Reduction of world population to below one billion by any means including war, pestilence, disease, starvation, and including man-made diseases, (AIDS, Ebola,) the introduction of live-stock disease, etc.
- Destruction of organized Christianity and Islam. (World Council of Churches, Reformed Judaism)

Again let us examine the afore-mentioned in context of the 21st century:

- The EC, NAFTA, FTAA, GAT, WTO.
- The Euro and the Dollar
- Environmental action, national parks, national monuments, rivers projects
- Brussels and the planned FTAA HQ in San Antonio
- Uncontrolled immigration
- Over 2600 [anti]-gun laws in USA, gun confiscation in Australia, draconian gun laws in Britain, Germany and Canada.
- Government takeover of large tracts of land in all nations, often with very poor compensation to the landowner.
- The gradual changes from voting for an individual to voting for a political party, which then appoints an agent of the party.

- Ebola, AIDS, recent TB outbreaks in England, hoof and mouth disease, basically man-made and man-induced diseases.
- The elimination of principles of faith, the inclusion of false dogma, the acceptance of perversion, the alterations of religious service, the continuous up-dating of all religious practice.

Anyone who has read this far and does not understand that, beginning with the French revolution and continuing on into the 21st century, all this is the truth, and has been taking place at an exponential rate in the last fifty years, should stop reading.

The, by far, greatest difference between the French Revolution and the American was that the American Revolution had a clearly defined and publicly known moral outcome goal. The French Revolution, on the other hand, had goals that were hidden from the populace, void of any moral or ethical tenet, that then brought the great excesses of self-driving horror, which lasted eleven years. The only other similar occurrences were the 20th-century Chinese Cultural Revolution and the Soviet empire's persecution of the Russian Orthodox Church, that are again leftist acts. The intellectual fathers of the French Revolution were Illuminist Rousseau, while the social and religious agitator was the Marquis de Sade. It has been said that the failure of the French Revolution is anchored in its lack of an outcome goal plan. I disagree with that theory, and am of the opinion that the plan was well known by its organizers. It was to create total chaos and, at the point of no return, to take over the reins of power and establish the first Illuminist state. As happens so often in history, they did not consider all possibilities – the little Corsican upsetting their plan.

Let me make clear a fact of history. No citizen of any entity can be said to enjoy freedom and liberty that cannot share in the day-to-day act of legislation within that society. Further, no person can be said to be secure in his property and the laws that govern unless those laws are understood and respected by him, and he has the ability through force of arms to protect his rights. (Britain, Australia, and soon Canada have outlawed private ownership of firearms.) One of the ways by which this evil cabal has gotten its way, is through the creation of law in such volume and of such complexity as to make law unintelligible. The application thereof is thus used as a means of selectively enforcing the created norms of that society upon those with whom it disagrees. (Clinton's use of the IRS against all political opponents.) This was first used in the French revolution and has remained one of the tenets right through today. Consider that Jimmy Carter the American president in his term in office instituted 86,000 pages of new regulations, that under the Clinton administration new IRS (U. S. Income Tax)[11] legislation that was supposed to simplify the statute in fact added 850 more pages to a law already consisting of over 2 million words. In Britain the Labor government of Tony Blair has acquiesced to the huge expansion of English common law through the incorporation of EC (Napoleonic Code) statutes. In any despotic government, such as the one planned by the Satori, where the power is to be vested in a small group of multi-millionaires, who retain for themselves the sole right of legislative action, only they will enjoy liberty and freedom. All others become serfs, and that is the exact plan.

Let me briefly explain another matter of the overall plan, which also made its first active appearance in the French Revolution. It began with the Marquis de Sade's book *Justine*. Bear in mind that de Sade was an Illuminist. It was the observation of the Illuminists that a moral and ethical society was very difficult to corrupt. In fact, it ís downright impossible. For several years they tried to find a solution to their dilemma. The plan that they envisioned, to create chaos, and through it attain governance over all of society, could not be implemented until a means could be found to destroy the religious, moral and ethical teachings that are the anchors of society. In other words they had to find a means of destroying the Roman Catholic Church. It was de Sade who provided the means to an end. Lust, sex and perversion were to be the vehicles used to undermine society's structure. Now I want to say that anyone who cannot apply this to our present circumstances must be brain-dead. Pornography is now one of the world's major industries; in fact, pornography just in America is a larger business by volume of sales than that of General Motors.

Sexual liberation became the by-word of the *Kulturkrieg*. The '60s proved to be the time that hastened it in this century. In America a publication called *Playboy* was the trumpeter of sexual liberation. Every month Hugh Hefner, the publisher and editor, or one of his cohorts, wrote a long column espousing his perverted philosophy, not much different from that of de Sade a hundred years earlier. In his "Playboy Advisor," another column, he perpetually admonished his readers to new and greater acts of non-conformity. In the beginning the effects of these icons on the perversion of society were not immediately obvious. In time, however, the issue expanded rapidly, with such publications in this century as *Hustler*, published by Larry Flint. This is the man who in the '90s defended Clinton's actions and was provided with information further debasing society, which he published. In America our Supreme Court has repeatedly found the right to sodomy, pornography, infanticide and pedophilia in the Constitution, an act that has surely made its authors turn in their graves, and supporting the contention that Illuminism has permeated the court since the 1850s.

What the Illuminati had struck upon was a very important fact of human existence. This law, and it can well be called that, is: man can serve but one master. By replacing God, morality, and ethics, with sex, innumerable people were seduced by sex, and thereby forgot God. The most immediate result was that, with God now replaced by sex, moral and ethical behavior no longer had an anchor by which society was grounded, and God was subsequently dismissed. Nine out of ten students in our public schools are unable to distinguish between right and wrong, preferring to shade all opinion in non-offensive gray. This is one of the direct results of the sexual revolution. It leads directly to one of the many-planned Satori ends: chaos, from which the New World Order is planned to be erected. It was not until the 20th century that Aldous Huxley, a renowned author and member of England's socialist Fabian society, an Illuminist organization, expressed clearly the proposition that sex could be used to implement social and political change. This change has accelerated in the last thirty years, primarily through Judicial Activism, the process by which judges illegally make law. It is a fact that the Supreme Court has for the last hundred years abrogated the separation of powers that is implicit in the American Constitution. Some of the reasoning offered by these judges is so pitiful as to make one cry.

What I have demonstrated above is a political and social outcome that is predicted in the writings of the Illuminati, and plagiarized by Karl Marx. There is a chain of events beginning, in the 18th. Century that is utterly predictable and can be found in documentation authored in the 20th. and 21st. centuries. Consider the issue of banking. The same interlocking corporations control every banking system worldwide. Every single supposedly national bank is in fact part of the same multi-national consortium and is private. The Bank of England, The European Central Bank, Crédit Suisse, and the Federal Reserve are all private. Furthermore mega-banks like BIS (The Bank of International Settlements), and the IMF (International Monetary Fund) are also private banks. Thus what you thought belonged to you, the people, or your government, does not. These banking houses have instituted a method of perpetuating and expanding their control through the custom of loaning money to governments. These interest-bearing loans must be repaid from collected taxes. In 2001 the average American, British, Canadian, or German worker slaves for from three to four months, not for taxation to benefit him or the society, but to pay the interest on loans made by their elected representatives from these banking monopolies. Thus slavery, which was universally outlawed by the end of the 19th. century has become institutionalized in the 21st., through debt instruments whose holders, the Satori or Illuminists, collect. Baron Rothschild, the head of the Bank of England, had predicted this before the War of Northern Aggression in the 1850s.

THE SECOND ACT

Socialism is a philosophy of failure,
a creed of ignorance and a gospel of envy,
its inherent virtue is the equal sharing of misery.
–Sir Winston Churchill

Address Joint session of Congress:
The world must be made save for democracy. Its peace must be planted upon the tested foundations of political liberty. We have no selfish ends to serve. We desire no conquests, no dominion. We seek to indemnities for ourselves, no material compensation for the sacrifices we shall freely make. We are but one of the champions of the rights of mankind....
–Woodrow Wilson, April 2 1917
asking for a declaration of war against Germany.

IT is an interesting side-note of history that the Russian court of the Czars conducted its business, as well as its social, func tions entirely in French. The consideration that Russia was the second great experiment of an attempted takeover of a government by foreign forces of evil should hardly be surprising, considering at least the French connection, and the previous French revolution. Moreover the Czar of that time was no Katharine the Great; in fact, he was a decidedly untalented ruler.

By the time of the Russian revolution dramatic changes had taken place in European society. The results of these changes were the industrial revolution, which had begun in England around the turn of the century. This change must not be underestimated in its impact on society. It brought with it great social upheaval, and the gradual urbanization, which was to change Western society from an agrarian-based to an industrialized urban-based one. While the rest of Europe was in the throes of this social turmoil, it was just beginning in Russia, but only in the European cities closest to the West. Greater Russia remained primarily a peasant society ruled over by landed gentry. This shift, which is still taking place in most third-world nations, can be visualized, in present circumstance by looking at places like Rio de Janeiro in Brazil or Caracas Venezuela and the devastating social effects this is having in the present. The action taking place in Russia of that time was no less dramatic. Millions of people moved from the country to the major Russian cities of St. Petersburg, Moscow and Kiev. Without housing or immediate employment they became the cannon fodder of Mr. Lenin's revolution.

Communism is both a social phenomenon as well as a political system, which advocates that all property is a communal asset. In other words, it reduces man into the realm of insects, upon which the communal aspect of Communism is actually based. In its doctrine it proposes that every member of the society must work for the state, and will then be rewarded in accordance to available assets and that persons needs. If we return to the previous chapter we will find Prof. Weisshaupt's Illuminist ideas amply demonstrated. This then by necessity bring us to the requirement to examine this proposition in the light of available evidence as to its value as a method of operating a national economy – and the more obvious use by Illuminism of Communist philosophy to bring about their desired end product. In demonstrating to a class I taught on socialism/communism I asked every student to bring in moneys they would earn the previous evening. I then added all the funds together and divided it by their number of students and paid it out. Those who got more were delighted those who got less were disgusted. This is exactly what those two systems are, in a word unfair.

Communism and socialism represent man's greatest economic and socially failed attempts in management of himself. There is in fact today not one single society that ever succeeded under this form of management. Every last case of starvation, in any society, can be demonstrated to have come out of socialist political theory. This then is the paramount reason that Illuminists utilize Communism/socialism as their prime motive force. The most pronounced examples in the latter half of the 20th century have been in Eastern Europe, the Soviet evil empire and Africa, where the Soviets can be shown to have had undue influence. As always, greed paid a great role in Africa, where Soviet agents instructed native black population that it was not fair or just for the "whites" to have the bulk of the wealth, even if they alone produced it. This was nothing less than a simple attempt at replacing Western European exploitation with Soviet exploitation.

The Republic of South Africa and Rhodesia are places with which I am more than familiar, having had a subsidiary business in South Africa from early in the '70s until the mid '80s. It is useful to understand that when white settlers came to *Kaapstadt* the only indigenous blacks in all of what today is South Africa were pigmy bushmen numbering less than 40,000, and Zulus in the central highlands. The pigmy's are now almost extinct. All the Blacks who now so uncompromisingly claim "Africa for the Blacks" are in fact immigrants who arrived after the whites to seek employment with whites, and a better standard of living working for the Boers than they had in the Congo under Belgian rule. In Rhodesia the situation was different. The indigenous black population was in the Stone Age when white settlers began immigrating over 200 years ago. The whites built up the most successful export-driven economy in Africa. Rhodesia exported thousands of tons of food every month. Today that nation, under the Communist Robert Mugabe, installed at the pleasure of British Illuminists, imports most of its food, is one of the poorest in Africa, and has established a state of total lawlessness. I was in Rhodesia in the '70s it was a true marvel; blacks had the highest standard of living on the continent. The society was almost crime-free, everyone had good food, and there were more jobs than people to take them. Today, under Communist rule imposed at the insistence of the British labor party, starvation is rampant, the society is a hotbed of crime and murder, towns and cities are filthy hovels, and most of the food available is imported.

I traveled to Southern Africa frequently; in exports it was one of our better markets. By 1978 we were exporting annually well over $250,000 to RSA from America, with another $ 50,000 from South Korea. We had secured the Sam Yang tire franchise for RSA, having worked out a deal with the RSA government to set up a totally black tire sales and distribution network in South Africa. We thereafter taught our black business partners how to sell the maximum for which we had attained annual import permits, making them very wealthy men. Regardless of what you have been told the ANC[12] was and has always been a Communist organization. The ANC secretary at that time was in fact the head of the CPSA[13]. I do not care what the media or any of the morons who claim to be experts on this topic has told you. I will tell you unequivocally that the standard of living, education, personal safety, property rights, employment, and freedom to act have all gone down-hill from the day the ANC took over, and that applies equally to blacks as well as whites

– while the situation in Rhodesia, now called Zimbabwe, is too depressing to even address. And I want you to understand I am not speaking of white values; I speak of the black population of what were once great nations. Americans, and Englishmen in particular, have some weird ideas when it comes to government; there is this ludicrous idea that the value of casting a vote in some rigged election is of greater value than eating three meals a day, or having the ability to walk down the street without being robbed or raped. That, as any Southern African black or white woman, over 70% of who have been raped in the last 10 years, will gladly tell you, is not the case. The RSA in the time of a short ten years has seen its standard of living crumble, the safety of its citizens eliminated, its exports, except for raw materials, decimated; every single citizen of the country is worse off now than they were under the previous white republican governance. I won't even go into Rhodesia, now called Zimbabwe, except to say that what Mugabe accomplished with the help of the British makes ethnic cleansing in greater Serbia look like a church picnic in comparison.

Why is Communism/socialism such an utter failure? Fortunately this is a very simple question to answer; it runs contrary to human nature. If that is the case, one must enquire as to the cause of its popularity, and why so many appear to be enthralled by it? Human nature is simply the behavior of man in always seeking the most effortless way to attain any planned goal. This is not laziness; to the contrary, it is intelligence. No human wants or desires to use any more effort than essential to achieve the goal intended. Because the Communist/socialist philosophy is centered in-group, action each member will do exactly what is required to attain the goal and no more. There is no achievable benefit to be gained by exerting additional effort.

This, then, is also the explanation of its popularity with so many people. Those who are not self-starters, those who seek only to get along, those uninterested in personal achievement, will invariably support a system that penalizes success and rewards complacency. There is one other element that must not be overlooked. Elected politicians are in every instance looking for a constituency group who will support their continuance in office. Socialism is the simplest way to develop such a constituency. Promise everything free, and they will vote for you in droves. The fact that everything promised by any politician must first be obtained, through taxation, is almost always overlooked by those who vote for it. If not overlooked, the attitude is "I'm not paying for it, I don't make enough; others are paying and I reap the benefits." Slothful and lazy or ignorant people, who hope to derive benefit from the labor of others, almost exclusively support socialism.

What simpler way to expand your individual support group than to promise them a chance at the public trough next to yourself? Thus socialists have constructed something called entitlements: a better word would be bribes for voters. Then they expanded that concept to group entitlements, whereby entire selected segments of the supporting populace get something for nothing. This was further expanded into provision of grants to communities, associations, and special interest groups. Then came support for class-action lawsuits by which industries (tobacco, per example) have been looted to the benefit of the public trough. Please refrain from the ridiculous platitudes about the health dangers of smoking; even a four-year-old could figure that one out. It is through these simple processes that our society is being forced into changes, which are in accordance with Illuminist plans. The unqualified lie of socialism rests in the precept that the government, under the auspices of your elected politician, is the provider of all these granted goods and graces. This is the trained lie that is the socialist philosophy. Everything government has, no matter what kind of government it is, comes from the people. Government does not produce, people produce; government does not make, it takes – in the form of taxes, fees, licenses, and charges made to individual citizens, and their businesses. In a true Communist state the government is the producer; this however, changes nothing, the people still *do* and provide the labor. All that is achieved is government management of the asset, and we all know how poor governments are at managing anything. Furthermore we need not go much further than the tax structures of all Western nations, and we can return again to Prof. Weisshaupt's ten points to see the graduated income tax. This totally unfair system taxes those who work more, produce better, apply themselves more studiously, and are taxed at a higher percentage rate. This is the crux of socialism, and Illuminism. The only remaining element on those who support this premise is what I call the do-gooder premise. There are those in society, usually people who came by their wealth with ease, in most cases by inheritance, or film actors, who believe that it is unjust that they have more than others and thus desire to help the unfortunate. Teddy Kennedy, Al Gore, Charlie Schumer, Dianne Feinstein, Julia Roberts, Alex Baldwin are such people. Never, ever do these do-gooders offer or give any of their personal wealth to those less fortunate; no indeed, what they want implemented by government is to give your hard-earned money impounded through confiscatory taxation to those people. Al Gore gave less than $ 400 to charity in 1998.

It has not escaped my attention that the bulk of the supporters of Marxism in western democracies are Jewish. These people are, however, not religious Jews; quite to the contrary, they are Zionists.

To begin with, it is imperative that you distinguish Judaism from Zionism as two separate and very different beliefs. While religious Jews believe in one God, and the first five books of the Bible, which they call the Torah, along with the Talmud, Zionists are in almost all cases agnostics or atheists. Zionist support of Marxism is directly traceable to the foundation of modern Communism in Russia, and the fact that the Russian Revolution was an imported foreign Zionist-lead act. Karl Marx was a Jew,[14] one of whose closest associates was Moses Hess, who is considered the father of modern Zionism.

Proof of the pudding as is said is confirmed by Readers Digest when they listed the eleven top leaders of the American Communist Party ACP. Among these were; Jacob Satchel, Gilbert Greenberg (alias John Gates), Arvo Mike Hallberg (alias Guss Hall) Irving Potiash, Philip Carl Weinberg Philip (alias P. C. Winter).

Another factor relinquished to revisionist historians is that the very Zionists who are assumed by many to be the icons of capitalist enterprise financed the entire Russian Revolution. Jacob Schiff was at the time one of the wealthiest men in the world; he owned the NY banking house of Kuhn Loeb & Co. That firm also had very close ties to the Rothschild Empire of Europe. He began his opposition to the Czar in 1904-05 by financing the Japanese in the Sino-Russian war. He did this with the sole purpose of weakening the Czar's position in Russia. It is known that about $20 million was provided to the Japan from various Zionist sources, a very large amount in 1904. These included, among others, Jacob Schiff, Kuhn Loeb & Co, the Rothschild banking houses in London, Paris, Vienna, and Frankfurt, along with another Zionist banking empire in Sweden.

Marx advocates the violent overthrow of all governments by the proletariat (workers) so as to shatter capitalism and create the utopian workers' paradise by a dictatorship of the workers. The Satori has seized on this as a way to institute turmoil and chaos sufficient to bring them to power after the assumed by them failed proletarian revolution. If we now examine present-day Russia, which is run by an amalgamation of crime syndicates together with various Marxist elements, we must conclude that perhaps they will succeed. At the time of the Revolution, Russia was a constitutional state; the Czar had in fact abdicated. Lenin then, by violent means, became the guiding leader of the revolution. Lenin was a Zionist who spoke Yiddish at home. He transformed Russia into a hellhole of unimaginable terror. At the very beginning Lenin set out the rules by which his state was to be managed, these were:

1 The State would control everything
2 The Communist party as the arbiter of all things
3 The economy would be centrally controlled
4 All property belonged to the state
5 All religion would be eliminated, especially Russian Orthodox Christianity
6 The state would be totalitarian and run by the general secretary of the Communist party, which just happened to be Lenin.

The hand of Adam Weisshaupt is more than just obvious in Lenin's rules. I am personally able to shed some insight on Lenin; when he lived in Zurich he was a deadbeat renter of an apartment of my grandfather, who threw him out onto the street for his extensive debt. Lenin flatly refused to work in any occupation to pay off his debts.

Well, so much for the workers' utopian paradise. It is a proven fact that during the entire life of the USSR no more than 5% of the population was ever allowed to vote or participate in any government function. Life expectancy, which was under the Czar the longest in the world is now 70 years later the shortest. In the foundational phase of the new state two things were required for participation, Party membership and being a Zionist. This remained the over-riding prerequisite until J. Stalin became the dictator. Now for those Zionists who disagree let me just say who the principal associates of Lenin were:

Trotsky – *real name* – Bronstein

Zinoview – *real name* – Apfelbaum

Kamenov – *real name* – Rosenfeld

Sederdov – *real name* – Aptheker

The names are self-indicting. But not only in Russia, in the entire world the principal architects of Communism were Zionists: in America, Emma Goldman, in Hungary, Bela Kun, in Germany, Rosa Luxembourg, and so on. What had taken place? The Illuminists, who in the previous century had infiltrated the Rosicrucian and Masonic orders, had now taken over Zionism.

Of considerable interest are Rosa Luxembourg and her associate Karl Liebknecht. These two people indirectly had much to do with the assertion of the Nazi party in Germany, because of their radical social and political speeches. In fact, they were so radical that the Russian Zionists did everything in their power to attempt to dispel their enthusiasm. Both were arrested by the *Freikorps*, some say under the direction of a Lieutenant first class Canaris, the liaison officer between the *Freikorps* and the KPD and GKSD of the German army, later to be made head of the Nazi *Abwehr*. I have some inside information on these matters because my half-uncle was an adjutant of Canaris; his name was von Wettstein – I keep in touch with his son in Hamburg.

Trotsky lived in Vienna, Austria before the revolution, where he had some very interesting friends. He often frequented the Café Central[15], the favorite haunt of Baron Rothschild. They enjoyed each other's company and were often seen playing chess. What would the richest man in Austria and a man of no financial means, consumed with the idea of destroying capitalism, have in common? They were both ardent Zionists.

Lenin's revolution was not Russian at all. Of the 384 original commissars, 13 were Russian, 15 Oriental, 22 American, and 300 were Zionists.

In 1917 Lenin made up a quasi-cabinet; there were 24 members, every one of them being a Zionist, all of them adopting Christianized Russian names. By 1935 the better-organized "Central Committee" remained a Zionist operation, with the exception of three men who were, however, all married to Zionist women. These three were J. Stalin, S.S. Lobow, and V.V. Ossinsky; all of the remaining 56 Central Committee members were Zionists. Also of note is the fact that an inordinately large percentage were not Russians but immigrant Zionists from all over the world, including America.

Commissars are political officers employed by the central committee of the Party, whose job it is to see that the proletariat follow the party line. They are active in both the civilian and military sectors. Every Soviet military unit had a commissar who shared command responsibility with the ranking officer, not at all different from the Gestapo used by the Nazis. They are both socialist systems, and if the leaders of socialism understand one thing, it is that in short order people hate the system, and as a consequence they must have secret police everywhere. If there is one thing military officers despise, it's a political officer interfering with their responsibility. You may have heard of the Nazi *Sonderkommandos* on the Russian front who systematically killed Jews. Actually they systematically killed Zionist commissars who were pointed out eagerly by Soviet soldiers and officers. These commissars held a life and death power over everyone; it was they who ordered, and saw to, executions, and who were responsible only to the central committee of the Party. It was the Communist commissars who murdered the entire Polish officer corps. To now understand the strong support of the Communists by the Jewish community of the West you must understand that, because of the Zionist nature of the makeup of the leadership, Jews and Zionists were virtually immune from actions by the commissars. It is therefore a reasonable conclusion that the Illuminati infiltrated the Zionist movement at the turn of the 20th century and then joined with the Communists. Bear in mind that the basic tenets of all three organizations are identical. If we now take the leap to modern Israel we can see the creation of something called a kibbutz, which is a Communist agricultural or industrial co-op.

More than that, the Soviet state was extremely pro-Zionist, to the point of making the ownership of the *Protocols of the Elders of Zion*[16] a capital offense. Under enforcement by the Zionist commissars, anti-Semitism was classed as a crime against the state and as counter-revolutionary. All accused were promptly sent to one of the camps in Siberia or executed by the commissars on the spot.

At the time of the Revolution of 1917 the American embassy in Moscow had an intelligence officer by the name of Capt. Wilson. It was Wilson who initially sent repeated reports to Washington stating that; "the entire Bolshevik Revolution was guided and run by Jews of an aggressive nature." The American ambassador to Russia at that time was David Francis – his reports stated; "The Bolshevik leaders in Russia, most of which are Jews, and 90% returned exiles and foreigners, care little for Russia or any other country but are internationalists." That, by the way, is a pretty fair explanation of Zionism. A British communiqué forwarded from London and emanating from the British legation in Moscow was more blunt; "There is now definitive evidence that Russian Bolshevism is an international movement controlled by Jews." The reason for the use of the word *Jews* is that in 1919 Zionism was not a well-known movement.

What I have been trying to do is to make you understand the very close relationship between Communism/socialism, Marxism and Zionism. There is great historic significance to this relationship in the 20th century. Virtually no historian will touch the subject, due to the inordinate power of the Zionist lobby in politics, book distribution, and the review of all printed books by a media that is almost totally controlled by the same people. Not only is it impossible to criticize any Zionist, doing so in many instances has resulted in death threats to those making them. Not only that, but I also know numerous historians who have found themselves threatened, sued in the courts without cause, and slandered through all sorts of diabolical means. In many nations it is illegal to challenge any Zionist dogma. Germany, per example, has sent scores of historians to jail simply for challenging the "six million" fictions.

Alexander Solzhensyn, in his book *The Gulag Archipelago*, lists the commanders of the Soviet concentration camps in Siberia, camps that murdered well over 35 million people during the Revolution. Aaron Solts, Yakov Rappoport, Lazar Kogan, Mstvei Berman, Genrikh Yagoda, and Nafataly Febkel, all, every one of them is a Zionist. The population of the camps was 99.8% Christians and Muslims. During the total time lapse of the 70 years that the Communists ran Russia, 900 Christian churches were destroyed, and over 66 million people were murdered.[17] This makes the much-touted Jewish Holocaust ® seem small in comparison.

You may well wonder why I would spend such an inordinate amount of text on what superficially may well be considered a side issue. The reason is that it is not a side issue at all. Zionists are a political power far beyond their numbers, who miss no opportunity to bring their leftist, socialist concepts to the forefront. Also, as noted above, there is a close relationship between Illuminism, Communism, and Zionism.

Freedom requires
Eternal vigilance

We are not only confronted by a beast of
mythical proportions

The true cause of our dilemma rests in a
society that is self- indulgent, lazy, disinterested, and materialistic.

Unless the efforts of patriots succeed in
awakening our populace to the events
planned for them freedom and liberty, economic as well as social will be relinquished
to the dustbin of history; *just as
George Orwell predicted in his book* 1984.

THE END PRODUCT

In human events, the power over a man's earnings is the power over his vote.

–Social Security Pamphlet 1936

After the first three years—that is to say, beginning in 1940—you will pay and your employer will pay, 1,5 cents for each dollar you earn, up to $ 3,000. a year. This will be the tax for three years, and then, beginning in 1943, you will pay 2 cents, and so will your employer, for every dollar you earn for the next three years. After that, you and your employer will each pay half a cent more for three year, and finally beginning in 1949, twelve years from now, you and your employer will each pay 3 cents on each dollar you earn up to $3,000. That is the most you will ever pay!

Ho Ho Ho...

IT may appear strange to write a book to demonstrate the goals of an organizational movement and reveal its plan, the plot of it all, at the beginning of the book. It, however, seems to me that the following chapters will be easier to comprehend once you understand what the movement's goals are. All of you have heard George Bush Sr. mention "The New World Order," and "New Beginning," and "A Thousand Points of Light". It will behoove all to remember that G. Bush Sr. is a member of The Order (Bones,) as was his father and grandfather and his son G.W., The Lesser, as is also John Kerry (Kohn) the Democratic Senator from Mass., who was also in the presidential race of 2004. The Order is American Illuminism, and all the three phrases above are pure Illuminist constructs. It is important historically to understand that these phrases are not the product of the 19th or 20th centuries. Napoleon Bonaparte, Benito Mussolini, Joseph Stalin, Lenin and Marx, as well as Adolph Hitler, all used the phrase New World Order. Although the origin of the phrase is somewhat obscure, I credit it to Illuminism and Adam Weisshaupt.

Present historic events differ from past history in that we cannot see what results will take place due to them. Having said that, history is a great teacher and in many ways history does repeat itself. By examining occurrences of previous centuries we can apply cause and event to our time, and predict with reasonable certainty what the outcome might be expected. I do not mean that we can accurately predict what is to take place in the future; what I mean is that general trends produce similar outcome. So it is that I have lived through two historic events and studied a third, all of which had the same goal, and all of which were supported by similar organizations.

The immediate counterpoint now brought by establishment historians, who lack the courage to report history honestly, as it actually took place, is that of "just another conspiracy kook." When you read a history book, have you ever read the details of how the conflicting sides were financed? Who paid for the armaments? Who, on both sides, made financial gains from the occurrence? Who was the beneficiary of a war? What people were involved, and benefited in the establishment of policy? Hardly, most historians persistently avoid those issues. Just per example, why in the Second World War, did the Allies strenuously avoid bombing any of the coal-to-fuel plants that allowed the Axis to continue the reduction of coal to liquid fossil fuels?

I do not intend to provide lengthy evidence of this chapter. Anyone wishing to authenticate its content can do so with ease by simply scouring UN, American State Department, and government documents from around the world. In addition, all that is really required is to listen to the movers and shakers carefully and analyze their prognostications. What I will tell you is based on over ten years of research. This book is not opinion, nor is it fiction; every statement is verifiable without difficulty. I want to state clearly that we are at the verge of repeating the actions of France, Russia and Germany as they occurred in the French, Russian and German revolutions. Each was different, but each produced a socialist dictatorship. Hayek said that he thought that socialism had finally been discredited by 1948; I think not. Socialist mentality, which has been so strongly established in the minds of almost everyone, is alive and well. In this materialistic age it has become the vogue to expect free services from the state, and that is the essence of socialism. There are two powers at work: first, the possibility of getting something for nothing, and second, the politician who provides something in exchange for constituency support.

The fact that in all cases the state obtains what it gives from the labor of the people is strenuously overlooked. These are wealth redistribution schemes, and are therefore pure socialism. In the 1930s considerable effort was made by governments in Britain, Canada, and America toward centralized national planning; exactly the same kind of planning as was then in use in Russia, Germany, Italy, and Japan. Can you remember the war we fought against those socialist states, and the ensuing cold war? Socialism in all cases has been proven to revert, sooner or later, to totalitarianism – something that is also true of democracies. America, by the way is a constitutional republic, or at least it was that. The reason for this is that all socialist governments promise their citizens services, which they are in all cases unable to provide. Then out of necessity to stay in power they establish a secret police; Gestapo in Germany, Brown shirts in Italy, commissars in Russia, and as this took place the totalitarian state was established. The purely socialist state of the last century has in fact been replaced by the "Welfare State" of the twenty-first century. It comprises a jumble of state bureaucracies that have attained a direction of their own without legislative or citizen input. The goal of this bureaucracy is totally self-centered, its only true interest being self-preservation and expansion. Thus it has developed into a system, relying on administrative coercion as a means of bureaucratic self-protection. Legislatively, in all two-party states the political machinery, i.e. the "System," fully supports the bureaucracy and *vice versa*. Thus in all republics ruled over by this "System" the elected legislative bodies have instituted laws at such fierce speed that even officers of the court are unable to follow its continuation. This then allows the bureaucratic institutions to utilize selective enforcement to terrorize the general population.

There are a number of things in common between the socialist creations of the 20th century, the EU, NAFTA, and the USSR. All of these have Illuminist roots. For 70 years the world shuddered under the Soviet "evil empire," an expansionist state that was swallowing up one country after another. It was their intended and advertised plan to spread their form of governance to every nation in the world (under their rule) whether they wanted it or not. In their terrorist implementations they resorted to war, torture, murder, assassination, extortion, deportation, and enslavement. Over 66 million of their own Russian citizens were murdered over a 70-year time frame in hopes of achieving their goal. Often it seemed that they would succeed. They failed utterly. To clarify, let me state that all the evil governments of the 20th century were socialist. These were: The Soviet **Socialist** Republics, The ***Sozialisti*** of Italy (Brown shirts,) Mussolini's National **Socialist** Party, The National **Socialist** Workers Party (Nazis), the EC[18], now called the EU[19], 15 member states, **12 of which have socialist governments**, and lastly **NAFTA, which is totally run by socialists.** These have recently been expanded to an entire group of East European national every one of which is ruled over by socialist governments. All of these share a certain commonality. [EU, NAFTA, the proposed FTAA, USSR]

All are ruled by:

1 Un-elected bureaucrats.

2 None of these party- (System-) appointed people could be removed from office.

3 Once a state is a member of the association there is no structured way to withdraw.

4 Organization rule usurps the constitutionally established member states.

5 Corruption becomes systemic, and organized from the top down.

6 A total aggressive expansionist system is used to coerce expanded membership by new states.

7 The development of a centralized secret police organization.

8 Elections are changed from voting for an individual to voting for a party, which then appoints a legislator.

9 An organization-controlled professional military.

The point we must now engage is the reason for this similarity, or why would these superficially different organizations have so much in common? In a word, there is a centrally controlled system that makes the rules, and implements the treaties and agreements, to see to the fruition of their plans.

The primary thread of similarity between all of the aforementioned associations is that all are either totally socialist or controlled by socialists. In the case of NAFTA and the planned to be implemented FTAA[20], critics will claim that the member states of NAFTA (Mexico, Canada, and America) are not socialist states. Point well taken; however, Mexico is a narco-republic totally controlled by a very small monied class, whose allegiance to the ruling class of America is absolute, Canada is a constitutional monarchy totally controlled by its bureaucracy which in turn is given direction by the Canadian Council on Foreign Relations, an affiliate of CFR, NY, both of whom are associated to RIIA[21]. The Unites States, like both other members of NAFTA, are ruled over by a controlled party System (CFR, TC, Bilderbergers)[22] in which both politically opposing sides represent, and are controlled by, the same group of manipulators (Satori) that represent the monied multi-national elites. These elites turn NAFTA and FTAA toward socialism in order to achieve revolution, which they intend to win through their control of the police and military functions of all member states. They do this in no small part through international treaties like WTO, and GATT. This entire cabal is manipulated through internationally arranged treaties (GATT, WTO, EU, NAFTA, FTAA,) whose sole purpose is economic control of individual states and state affiliation to a controlling corporate multi-national group. This group, through their secret and semi-secret organizations, (CFR, RIIA, TC, Bilderbergers, Bones, etc.) that they control, influence and direct the governments of all the states in which they are operative. Thus we have the development of the EU "Rapid Deployment Force," the participation of all member states in NATO[23], and the American and Canadian change from a citizen participated (draft) military to a professional, and then UN integrated, military force. As mentioned before this is the total development of an insect like governance in which the state is the ultimate power and the individual is powerless.

The outcome of all this is already written in all history books for anyone to look up. Every previously instituted state based on these principles went through the identical circumstances.

1 It developed a powerful secret police/military, in response to its inability to deliver promised socialist largess.

2 It located a fall group to blame for its failure.

3 It instituted massive arrests of all opposing factions.

4 It centralized planning.

5 It attempted expansion through coercion, war, or threat.

6 It collapsed.

There are no exceptions: every socialist organized state that did not shake off these socialist plans buckled. It is the plan of the Satori to bring member organizations such as the EU and FTAA to this point of failure, and at the peak of that coming revolution to ride in on their white horse and save man by offering their solutions. The revolution is by that time anticipated to have reduced the world population to their announced one billion.[24] The military/police of that time being completely in Satori hands is the anticipated means. A consortium of multi-national businesses is orchestrating this, in conjunction with the bureaucracies of government. It is Illuminism.

The concept in Western democracies, which have two-party systems, that, "my elected officials see to my needs, desires, and wants, and look after my interests" is silly. Elected System politicians are beholden to the Satori who see to their needs, finance their re-elections, and provide for their pleasures. They do as they are told, or find themselves promptly out of office.

There is a basic difference between the ways a socialist or totalitarian state functions and the role of operation of a free republic. In Socialist states all aspirations, plans, production, and social bearing are made subservient to the state. I call this the insect mentality. To accomplish these ends the state develops the machinery of a secret police to enforce its edicts and demands. Furthermore, the state develops central planning of all economic functions so that it can point to outcome goals, which they then tout as their successes. Such goals are invariably altered with time, so that the outcome can reach the thereafter-announced promised result.

In a free society all planning functions are left to the free market. Supply and demand regulates output. And the bureaucracy is maintained at the smallest level possible. No secret police is required, and citizens have the option to act, both socially and in their occupations, as they themselves desire.

I should now point out that my detractors would say that Britain had seven years of socialism and Sweden well almost eternally, and neither has produced a totalitarian state. True enough, but what happened to the people of those nations while under socialist rule? Britain's primary product was what they called the "brain drain;" my wife was a product of it. Anyone with any gumption, education, or desire for self-improvement emigrated to open- market societies. Those who remained became mere puppets of the System; it became worse and worse, finally people had enough and voted in Mrs. Thatcher, who reversed the entire socialist mega- state and influenced even the socialist leaders – to the point of reversing their entire dialogue. This in fact may be said to be exactly what began, but did not finish, under Reagan in America.

Sweden, at the beginning of their socialist experiment, was the largest producer of ships in the world; they were an industrial model, world leaders in any number of industries. ACEA, the largest firm in Sweden, merged with BBC of Switzerland, moving their headquarters there, Saab Scandia sold off its automotive division to GM and now produces aircraft for the Swedish and Austrian air force. There is no remaining Swedish shipbuilding industry. The country is truly depressing; taxes are so high that people can't afford to go out to dinner. The nation has no morals; as in America, pornography has become the largest industry. Having done business with Swedish firms, I can tell you from personal experience, and from numerous visits, that this is no model anyone would wish to emulate. In the '80s my firm was involved with a Swedish company, and I noticed an inordinate turnover of personnel in their sales and engineering force. When I then queried one of the engineers about this, he explained that exactly half of his direct earnings went in taxes to the government, and that when he did not work he was paid half of his gross salary. The predictable outcome was that people worked for a year and then loafed until their unemployment benefits ran out, whereupon they went back to work. After all, why not? By doing so you gain or lose nothing.

The inescapable truth is that the New World Order crowd's plan of operations is to establish a socialist world under their control, and then to implement, through their control of all state functions, feudalistic governance with themselves at its head.

The end goal of the New World Order is:

A totalitarian feudalistic state managed and controlled by a very small group of men,*

socialism being only the means to an end.

It is the intent of these people to rule over a planet populated by about one billion citizens; that indicates a reduction of the world population (2003) of six billion people. They plan a single currency controlled by them. They plan a government that is not representative of the people.

There is not intended to be any freedom; all means of communication will be controlled by the state. Every member of society will be issued a number that is to be implanted in the body using RFID[25] technology. Society will be continuously monitored, using the system called CCTV,[26] now in use in England, which was tried and removed under public pressure in Florida's Ybor city (part of Tampa). People are to be dumbed down by specializing education toward technical job applications; in other words, education is to be restricted to knowledge as required by the industrial system operating in the citizens' general region of residence (America's School-to-Work program.) This book will clearly demonstrate the methods presently used toward the achievement of those goals. All this leads us back to the points of

Adam Weisshaupt's Illuminati; over and over again we see that guiding hand representing the backdrop of the plan.

Illuminism, Communism, socialism, Zionism
and the N.W. O. are one and the same.
All the "isms" are simply the means to an end.

Once the "isms" fail, as they must, a
revolution is to take place. Not unlike
those in France, Germany, and Russia, in
the 20th century.

By that time the Illuminati plan to have total
control of the military/police organizations,
and to have disarmed to general public,
and thereby take over.

HEALTH CARE

If education is the primary Illuminist venue, then health care is the second.

The most dangerous tendency of the modern world is the way in which bogus theories are given the force of dogma.

–Jean Daniellou:
"The Lord of History," 1958

MANY people are of the opinion that the concept of state-sponsored health care stemmed from the Fabian socialists of England, or from the published works of Karl Marx. This is in fact a serious error, because the thesis of government support services including health care is with certainty almost as old a recorded history. Who first realized the basic idea as a ruler to utilize health care as a vehicle to gain popular support by offering free or subsidized healthcare services will probably never be known. The concept, however, of state sponsored health-care guarantees has been the hallmark of every Illuminist-tainted government of the 20th century.

The dispute in the United Kingdom in their May, 2001 election campaign debates illustrates this well. The entire debate was centered on only three issues, which were health care, education and crime. The very first and primary issue was health care. The Labor party, socialist champions of the "working classes," had changed the way people waiting for health care services were counted. They accomplished this by clever manipulation of statistics, by simply beginning the count with the specialist rather than with the general practitioner. This commonly used method of skewing government-reported statistics resulted in a reduction of the waiting lists of citizens by 100,000. The actual number of paid-up recipients awaiting services was at that time just over 380,000. Waiting times, depending on such obscure factors as age, could be over one year. A good friend awaiting heart by-pass surgery at age 56 died waiting for service. My father-in-law died while waiting to see a specialist. Other British friends have all opted for private insurance coverage, opting out of the state health care system; they at least are still alive. In the debate both Tories and Labor did not debate the issue of, should there be no waiting time? Instead opting for a discussion as to how many citizens should be on the waiting-for-service list. This is how two-party systems are able to skew the debate through the use of the Hegelian dialectic, boiling the issue of debate into two unrelated and false questions, thereby avoiding the actual concern. This is the primary means by which Illuminists and the N.W.O. control the debate and the outcome on all issues.

When we listen to the American Democrats we would assume that health care, in the form of the welfare state, was the bright and new invention of Hillary Clinton. In her and her friends' conception, health care is a device of immense complexity that can only be solved by the state, with its vast (confiscated) resourses. The general public, and the media lap dogs of the "System," overlook the fact that the state has no income, and that any derived and distributed benefit must first be confiscated from the people in the form of taxes, license fees, etc. The more serious fact that the state, through its bureaucracy, is the most inefficient vehicle to administer such largess is strenuously overlooked. In demonstration of government's poor ability to manage we must look no further than the American Social Security administration, whose Ponzi scheme consumes 30% of the collected taxes in management and administrative burden. Of note is the fact that private insurance carriers at maximum consume 7 to 8% in administration, and develop an interest income on invested funds to boot. A close scrutiny of the FDA[27] also demonstrates the very same incompetence of management. Considering that this agency is responsible – due to their horrific management – for more deaths in America than automobiles, guns, and heart attacks combined, provides an excellent understanding of just exactly what government management is all about. Yet a further demonstration is provided by Hillary's health care fiasco of the '90s, which illegally instituted group that wasted over $25 million in an attempt to socialize 17% of the American economy. They provided not one single positive result, and in their deliberations purposely excluded nurses, doctors, health insurance companies, (anyone who had any inkling, even slight of the issue) in the impaneled secret task force. The Clintons are both socialists to the core.

Many governments of the past had come to realize that the "Welfare State" might be used to begin the expansion of government into the "Police State." This in fact is the long *Road to Serfdom* process of the usurpation of individual rights supplanted by "group rights," which are the trademark of Illuminism. The rulers thus take the "God-given Rights" as in the American Bill of Rights and supplant these with their own man-made rules. In the 21st century this would not only be health care, education, and growing crime rates, but also laws such as The Patriot Act and Homeland Security Acts, which violate our Constitution and almost the entire Bill of Rights. For any still questioning my thesis, the examples below of individuals who implemented universal healthcare should be interesting:

Otto V. Bismarck	German Chancellor	1884
Franz Joseph I	Austrian Emperor	1888
Franz Joseph I	King of Hungary	1891
Nicholas II	Czar of Russia	1911
Lloyd George	Prime Minister, UK	1911
W. S. Churchill	Prime Minister, UK	1945
Vladimir Lenin	Dictator	1922
J. V. Stalin	Dictator	
J. Pilsudski	Dictator, Poland	1920
A. De O. Salazar	Dictator, Portugal	1919-33
Benito Mussolini	Duce, Italy	1932-43
F. Franco	Dictator, Spain	1942-45
G. Hirohito	Emperor, Japan	1934
H. Vargas	Dictator, Brazil	1944
Juan Peron	Dictator, Argentina	1944
A. Hitler	Chancellor, Germany	1933-45
J. B. Tito	Dictator, Yugoslavia	1947*

In the 16th century France's Henry IV promised his citizens a chicken in every pot. With him began the process by which rulers called themselves the "Servants of the People." This fallacious cry, (look at their incomes!) has been assiduously taken up by the N.W.O., in fact in every instance when they plan the enactment of yet another of their draconian socialist schemes we are all subjected to one of the following two quotes: "It's for the children" or "It's for the poor." We've heard all that before, remembering LBJ's "War on Poverty," into which black hole we have, by this century, dumped over $4.7 trillion without any benefit whatsoever. Do consider, every time a politician promises you something… from where is he getting it?

In the 19th century we can clearly see the foundations of the place from which the social governmental responsibility theories were hatched. In the Weimar Republic of Germany we can identify our starting point. In fact the phrase "welfare state" stems from the German *Wohlfart Staat.* Interestingly the phrase "police state" also comes from German as *Polizei Staat.* Bismarck, not FDR, was the founder of the modern concepts of state welfare. Those Bavarian Illuminists, who behind the scenes have been so active, brought it to him. He was led to believe that through a mild form of socialism he could establish an economic and social control that would strengthen his reign. Industrialization had elevated many, in income and status; into the newly emerging class we call the middle class. The ruling elite of the 20th century has looked upon this class with disdain, suspicion, and fear. In the German-speaking world an entirely new form of humanitarian governance developed under the tutelage of the Junkers. That system, called *kameralist*, taught that there existed a method of civil government whose specific purpose was the attainment of a welfare state structure. In other words the replacement of civil social welfare, by citizens, was to be supplanted by government. Such a system removes personal responsibility, and community effort, in caring for ones fellow citizens, placing that burden with the state and absolving individuals from civility, charity, and communal responsibility. It represents the core belief of Illuminism, Communism, socialism it destroys community. It is planned to turn into the *Polizei Staat* (Police State) at its pinnacle.

As in fishing, the hook must first be set. Setting the hook is the process of offering the citizens free services for health care, usurping previous channels and self-reliance. It is important to remember that one of the issues of the Illuminist movement copied by Marx is the elimination of religion, which as the Communists say is the

"Opiate of the People." Bismarck was one of very few people who clearly understood the variance between a free economy, the welfare state and the police state. The first step when entering this venture is to offer people services from the state at no charge, thereby usurping previously established channels for them. This will displace organized religion and place the state in a better light. It will transfer the social and emotional bond and faith in God to the state. Secondly, this will destroy the family unit by substituting state for father. Through this a dependent class of citizen develops which will then, out of self-interest, support the state and the political structure. Any fool will understand that the state lacks the resources to expand these promised services to the total population, and will eventually have to economize by reducing services in some manner or form. It is a fact that this unbroken cycle can be witnessed in every socialist state throughout history. In America, per example, Social Security age limits have been increased, the benefit has been subjected to taxation, accrued interest in held deposits is not computed, and employer's payment portions are not counted – worst of all, as the currency is inflated through the unprecedented expansion of fiat money, whose buying power thus declines, cost-of-living increases are kept under 40% of the actual inflation rates. In the final act of this Ponzi scheme the institutions of police and military are merged, and employed to quell the citizens' dissatisfaction with the reduction of services. At this point one must recall that police and military functions differ greatly, in that police protect and serve while military seek to kill and destroy; through this variance the merging of these functions is always a disaster for the indigenous populations. In this final act a scapegoat is identified, who can subsequently be utilized as the party to be blamed for the curtailment of services, and to channel anger away from the state and toward the intended victims. This can take varying directions in the form of an event (war, drought, flood) or in blaming some social group that opposes the state, (Jews, Blacks, Patriots, Constitutionalists.) In the past as well as the present this can quickly be identified; Israelis blame Palestinians, Boers blamed blacks, Bolshevik Zionists blamed Orthodox Christians, the Bush administration blames terrorists and patriots. This last assertion, blaming terrorists who are the creation of one's own policies, I find particularly galling. It can be shown that in every instance of this Illuminist-implemented socialist system, the state in the end resorted to force of arms to maintain its, by that time, illegitimate position.

America, with the passing of the Patriot Act and the Homeland Security Act, along with numerous odious EOs[28] and legislative acts, can now be considered an empire. In violation of the Constitution, the "federal" government has armed over 300,000 bureaucrats, including tax collectors, park employees, farm agents, environmental officers, and numerous others who have no law enforcement function whatever. We see in this occurrence the early development of the military/police structure that will undoubtedly be led by FEMA[29] when required by the powers in charge. The laws so far enacted in the Bush-the-Lesser administration violate virtually the entire Bill of Rights along with the original Constitution. The "separation of powers" implemented by the founders no longer exists. One bad by-product of this is the ever-increasing tax burden, which is growing at very great rate due to the under-reported dollar decline associated with inflation. Americans are, as of this reading, taxed as an average family of four at the rate of 49.2% – a percentage of taxation that is, like everything else from government, falsely reported.

It should be pointed out that when examining the value of currency the following result is found:

Dollar value Jan. 04 to Dec.-04

	'03	'04	%
Pound	1.70	1.89	-10.6
Euro	1.17	1.37	-13.4
Swiss Fr.	1.33	1.56	-17.3
Average Dollar decline			**-11.9%**

Hard assets			
Gold	3.85	149.00	-16.6
Silver	5.10	7.60	-49.
Palladium	744.	860.	-15.6
Average dollar decline			**-27.1**

Combined currency and hard asset average decline
19.35% [actual rate of inflation]

The primary official purpose of all this expanded police authority is, we are told, our protection from terrorism and crime. That is falsehood. The enforcement of FDA labeling laws by jack-booted ski-masked thugs has nothing to do with crime. The very obvious lack of border security and the fact that America now has 340,000 illegal immigrant felons, 22 million illegal immigrants, and untold millions of legal immigrants more than supports my statement that law enforcement is not the object of the government. Consider that the two largest business enterprises in America are drugs and pornography, and that government is not only involved with both, but in the case of drugs most certainly in on the take. Or perhaps someone actually believes that the FRS (our banking monopoly) does not know who is transferring $850 billions in cash in and out of the country annually. Neither the EPA nor the FDA has anything to do with violent crime, so why do these people need to be armed? Does it really take a gun to enforce labeling laws, or to fine polluters? If the state were in fact concerned with terrorism, as they claim, they would close the borders, rounding up illegal felons, and deport illegal felons. In fact all these issues are merely excuses by government to expand their police authority over legitimate citizens – in other words, the beginning of the police state.

What Bismarck accomplished was changing the old authoritarian *Junker* class into accepting a quasi-democratic, and well-organized, bureaucracy based on an Illuminist welfare state. Citizens of Germany were enthralled with this new form of governance, which was to expand to all European nations by the 1940s. Its clones were the Italian, Portuguese and Spanish examples, brought in by Mussolini, Salazar and Franco. Later it made the ascendance and expansion of the Nazis easier, as they not only accepted the Bismarck model but also expanded it substantially. In all these models the police state followed behind.

One of the first to warn about the welfare state was Prof. Lujo Brentano, who warned as early as 1880 that "adventures into state controlled medicine will ultimately lead to a 'Neo-welfare-state' and is not about providing the citizens any service, but in fact a means for the state to control the private citizens' vote, and the socialization of the state." This is not a very difficult prediction to make, since the average cost of health care is between 14 and 20% of any national economy.

The most remarkable fact, when we review all past social welfare schemes, which deal with the medical establishment, is that in every single case private insurances, which invariably parallel the public ones, are substantially less expensive, serve their clients better, and react faster. Notable also is the aspect that private carriers consume between 7 and 9% in management and administration burden, and the government agencies between 20 and 40%. Significant in 2004 is the British government-instituted health care, which now has a parallel private competition, which is preferred by those who can afford it – an overwhelming 84% of the population. This is due to better service, no waiting lines, no age discrimination, and better competence by the medical practitioners.

One must clearly understand that all this health care welfare propaganda, and that is exactly what it is has nothing whatever to do with health care and everything to do with political power and control. Let us examine the Weimar Republic one more time. Germany's NSAP[30] was able to garnish only one third of the vote. Ten percent were Communists, who violently opposed a competing socialist system. The huge German middle class, who had been seduced by the offer of free medical service, a WPA[31] work program sponsored by the national government, did nothing. Why? Why do Americans, Britons, Germans, Frenchmen, and Canadians do nothing now, as they see the very same process-taking place in their respective nations? The answer to that lies in the system of government benefits, which are offered to groups as well as individual members. In the Weimar Republic the government catered to the unions; our government caters to unions. The government catered to industry by instituting higher tariffs; our government pursues the road of no tariffs (Free Trade) so that industry that is no longer regulated is able to increase profits by exporting production and labor. At least one party in America is the captive of labor unions, and exactly the same is true in Britain Canada, and France. Big business, i.e. multi-nationals, through their NGOs[32] control the entire cabal, having instituted government-regulated trade (through WTO, GATT, EU, FTAA, NAFTA) by having sold the public into believing that Free Trade is to the general benefit, when in fact all it has done is remove well-paying manufacturing jobs to third-world locations, allowing the multi-nationals higher profit margins. Reality in America is the loss of 3 million manufacturing jobs, over 2500 manufacturing plants, and 4 million indirect manufacturing jobs – the indirect job loss being the result of domestic as well as foreign manufacturers building plants in Mexico rather than in America.

We see from the Clinton impeachment trial that Americans do nothing even if proven treason, perjury, and theft are obvious. Like the German middle class of 1933, we are suckered by the System into a lulled belief that everything will be OK in the end. The fact that we have, as a nation, been slipping down the slippery slope of economic decay is just the more obvious. Once state paternalism is established, and the number of government employees, military, bureaucrats, teachers, state employees and all the rest, accounts for 50% of total employment it's over, the system becomes self-perpetuating. This is exactly how the Nazis took control of the Weimar Republic. It is the means utilized by the System operators of all two- party states to remain in power. This is one of the means used by the Illuminist movement to maintain their control of societies.

The turbulent times of pre W.W. II sped up social engineering. The basic structures put in place by Hitler, Mussolini, Salazar, Franco, Churchill and FDR set the foundation for the coming police states, or bankruptcies of the economies that had been implementing them. And don't think that the American economy is not bankrupt; consider a $24 trillion national debt. We also saw the efforts of the socialist and Communist movements in their relentless *ferstaatlichen* (placing the government in charge of everything) as the prime movers and cheerleaders of the efforts.

Lenin is the 20th century's most prominent proponent of health care, cradle to grave. The catastrophic effects of the Soviet system of health care can now, in 2004, be seen; the nation has the lowest life expectancy in the world, at 50 for a male. This is the nation that under its previous government (Czar) had the longest life expectancy. Average life expectancy for males in industrialized nations now averages 20 years longer than in the USSR – so much for socialized health care. Worse than that is the fact that the Soviet system was instituted in scores of subjugated nations, resulting in almost one billion people having become dependent on the state and now lacking the self-reliance or initiative to see to their own care. The unilateral collapse of the Soviet socialist system, and the inevitable inability of people to look after themselves following 70 years of state care, have resulted in total failure.

It behooves us to examine how this most benevolent of Soviet plans was applied to its citizens. Propagandists for Communism inform us that they were all covered from cradle to grave, and that the only reason for the present malaise is the improper application of socialist planning. Rubbish! From 1922 to 1938 the Soviet government nationalized everything. Then they instituted a 6.5% payroll tax for health care, in fact an overall 25% tax for social services to be provided by the state. The national budget was used to cover all the huge losses of the system. In 1938 the health care portion of insurance was increased to 8%. When this proved incapable of covering the enormous losses, they instituted a tiered system of health care availability dependent upon a government grading system. Benefits were severely curtailed to the average worker; only Party members (less than 5% of the population) continued to have full coverage. Shortly after that Social Security (retirement) benefits were re-graded to 50% of average income, from 100% of average income. Government officials, however, continued at 100%. This seems awfully similar to the congressional retirement benefit for our elected representatives and un-elected bureaucrats in America. Health care became a very good deal for the elect few and a very bad deal for the general population. Birthing care, per example, was eliminated for any woman who had not in the previous seven months had a full-time job. This is a violation of the old Soviet constitution, but then their leadership cared even less about that than does ours. As in any autocratic dictatorship, the upper echelon had dachas in the Caucasus, spas in the Crimea, and any service that could be thought of, including stores with Western goods, while the balance of the population lived in abject poverty. This is an important point, because it underscores what I have said from the very beginning; namely, that social services are offered only as a means to an end, have nothing whatever to do with benefiting any of the citizens, and are put in place for the sole purpose of creating the developing police state under which all is controlled by those who instituted the welfare state to begin with. When all this comes asunder the Illuminati will be waiting to take over the reins of power.

It may be useful to examine the general effects of the socialist state on a nation's economy, and how that impacts on individual citizens' personal standard of living – perhaps "general welfare" would be a better gauge? Bear in mind that in the Free Trade scenario pushed by the Illuminists the cost of manufacture becomes the prime mover of multi-nationals in deciding where to manufacture. Due to social costs Germany[33] has, for the seventh year in a row, the highest cost of manufacture in the world: in 2002 this was $27.98 per hr. This was followed by Norway at $26.00 and then America with $18.89 This gives rise to the question, do the citizens of those three nations have a better standard of living now than they did 25 years ago? The resounding response is, No! People in all three nations were much better off 25 years ago than they are today. The great majority of households did well with only one parent working. The buying power of the earned income was substantially higher. Crime was lower. The drug epidemic was only on the horizon and pornography was illegal. An average annual income allowed the purchase of one half of a one family house and approximately two and one half cars, based on total income. Today, in all nations listed above both parents must work, the cost of a home has risen to the point where on average it would take four years of labor of one parent to purchase a home, and the figure would be two years for a car.

If we go back to the '50s the matter becomes much worse. While the welfare state has grown, taxes have increased six-fold over the 25-year time frame, health care has dramatically increased in cost but not improved in service, all services offered by the state have drastically deteriorated. The cost of the welfare state is totally born by the taxpayers, with the cost of taxes showing the greatest increase over the total timeline. In America, for example, the total tax burden from 1950 to 2004 has increased by just over 600%. It is my proven assertion that the lowered standard of living is closely related to taxation, and that increased taxation is caused by welfare-state policies. Furthermore, that these socialist, Illuminist stratagems are the sole cause of the dwindling standard of living in industrialized nations. A reasonable point of comparison would be Canada. Since Canada implemented their draconian health care system, the Canadian dollar has plummeted against the American dollar by over 40%. This in turn has made goods and services 40% more expensive. If the health care were, on the other hand, implemented by private insurance carriers faced with competition, the overall cost of providing the service would be about 25% lower. This is firstly because there is no competition, and secondly because of the inherent bureaucratic manner in which governments function. Now I ask you, does anyone truly believe that individual Canadians are better off paying 25% more for health care in order to support a bloated mandarin class of government officials? The population at large because of its complication, and the fact that most of us are far too busy keeping food on the table even to consider the issue does not usually address this question. That is exactly what the Illuminists want.

Under no circumstances do I want to give the impression that health care should not be available to all, but simply to establish that the government is the very worst provider of services to individuals that one can even imagine.

We can clearly recognize that the concepts of socialization of health care services under governmental authority are a wholly European concept, one that is foreign to America. Americans of the past were for the most part rugged individualists who had little interest in government largess, preferring to take care of their own. When the bankers brought about the Great Depression and then had their man Franklin D. Roosevelt elected, they had him begin the creation of a modern welfare state in America. The model used by FDR was the Fabian one imported from England, due to FDR's unreasoning hatred of anything German. The Fabian model was, however, based on the German model of Bismarck, which in turn had been brought to him by the Illuminist movement.

One must understand that this concept is a wealth re-distribution scheme, which is socialist in nature, and Illuminist in origin. This then is where Lenin comes into the picture, closely followed by other socialists like Salazar, Franco, Hitler, Mussolini, Vargas, Peron, Tito, Stalin, FDR, Carter and Clinton. The only difference between socialists and Communists is that the Communists are in a hurry; the end result espoused by both is identical. Our 21st century legacy is the EU, three quarters of whose membership is made up by socialist states. Certainly no one can dispute that Germany, France, Britain, Italy, Spain, Austria, Greece, along with all the new East European states, are socialist. In this case, the newly elected member states of Eastern Europe are in fact less socialist than the old-established ones. Socialism fails due to the dis-incentives, which are implicit in the system of penalizing success, hard work, and inventive production through graduated and rising income taxes, on individuals as well as business. This results in lost opportunity, reduced research, lowered expectations, lower industrial development, reduced employment growth, and finally less income for government – despite higher taxes for the public.

Health care may be considered a dilemma because the Illuminists have successfully utilized the Hegelian Dialectic; they boil the debate down to false issues that were made by them. They structured the debate into A) Will the state provide health care to all, or B) Will there be no health care for the people? Anyone who examines the issue will see that this structure is specious. There are not merely two possible arrangements but many in the real debate:

1 Government health care for everyone, cradle to grave.

2 Government partial health care for those who need it.

3 Private free-market health insurance for those who want it.

4 Private health care with a co-pay option.

5 Government-mandated private coverage.

6 Government and private co-pay and un-insurable coverage.

In my opinion, health care coverage should be universal for all citizens on an equal basis. By "universal" I include government employees and elected officials, who presently have a system that is taxpayer-funded and exceeds even private carrier coverage.[34] Employer coverage, the process most commonly used today by working people, is a very bad solution, because there is no direct interrelationship between the recipients and the payer. This causes overcharges, unnecessary services, and larceny. The individual covered by the insurance should have a minimum co-pay responsibility for the first $1,000. Employers should not be allowed to provide coverage. The total amount of health insurance cost should be 100% tax-deductible. All carriers should be private insurance companies. For those unable to afford the cost of insurance, the government should co-pay the cost of their policy, but not without a penalty for every service provided. Self-induced problems caused by smoking, drug usage, alcoholism, and other such should be excluded from all insurance. This is what is called a "*Laissez-nous faire!* [Let us do it!]" solution. It would reduce health care costs by 40% at a minimum. Once people saw and reviewed their bills, all the false billing, overcharges, etc., would promptly stop. The practice of requiring hospitals to provide services for illegal immigrants must be ended immediately; anyone coming into the country must by law be forced to purchase short-term health insurance for the intended and announced stay of duration. This will halt the financial hemorrhaging of hospitals, particularly in the Southwestern and Southern states where Mexican paupers are bankrupting them.

Having had numerous experiences with hospitals, because my wife is a RN,[35] I can testify that, at least in Florida, hospitals miss-bill, inflate charges, are swamped by Mexicans seeking health care without the means to pay, and are very poorly managed. In a billing to my family, when it came to push and shove, the hospital, under threat of legal action, reduced our bill by over 70%, all of which were overcharges and charges for services not rendered. An insurance carrier would simply have paid, and then increased the premium prices.

Government is much too inefficient to oversee health care for 300 million people. Consider for a moment Social Security. This government-administered program is the greatest rip–off in man's history. In my own case I confronted a friend who is an insurance actuary, asking him to tell me, based on what I have paid in to SS and what my employer paid in and the interest accrued, what monthly benefit I would obtain at retirement age. Accumulated payments, including interest, amounted to just under one million dollars: based on an interest rate of 4.5% and a life expectancy of 84, he told me I would get $3,450 per month and, after death, my family would get the residual left over returned to them. SS pays me $1,106 per month, and when I keel over my family gets a $300 death benefit. I rest my case.

Health Care in Britain

A SOCIALIST MODEL

After arduous lengthy in fighting and debate, Lloyd George succeeded in 1911 with his national health care plan. The resulting insurance scheme funded through taxes, provided cash benefits, with some medical services offered. It covered politicians, citizens, loafers, and workers, but just like the Hillary-planned health care fiasco, gave no consideration whatever to doctors, nurses, or insurance carriers. Predictably, management and operational costs in England rose to 17%, while in Ireland to 20%. Private carriers in the UK at that time operated their plans on an overhead cost of from 8.5 to 9.3%. Benefits were poor, and the national improvement in health care touted by George went the other way. Doctors were furious and many chose the route of departing for other Commonwealth nations, an act to be repeated in the '60s. The entire fiasco led to the Beveridge plan, a cradle-to-grave plan that had great popular support due to the failure of the George plan. This was at a time when the Fabian socialists were popular, and the Soviet model was touted as the great leader to follow in health care. A barrage of false propaganda by Stalin as well as Labor hid the true facts of the Soviet system. Does this ring a bell with anyone? What about the Kennedy/Kastenbaum health care legislation? What about Gingrich's tacit support of bi-partisan healthcare? What about the phony health care bailout in the '90s by the Republocrats? I find it truly amazing that not one single journalist had the guts to blow the whistle on these repeats of past history. With the 1945 election Churchill was out and Labor was in; to accomplish this feat they had prior to the election offered what even Lenin refused to give, complete medical care for everything for everyone – including foreign visitors – from cradle to grave paid for by government. (Well, actually, the taxpayers, but that's not how they structured the campaign.)

This led to the "Brain Drain" in which England lost all their best and brightest, who opted to move out to America, Australia, South Africa, Canada, and New Zealand. It also led to the longest-serving Tory government in British history, in which Mrs. Thatcher not only reversed the direction of nationalization but also sold almost all the industries that had been nationalized, and scrapped the health care system as structured by Labor. She succeeded in reversing the terrible decline that had been foisted upon the country by the Fabian/Illuminist alliance and which can be placed at the feet of socialized health care.

Through this we can see that the concept of nationalized health care traveled from Germany to England and from there to America. We see that it has caused a decline in medical services, and the decline of every national economy that installed any such system. We see that it is one of many instruments used by Illuminism in order to bring nations down, so that they can be incorporated into the greater Illuminist cabal. We see that it is the model pushed by Ted Kennedy, Diane Feinstein, Nancy Pelosi, Charles Schumer, Tom Lantos, and any number of socialists under the sway of the Illuminati. In more exact terms the results of national healthcare are:

1 The lowering of medical services quality.

2 Substantial overall cost increases in medical services.

3 The inability of government to sustain the promised service.

4 The application of the political class to use health care in development of a dependent class, used then to perpetuate their positions.

5 The degeneration of services.

6 The development of reactions.

7 The empowerment of a police class to stem opposition by the people.

8 The development of a scapegoat to blame for the failure of service.

9 The development of the police state.

10 The drastic reduction of services to the population, while at the same time increasing services to the governing class.

11 Severe shortages in medical profession employment (doctors and nurses).

12 A secondary and parallel system for the elected and bureaucrats.

When you think on the issue of health care you had best consider the effect that it has had on other nations, and who is in fact behind the entire idea. Look to our neighbors to the North, who, waiting in line for almost any service, choose to come across the border to get their treatments. Look to England, where untold people die waiting in line for services up over a year, and where many services are allocated based on age. Look to Russia, where the system longest in effect has resulted in a life expectancy that is 25 years shorter than in other places. In all three aforementioned places the quickest-growing business is private insurance health care. Sure, free health care sounds great, but it is a lie, and if you have to wait until you are six feet under to get the promised service it is useless.

Illuminist plans to take over the world are not centered on any one single issue. Many unrelated issues and systems come into play. Health care is but one of these. The plan has been hatching for over 200 years and it is only in the 21st century that we can begin to unravel their nefarious plans. The puzzle is on the table and all the little parts are beginning to come together. So, soon, you will see the entire picture.

ILLUMINISM IS LIKE A PARASITE.

It attaches itself to some movement, takes it over and uses it to pursue its goals.
It managed this in the French Revolution, through Masonic and Rosicrucian bodies.
Not until Dec. 3rd, 1913 was the Masonic Grand Orient of France able to purge Illuminism from its ranks.
It did it again in the Russian Revolution, through Zionism, which it controls even today through its affiliation with Communism.
It is doing so today through Zionism, in Gulf War I and Gulf War II.
Its most recent action is the 4th generation war, which we call terrorism.
The American branch of Illuminism is called Bones, The Order, The Order of Death, and 322.
The Order is seated in New Haven, CT., at Yale University. Their home is called the Tombs.
Bones' annual meeting is held at Deer Island, located in upstate NY.
The Order is incorporated in Connecticut.

FAIT MONEY, ECONOMICS AND TAXES

> *22.6% of all the taxes you pay finance the monopoly we call the FRS (Federal Reserve System.) The FRS is the banking monopoly granted to the Illuminists by Congress.*
>
> –Non Vox Populi

IT is a logical journey for any discussion of the Illuminati to examine closely the financial markets, banking monopolies, fiat money, and government's collusive involvement within that sector. I am not alone in my opinion that we are at the beginning of the end of the financial structure that was set up, in my home state of New Hampshire, at Bretton Woods so long ago. The indicators of its imminent worldwide collapse can be found everywhere. I don't want anyone to suffer the false notion that these things are not contrived, or that they could not be prevented by the proper application of reasonable economics. The fact is, however, that the powers that be have no interest in either preventing the coming economic collapse, or saving your personal assets from the humongous losses that are already rolling down the pike. Unfortunately, this is a dry topic, which is the reason that so little of it is reported in the media. Even financial publications, like Barons and *The Wall Street Journal,* rarely, if ever, produce any articles that deeply review the economic issues we face.

The creation of government debt, which in all nations is stated to be due and owing to the international banking cartels, is an outright lie. If we examine the creation of any of these national banks (FRS, ECB[36]) we see that upon their founding, the national treasury of the country in which they were created provided the funds for them to back the fiat currency that they issue. In other words, *the bases of their ability to issue paper money, the gold and silver, are the property of the citizens of that country.* In no instance do the balance sheets of any of these banks reflect that reality. So, by sleight of hand, they have converted the people's asset into their own asset. They have stolen the people's hard assets, and then issued paper, which they have continuously inflated. Inflation is caused by only one occurrence. If you issued paper (fiat) money, which in all cases was backed by some hard asset, then you would issue a silver or gold certificate dollar; if you, however, then issued a paper dollar, you would have to place a silver dollar into a storage vault, so that the paper (fiat) bill had value. The United States has sold off its entire silver holding and reserves. A one-ounce silver coin in Feb. 2004 sells for between $6 and $8, depending on the quantity purchased. We are not speaking of collectible, numismatic coins but only bullion coins. This then indicates that the value of the single dollar bill has been inflated, in just the last 39 years, by about 800%. But that, as they say, is only half the story. Since all the stored silver (the property of the people) has been sold by the FRS, they have realized a profit in the billions, money that has never been repaid or even entered in the books as credit to the people. And then some fool in government speaks of "insider trading!"

When Congress spends more money than they collect in taxes, a common occurrence, especially in the Bush the Lesser administration, is to borrow money from the FRS. To be honest, the FRS has no money; all the money that they have has been issued as paper money and is in circulation. So, how can you borrow money from someone who has none? This is in fact a simple deception carried out by the FRS. They simply offer to sell loan instruments that they call bonds, savings bonds, treasury notes, or what have you. They sell these based on an interest rate, which is tax-exempt for the purchaser, and naturally with a nice profit for the issuing bankers. So they borrow money to issue money, and then based on that loan print up more paper money. Why don't you try that? They would have you in jail in a New York minute. In any event this entire Byzantine cabal bases the currency in circulation as valueless and backed by debt, which is in fact less than nothing.

Now we can examine where the taxes collected from the average American go:

1	Military	26.2%
2	Debt service	22.6%*
3	Health care	19%
4	Income security	5.5%
5	Veterans Administration	3.4%
All the rest are under		**3.3%**

- How much have taxes increased since Gulf War II?
- Since 2000 tax collected from Americans has risen by $110 billions. (The big tax cut?)
- How serious are these bankers and elected crooks about correcting the problem?

Not at all serious! In 1982 the Grace Commission, presented to the government a detailed study of 21,000 pages. The private sector funded commission spent $76 million of their own money to produce their voluminous report. The Grace report made 2,478 recommendations for curtailing government spending, which, if implemented, would have saved the taxpayers of America $424.4 billion dollars by 1985, without curtailing a single government program or service. In the letter presenting the report to then sitting President Reagan, Grace told him that one third of the taxes collected was wasted, one third of taxes due was not collected, and one third was sucked up by the banking monopoly. So, according to the Grace Commission, none of the money collected in taxes funds the government at all. How many of the recommendations were implemented? None, not a damn one! This more than proves the case that the Illuminists have set up a system to fund themselves out of the taxes you pay. It is accurate to say that a full third of all taxes paid go to the banking monopoly as debt service. Thus we are all funding our own demise.

The IMF (International Monetary Fund) is a creature that came out of the Bretton Woods conference held on July 12, 1944. The name comes from the place in NH where the meeting was held, in the White Mountains, far, far away from the prying eyes of the public or the media. The name of the conference was the United Nations Monetary and Financial Conference. The resulting horrible international monetary policies were adopted by the United States in 1945 as: Title 22, Section 286, of the U.S. Code. This is where it gets really Byzantine. Taxes collected name the Treasury as the payee. The payments then go to the Federal Reserve Bank, a private corporation, and the only business in banking that has never been audited since its founding in 1913. From there the money goes to the International Bank for Reconstruction and Development and is deposited into an account called "Quad Zero." It is from this account that funds are distributed as per 22 USC 286 and CFR 11 Section 214.7.

According to the smoke-and-mirror U.S. Bureau of Public Debt, Americans at the end of 1984 had a total public debt of $7.1 trillion. Today's public debt, according to me, is $24 trillion. You may well ask how I came up with that number, and it is not difficult to work out; all you do is add together all the IOUs in the various agencies, Social Security, Highway Trust Fund, Patent Office, and so on. Then you add all the numbers together. The number reported by the Bureau of Public Debt reflects only the actual amount *minus* the outstanding debt to agencies that have had their income placed in the General fund.

Next it is vital to understand the basically corrupted Income Tax as constructed in America. First, it is a tax that is progressive, the more you earn the higher the percentage of taxation. In other words, in accordance with the Illuminist doctrine, we tax incentive and industry. The advice here is, don't excel or you will be punished. This is the very rule that was adopted by Marx and published in his Manifesto. The theory put forth by the left, that it is only fair to tax those who are wealthier more, is specious; they automatically pay more. Consider that if you make $10,000 and have a flat tax of 10% you pay $1,000 in tax, and if you make $100,000 you pay $10,000. Why, except to penalize industry, would anyone propose to tax the $100,000 at a higher percentage? The greatest lie in this system, however, is not in the graduation, but instead it's inflation. It hurts every taxpayer regardless of his tax bracket. The system automatically collects a higher percentage of taxes every single year; the exact increase is the effect of inflation. As the currency is inflated your earnings increase, and thus raises the percentage of taxation. In actual terms this works out to an average annual increase of from 3.5% to 6%.

The largest portion of the budget is the military, which accounts for 26.2% of the national budget. We are speaking of some astronomical amounts of money here. The current Zionist-instituted war in Afghanistan and Iraq has, just since the initiation of Bush the Lesser, cost us $500 billions. I'm sure everyone remembers the $87 billion The Lesser demanded and received from Congress for Gulf II, but who remembered the $67 billion that had already been appropriated before, or the $20 billion sent to Israel, or the billions sent to all our wonderful allies and partners? This war is about one thing and only one thing, the elimination of the only military contender of sufficient prominence to challenge Israel in the Middle East. Everything else – WMD's, nuclear technology, yellowcake purchases from Niger, mobile weapons labs, chemical weapons, bacteriological weapons, ICBM's, CBM's – all are lies.

This then brings us to the number two issues in finance, namely our staggering deficit in trade. Ever since the Illuminists concocted the "free trade" Trojan horse, Western economies have declined. America's trade deficit in 2004 is anticipated to reach the overwhelming amount of just over $550 billions. Together with the Iraq war, that works out to a total of one trillion dollars. I am absolutely convinced that the free trade scenario is a well- thought-out plan by the Satori, utilizing the British model of the early 20th century, when free trade was responsible for a 25% decline in the British economy. First off, there is no such thing as free trade: what we have is government-controlled trade. The control vehicles are EU, NAFTA, WTO, GATT, and the coming FTAA. The originating agencies of these treaties are the NGOs who so vehemently wanted them put in place. Why? That is simple. Large corporations, and we speak here of multinationals, have a common competitor – small business, family farms, and independently held corporations. They, through their inefficiency, are unable to compete with these smaller entities, and have thus come upon a plan to destroy them. Simply, they have instituted free trade through government mandate; they are thereby able to move all their production facilities to the lowest-cost- labor locale, and thereby run independents out of business. This process is not unilateral, in that it takes place in various venues. Communications, which these people have desired to control, is one such item. In 1998 they had the Communications Act passed in congress during the Clinton administration. This law has permitted the consolidation of radio stations to the point where, by 2003, 800 independent radio stations had been gobbled up. Local programming is gone; telephone lines pipe in programs produced in the media centers of NY and LA. Similarly during the first Clinton administration over 600 independent banks were eliminated and bought up by the larger international banks. Not excluded from it is distribution, where other monsters like Wal-Mart and Kmart are eliminating family-owned retail business.

Let us review some recently published financial information. The FRS issues quarterly reports on a topic they call 'Financial Aggregates.' What this actually is is the national credit market debt. This includes all types of borrowing, corporate as well as personal. We will review the numbers from 1952 to 2001 third quarter. Beginning in 1952 we find debt at about $40 billion, and until 1974 it remains at reasonable levels, under $100 billion. By 1975 a veritable explosion of debt begins, a meteoric rise from $100 billion to $30,000 billion in 2001. Consumer borrowing had simply gone berserk. In November 2001 borrowing had increased by $19.8 billion, or 14%, above the previous quarter: this is the largest monthly increase recorded in financial history.

While Americans were on a borrowed money-spending spree in all reality completely beyond any reason, 'Corporate Equity' or the financial category of the value of stocks went in the opposite direction. NASDAQ capitalization, which consists of the number of outstanding shares of stock times the per- share value of the stock, went from $6.7 trillion down to $2.9 trillion from March to December 2001. That's a period of nine months and a drop of over half. In that same time frame, the NYSE capitalization dropped from $12.9 trillion to $11.7 trillion. This indicates that total corporate value, which had been $20.1 trillion prior to this cataclysmic decline, fell to $13.7 trillion, or an overall equity loss of $ 6.4 trillion.

In order to prevent rapid market contraction, i.e. the bursting of the bubble economy, the FRS under Mr. Greenspan's leadership inflated the dollar at heretofore uncalled-for speed. Again we learn from the FRS that their Monetary Aggregates – that means the money supply – shows an increase, from 1974 to 2001, from about $50 billion to just over $8000 billion. That means that the Bank increased the money supply by $7950 billions, or 160 times. That was the cause of the '90s stock market bubble, and the subsequent collapse, in which Mr. Greenspan's friends made a killing. .

Notably, the rapid rise in the values of shares of corporate stocks worldwide during the '90s was based not on value but on speculation, due to an over-abundance of capital in the marketplace. These increases were prevalent not only in America but also in GB, Germany, France, and Japan. Fueled by ever-increasing money from the banking monopoly, some firms attained values of 250 times earnings, while normalcy is more like six times.

Then, in the short period of thirteen months, the FRS reduced prime interest rates eleven times, creating the specter of easy money and priming the speculative bubble even more.

The above factors – namely the rapid increase of the money supply, the astronomical growth of borrowing, and the continuous reduction in interest rates – created the bubble economy of the '90s. A repeat of the well-practiced introduction to yet another depression, all managed by the Illuminist bankers and their Zionist allies. It is these market manipulations that allow central bankers to consolidate ever more of the economies in their hands. Don't forget the banking collapse of the '90s, in which the multi-nationals gobbled up over 600 private smaller banks.

Again, during the same time frame, American manufacturing, as reported by the U.S. Dept. of Labor, lost 21.5 million manufacturing jobs. This was due exclusively to GATT, WTO, NAFTA, and other international trade agreements spearheaded by the Trojan horse of "free trade". The most severe losses occurred in the machine tool sector – my plant among them – machine tools being the backbone of any industrial economy.

Insolvencies and bankruptcies, both business and personal, are at the turn of the century at the highest level ever recorded, and this is with a substantial tightening of bankruptcy law.

To see the mayhem worldwide, we need only look at the economy of Japan, which stagnated in the early '90s and has done nothing of any note since. Japan is at the verge of default; any slight catastrophe or the failure of one of their larger banks would trigger it. Worldwide, for third-world nations, the primary agents of this economic maelstrom are the BIS[37], and IMF[38].

The most immediate result of these agencies policies has been the debacle in Argentina, whose entire economy has collapsed. Argentina was the fourth-largest economy in this hemisphere. Several economies are on the verge of the same course, Turkey and Brazil among them.

All these actions are driven by derivatives, trading an option that did not even exist twenty years ago. These highly speculative and unsecured trades have instituted monumental losses in numerous financial institutions, including Citibank, Swissbank, and Chase.

One of the best-kept secrets of the financial manipulators is an often-unknown allowable act by mutual fund managers. Almost all mutual funds contain a clause in the articles of agreement with the investor that allows the managers of the fund to borrow money utilizing the portfolio of assets as collateral for the loans. Now understand this; they use the money invested with them to purchase stocks, bonds and other instruments on your behalf; then they go to a bank and borrow money using your asset as guaranteed collateral for the loan – just like your borrowing money from the bank and using your neighbor's house as collateral on the loan. Can you guess what happens if the loan is called? That's right; they have assigned your investment as collateral, and the banks have first option to liquidate the holding to make good on the loan. That this will result in an eventual total collapse of the mutual fund markets just exactly the same way as the stock market did in 1929 is a given. The only difference is that they did not call them mutual funds.

Now, to consolidate all these factors, we see a world economy that is at the brink of total collapse. The outlandish actions of the bankers that manipulate the entire system have created a bubble economy by inflating stock prices to many times their actual value. At the same time they have loaned inordinate amounts of money (guaranteed by your future taxes) to "Developing Nations" debts, which these countries cannot repay under any circumstances. Remember how Mexico and Panama both defaulted, and how the FRS and the Treasury bailed both out with your taxes? The Panama Canal Treaty bailed out Marine Midland Bank, per example. If you are to understand one thing out of this book, then let it be: BANKERS NEVER LOSE, THE ILLUMINATI NEVER LOSE, **you lose.**

All the actions of these globalists fly in the face of the reality of proper governance. The principles of natural law, which was the outcome of moral authority as incorporated in the Magna Carta and later the U.S. Constitution, clearly point to a requirement of those who govern to do so to "promote the general welfare of the population and its posterity." No person could possibly attribute any such notion to the Illuminists' plans. The globalist's view is typified by the writings of Zbigniew Brzezinski, Samuel P. Huntington and Heinrich Kissinger, who present to us the intellectual Illuminist proposition, which is the pyramidal feudalistic state in which people are reduced to an insect status with no rights of election, governance, or intellectual independence. (That all three are members of the CFR, TC and Bilderbergers[39] goes without saying.) The foundations of this plan are clearly visible in UN, EU, and NATO documentations, as well as in the text of NAFTA. The planned FTAA is only to be a further expansion of it all. Education worldwide presents us further ample proof.

All money globally is controlled under the same basic rules. These are; that all money is fiat, paper. That all money is basically unbacked by any hard asset, gold or silver. Those bankers are able through various means to inflate and deflate the value of the currency. That governments are induced to spend more money than they take in, in taxes, and that the bankers will then loan money at interest to the governments in question, the very same money that they got from the people to start with. That this outstanding loan is called the national debt, and be large enough to represent about

20% to 40% of the total tax collected in any given year. That government, on behalf of the banking monopoly, heavily penalizes forgery of the fraudulent worthless currency. That government uses the power of government to create a collection agency on behalf of the banking monopoly, and further to protect, and enforce laws as requested by, the banking monopoly, so that the issuance of the currency is a monopoly. I defy anyone to challenge any of the aforementioned facts.

It is my contention that for the last fifty years the entire world has been totally under the control of these people. Every issue that is scrutinized develops the same or a similar outcome. At the end of the tunnel is the ever-seeing eye of the New World Order.

By percentage we have damn little to fear from terrorists, but much to fear from our legislators, who abolish our freedoms under the pretence of protecting us.

Upon occasion I have been asked to
define Globalism.

My response is: It's just like the
death of Princess Diana.

An English princess with an
Egyptian boyfriend gets
Killed on a French highway in a German car
Driven by a Belgian drunk on Scots whiskey,
Chased by Italian paparazzi riding
Japanese motorcycles,
Being treated by an Indian doctor using
Pakistani medicine,
Which news is given out on American-
designed computers,
Built in Taiwan entirely of Chinese parts.

THE ASSULT ON FREEDOM

La Temposta di Mare

Speech:
And while I am talking to you mothers and fathers, I give you one more assurance. I have said this before, but I shall say it again and again and again and again: Your boys are not going to be sent into any foreign wars. They are going into training to form a force so strong that, by its very existence, it will keep the threat of war away from our shores.

–Franklin D. Roosevelt
Campaign address Oct. 30, 1940

NEVER in the history of our nation have freedom, lib erty, and free enterprise been under such an assault. Much the same is true in England; Canada and Germany have succumbed. The citizenry thinks much the opposite, and this is true to history; in 1933 the great mass of German people had no idea what was to be in store for them. The loss of freedom is a slow process, which in our case has been ongoing for a hundred years. Incrementalism is the proper way to explain the progression. No sane person could possibly consider this attack to be by chance.

Conservatives will oppose my statement, based on the premise that recent Supreme Court pronouncements have established new freedoms, nude dancing, pornography, and flag burning, unintended by the founders. Liberals will oppose me, saying that the "conservative makeup of the Court, and Congress has curtailed freedom of speech." To both I say, please consider Hate Crime legislation, or more accurately thought-police action. It is, in my opinion, ludicrous to consider nude dancing as an issue; frankly, who cares, as for pornography, the second largest enterprise in America, it simply attests to our inevitable fall from grace. Flag-burning being simple and simple-minded, not one of these has anything to do with free speech. Only our Supreme Court could find the issue of dancing without clothes, pornography or flag-burning to be an expression of speech. This is, just like bussing and other issues, merely a diversion to keep your eye off the ball.

Many of you have heard me on the radio or on TV discussing various issues with one or another talk show host. I have been doing radio since 1997. During the second half of the Clinton administration, Hillary was successful in silencing a great many people. She succeeded in getting her husband and Congress to implement the Communications Act. I can tell you at first hand that this one act has done more to stifle free and open debate on issues than any other action, of government or outside it, in our history. As my new book *Our Political Systems* had just come out in winter 2004, I did a mailing to all the talk show hosts who had interviewed me on their programs, many of them numerous times. The result was that almost half of these books came back as undeliverable. Much to my amazement, I found out that over 800 independent radio stations had been bought up by conglomerates. These do not produce local content shows; they instead run the stations as robots, with all the programming piped in from LA or NY.

Newsprint is not much different; from over 4000 independent newspapers at the beginning of the 20th century down to less than 200 at the turn of the 21st century. People will say, but now we have

TV; great, and how many independently produced news programs does that provide? Not very many, considering that almost the entire TV news programming is the product of a very small number of networks, which all get their information from less than six sources.

In news magazines we are no better off, with the four major magazines all tied to the same publishing empires as aforementioned. Thus we see the old axiom; they cannot make you think about anything but they can most certainly make you think about what they want. Or, those who report the news decide what the news is about. Through one of the simplest propaganda tools, omission, they direct what you hear and see, and thus what you think. Generally, news distribution channels have been merging into large conglomerates for some time. In the latter half of the 20th century, however, this has accelerated. Syndicates who own radio stations, TV stations, newspapers, magazines and so on now dominate the media. The *NY Times* syndicate; the *LA Times* syndicate, the *Washington Post* syndicate, Newhouse, and so on are the media moguls.

In 1994, a maelstrom media battle is forming up between Hollinger International, the owners of *The Jerusalem Post, Chicago Sun Times*, and England's *Daily* and *Sunday Telegraph, vs.* a takeover by Britain's Barclay Brothers. What we see here is the even more alarming trend of cross-national media monopolies, which will surely be supporters of all global and multi-national business. When you consider that the mega-banks all have their hooks into these diversified multi-nationals, through control of them by sitting on their boards of directors, you begin to understand the interlocking mechanisms that allow Illuminists to control entire nations and industries.

The many-headed hydra of political control function is well established with one of the most publicly talked-about issues. Campaign finance reform that has been on the political front burner ever since 1974 when The Federal Finance Campaign Act (FECA) made it illegal, under certain circumstances, to publish your opinions about candidates. In this heinous law, citizens or groups were prohibited from expressing, in a coordinated way, support for or opposition to a candidate. The amount of money gifts was restricted to a set dollar amount in any partisan effort. This amounts to censorship of the very people most involved in the campaign, and without any doubt is a violation of the First Amendment, which pornography, an upheld right, most certainly is not. The so-called 2002 bi-partisan – a matter always to be mistrusted – Campaign Reform Act expands the previous ill-conceived law substantially. In fact, this act should have been called the Incumbents' Protection and Re-election in Perpetuity Law. It imposes severe restrictions in content as well as in financing, on dissemination of information relating to candidates running for election. Now I ask you, why would anyone institute a law to prevent you, my reader, from learning exactly what your incumbent voted for, and did, during his term in office? Well, the answer to that is simple; if most voters found out exactly what the bums they elected in fact voted for, they would find themselves out of office pronto. Was it the intent of the founders of our republic to prevent you from finding out what a Barney Frank, Tom Lantos or Charlie Schumer did as your representative? I should say not. The only exception to this law is that newspapers are exempt from it. Once you understand that newspapers are overwhelmingly liberal and leftist, and that when this law was passed the liberals controlled the Congress, you begin to understand what's going on here. Frankly, it has nothing to do with campaign finance reform and everything to do with the perpetual re-election of incumbents. We can clearly see that the McCain/Feingold bill is a system-imposed perpetuation for incumbents. If this bill had had anything at all to do with reforming a totally corrupt system it would have: restricted financial contributions to all campaigns to only individuals; restricted the amount of contributions by families; denied political party funds to any one running for office; prohibited financial support from business and labor; restricted contributions to only people living within the running candidate's district, and severely punished all contributions coming from outside the country. It does not do any of these things. There is no question but that the only thing this reform does is to restrict the freedom of speech, for individuals as well as groups.

To prove my point all we have to do is to listen to some prominent Democrats on the issue; Rep. Jan Schakowsky (D., IL) "If my colleagues care about gun control, then campaign finance is their issue so that the NRA[40] can't call the shots." Or then we have Rep. Rosa DeLauro, (S., CT) Rep. Marty Meehan, (D., MA) Sen. Harry Reid (D., NV) and Sen. Dick Durbin (D., IL) all stating that it's about limiting negative ads by the NRA. The disingenuousness of these representatives and senators is reflected by the fact that the ultra-liberal Washington-based AIPAC Zionist lobby, with 150 paid staffers and a $15 million budget, makes the NRA look like a piker by comparison.

In December of 2003 the Supreme Idiots in *McDonnell v. Federal Election Commission* was unable to find a violation of the First Amendment in this law. So much for free speech, I cannot find a clearer violation to the First Amendment (in the Bill of Rights) than this law.

We have a government-licensing agency called the FCC. The Federal Communications Commission is the agency that licenses radio and TV stations, and assigns them the frequencies on which they must broadcast. They allocate frequencies based on the "public interest;" no one has ever defined what that phrase means, but I can tell you from first-hand experience that access is very restricted. Along with the aforementioned enactment of the Communications Act under Clinton, the number of radio stations, in particular, has diminished by numbers exceeding newly issued licenses by 800%. This amounts to a restriction of access for the public, and is in my opinion a governmental agency's violation of the First Amendment. By allowing centrally operated conglomerates to provide programming for up to 400 radio stations, none at all are served, certainly not radio listeners in any specific locality, who are no longer able to obtain local content in programming.

Another device is the Presidential Debate Commission. Composed of three Democrats and three Republicans, its only real purpose is to keep third-party candidates away from any planned debate. This reached the alarming point where in the debate to be held in Boston in '96 there were over 15,000 protesters. These were conveniently kept over one mile away from the auditorium by Boston police, MA State police, and National Guard, including three helicopters. When Ralph Nader[41], who had a ticket, attempted to enter the auditorium, he was forcibly kept out. Then in the 2004 election the Libertarian and Green candidates were arrested in St. Louis when they attempted to enter the debate auditorium. The Libertarian had a court order to be delivered to the Debate Commission who had prevented his Show Cause order from being delivered in Washington DC. Both presidential candidates were held in Jail until the debate (propaganda session) was over. Not only is this undemocratic, but also to exclude the Conservative, Constitution, and Libertarian Parties, all of whom had gained ballot access in almost all states, is a confirmation that America is no longer free.

The heavy hand of government was used extensively in the '60s Kennedy administration, when then Assistant Sec. of Commerce Bill

Ruder admitted using the heavy hand of government in implementing the "fairness doctrine" to force conservative stations off the air, or at least to change their programming. They used the legal system to make opposition to their programming rules so expensive that most stations simply buckled under. In fact, the FCC is one of those agencies without which we would be better off. When I lived in NH, well over 200 national radio stations and four TV stations had interviewed me as an author. Being fond of classical music, I often listen to PBS, and so I attempted to get interviewed by them. While scores of authors and poets from Russia to California were interviewed, I could not get on their station. Finally, in desperation, I brought a complaint to the FCC. I proved that every author they had interviewed within 12 months had been a liberal. I demonstrated a severe bias in local as well as national news. I showed numerous false or misleading reports on many issues. The FCC was uninterested.

If we go all the way back to the 1930s we see FDR giving his Fireside Chats (Communist propaganda) and the FCC actively preventing any republican contradiction, criticism, or even opposing view. It is here that the "Fairness Doctrine" comes into play. It only applied to dissent against the ruling liberals and the empowered establishment.

The unrelenting assault on American's liberties has been accelerated by the Bush the Lesser administration under the tutelage of John Ashcroft. It was Ashcroft who was one of the architects of the Patriot Act, the most onerous and unpatriotic articles of law ever instituted in a democratic state. In violation of almost the entire Bill of Rights, it is an affront to the republic. Under this law government may at their discretion; listen in on attorney-client conversations without a court order, impose gag orders on bankers after they have pilfered a person's account without a warrant, force a doctor to divulge private medical information on his client, arrest people without a warrant, while withholding their name, and not even identifying the arrest, arrest people under secret warrants, monitor e-mails and telephone conversations without due cause. Hold people in prison indefinitely in violation of the law. The list is in fact endless; it is more than an assault, it is imposed dictatorship. Since 9-11 the Justice department has issued 113 secret warrants – which, by the way, is over double the number of such warrants issued in the previous twenty-plus years. All this, in view of the fact that they are unable to locate 340,000 illegal convicted felon immigrants, and somewhere between 16 and 22 million illegal immigrants, leads one to understand just exactly how specious their supposed efforts to protect the public from terrorism really is. The fact that over half of all incarcerated felons in prisons around the country are illegal immigrants does not escape my attention either.

Annually a study is carried out in which a determination is made as to the state of freedom in America. The Heritage Foundation and the *Wall Street Journal* carried this out in 2003 as their 10th annual Economic Freedom survey. 155 nations were listed, and it was carried out before the enactment of the Patriot Act, based on previous year's data. The United States was tenth; North Korea was dead last. The fact omitted in the survey was taxes in America. We know that when we add all taxes together the average American family of four pays 49.2% of their total income in taxes. Can someone who has the government confiscate half of their income for purposes of the state be considered free? Added to this are property taxes, which all Americans who own their own home must pay. This is a tax on a personal possession by a third party who has no interest or stake in it. To make matters worse, they tax interest income on invested monies that have already been taxed. Additionally, America has a Capital Gains Tax. This is a tax on the gain in value of a holding. Consider; you pay taxes and with what is left over you buy a property, on which you pay property taxes. Then you go to sell it, and they tax you on the gain, if any, of the resale price. (They don't give you a credit if you have to sell at a loss.) What we have here is a tax on a tax on a tax, triple taxation. We are, as a people, nothing but slaves of the banking monopoly that is the sole beneficiary of our labors.

Tenth, in my estimation, is just not good enough, I want America returned to first; after all, we were first from the 1780s to the early 1900s. It was in 1913 that everything began to go wrong, the time we had our Congress – in violation of the Constitution – turn over the reins of finance to the international cartel that we now recognize as the Illuminati.

Since the late '70s government regulations have required private institutions and academia to punish speech that may be characterized as "hostile environment harassment." Just the consideration of such a law is stupid; the phrase aforementioned is so vague that it can be applied to anything and everything. It is no different than the Hate Laws now enacted in numerous jurisdictions, which amount to the "thought police" of George Orwell's *1984.* These actions attempt to restrain civil society to a standard imposed upon it by people who desire to rule it. Furthermore, the totally inequitable guidelines used to enforce these odious laws reflect a bias against all Caucasians, but especially Caucasian males. In the last ten years we have seen scores of murders by blacks of whites, some really horrific; not in one instance were the black racist offenders ever charged under "hate crime" statutes. It is relatively simple to see that this is merely another issue used to divide, and conquer, the general population through the expansion of racist legislation, and the anointing of a special group to the exalted status of victims.

It is through division of the electorate that the ends of the Illuminists can be implemented – that is exactly how it was done in France and Russia. This is again the group rights *vs.* individual rights issue. Our republican constitution does not, and has never, offered group rights to anyone. Group rights do not exist in law, and should not do so. If you have individual rights you do not need group rights; the only use that group rights serve is the separation of citizens into collectives that the implementers of them can then use to divide the opposition to make their plans come to fruition.

Behind all this we see PNAC (The Project for a New American Century), an organization that as far back as 1997 proposed the ousting of Saddam Hussein and the takeover of Iraq's oil. Richard Perle, Paul Wolfowitz, Douglas Feith, John Bolton, Elliot Abrams, and Dick Cheney were the neo-conservatives behind this proposal. Interestingly, Richard Perle is also a member of the board of directors of Hollinger International. They are all proponents of "total continual war," and all of them are comfortably ensconced in the White House. Oh, and by the way, they also propose war against Syria, Lebanon, Iran, Jordan, and anyone else who might possibly oppose Israeli hegemony over the entire Middle East.

Neo-cons, who claim the mantle of
Conservatism, are in fact a bunch of
Aggressive Zionists whose
Aims are more in favor of
Israel than of America.

TREATIES AND AGREEMENTS

Tum podex Carmen extulit horridulum. *

ANY consideration of how a secret third party is able to interfere in the governance of any nation must seriously consider the external (foreign) policy of that nation. There are forces at work both in the NAFTA[42] and planned FTAA[43], as well as in the EU[44], that are unknown by the people and are contrary to their best interests. In fact, it is my proven contention that a vast system of secret and semi-secret societies manages international affairs in the entire Western World. Without beating about the bush these are:

- RIIA The Royal Institute on International Affairs, London, U. K.
- CFR The Council on Foreign Relations, New York City.
- TC: The Trilateral Commission, New York City.
- The Bilderbergers: – Mostly NATO nations. World-wide, Europe.
- The Order [322, Bones, Skull & Bones, The Order of Death] Located at Yale CT

At the leadership of these organizations, represented though NGOs, (Non Governmental Organizations) may be found the members of the boards of directors of most multi-national corporations and academia, and they're international banking financiers. A large percentage of those directors are members of Illuminist organizations. Some of the private banks are totally Illuminist in managerial makeup. It is imperative to understand that in any publicly held large business the ownership of 10% of the outstanding stock certificates is more than ample for total control. The same is true of these organizations. While Illuminists may not even represent a plurality of the overall membership, if they direct the ideology and management, they in fact control it all.

An excellent example of that is the CFR's total control of American foreign policy. CFR members, since the presidency of FDR, have held virtually all cabinet positions, as well as the leading military ones, such as the Joint Chiefs of Staff. Furthermore, this has been under both political parties; should you locate one who is not a CFR member, then look to the TC or Bilderbergers for their involvement.

Those listed above are only the principal contractors for the Illuminists who are installing the New World Order internationally. In concert with the aforementioned, there are literally hundreds of auxiliary agencies, most of which are not even aware of the master plan, which could be considered sub-contractors of this vast spider web. These are such organizations as:

- The Runnymede Trust UK
- The Club of Rome Paris, France
- The Carnegie Endowment for International Peace USA
- The Carnegie Endowment USA
- Numerous environmental umbrella movements like:

- International Greens, Green Cross, etc.
  S. F., USA
- Green Peace – World-wide.
- Large international and national religious groups such as:

  The World Council of Churches

  The American Council of Churches

All these groups, which appear to have different goals, in fact work toward the same finality. If we examine the individual policies of these organizations in G7 nations it becomes readily apparent that, while most of these groups function within a national sphere, they in fact are international and have their individual counterparts in every nation. Thus the gun-control movement has a counterpart in every nation, as do environmental, social, economic, and political – as well as religious – societies. These then act as the driving force for domestic as well as foreign policy in all these nations. As Mark Twain so aptly put it: "Some men worship power, religion, or politics, but all worship money"!

It has come to my attention that all republics, democracies, and constitutional monarchies have one constitutional item in common. In all of these states foreign policy decisions, once legitimized by legislative action, become an adjunct onto existing constitutional law. In America this is founded in the constitution: Art. I, Sec. 10; II, 2; III, 2; VI. In fact any treaty ratified by the government becomes part of the constitution. It seems that this interesting fact has not escaped the Illuminists, who have devised a diabolically simple means of circumventing the will of the people. In the middle of the 20th century, after W.W. II, we saw a rapid increase in treaties, which, as the plan accelerated, began to become economic in nature. Previously, that is directly after the war, most treaties dealt with national or international security, or, as with the Marshall Plan, the rebuilding of a destroyed Europe. These new economic treaties allow certain insider's unprecedented access and control over the economies of all the nations involved. They also legitimize the plunder of national economies for the financial benefit of a very small number of insiders. The international treaties that facilitate this process are GATT[45], WTO[46], EC[47], EU[48], NAFTA and FTAA, etc. All are international in scope, and all affect every citizen of every individual nation involved. Thus we can see that the Illuminists utilize international treaties, which are then adjunct onto the constitutions of the individual member states, as the means to circumvent domestic law, in opposition to the desires of the people. No clearer example of this exists than Clinton's illegally enacted NAFTA, which in view of overwhelming opposition could not be legislatively passed, and was enacted as an illegal agreement. Another commonly used ploy is to submit an agreement or treaty to the public, have it fail to pass, and then simply keep re-submitting it, over and over again, until it finally passes. If all else fails, the law may be enacted by judicial fiat, based on some bogus interpretation of constitutional law.

Supporters of globalization will inform anyone willing to credit their mendacity that its enormous benefit is to *"create greater economic equality; in which the process has largely been successful"*. Well, they are in fact correct, but are examining only one side of the equation. If, as they state, economic parity is closer to a reality; then the other half of the question is, at whose cost? India's, as well as China's, economies, gross national product, and individual well-being may well have increased; but at the cost, not of the bureaucrats, multi-nationals, and mega-banks who support these policies, but rather of the individual citizens, family farms and small businesses of the nations of the economically developed world. It must be clearly understood that the beneficiaries of these international entanglements are a very small and limited group, while the losers in the process represent 98% of the individuals living in the G7 nations. This is undoubtedly the reason for all the widespread opposition to globalization.

The advocates refer to the outcome of the plan embodied in their false slogan of Free Trade as "spreading the wealth." You cannot possibly become more socialist than that. What was previously and is still done on a national level, through progressive income tax schemes, has been expanded and internationalized. Please do re-examine Weishaupt's ten concepts. They are succeeding on a massive scale by their forced de-industrialization of the developed world, and their concept that the future for the West lies in economies based on the "service sector." Let me inform you of one simple fact that was well understood by the American colonists, and was the root cause of the Revolutionary War of 1776 between the American colonies and Great Britain. What the colonists knew was that any nation without a manufacturing base is the colony of a nation with a manufacturing foundation. What these mega- corporations are doing, through their relentless efforts to increase their bottom line, is gradually turning the G7 nations into colonies of the new manufacturing world. That is most certainly how it will end. While these globalists shamelessly tout the success of third world economies that they claim to be helping, they totally ignore the havoc that they wreak on the labor, small business, and family farms of their own countries. As Mr. Jefferson so aptly put it, "bankers have no country."

Consider the last few meetings of the globalists, Seattle, 14,000 protesters, Quebec City, 34,000 protesters, Genoa, over 100,000 protesters, the World Economic Summit at Davos, Switzerland, caused riots, and massive destruction of property in Zurich when the Swiss police refused to allow rail passage to Davos. The economic summit of 2004, also held in Davos, caused considerable riots in Chur, the closest railhead that protesters were able to reach. Opposition to NAFTA in America has remained steady at over 80% even with unrelenting false propaganda, by controlled media as well as government, on the issue. In the EU, the most virulent organ, the Euro, has been rejected by the Danes, and is opposed by over 75% of the British populace, whose government dare not put it up for a national plebiscite in fear of a repeat of the Danish rejection.

The consideration of the touted Illuminist idea of "spreading the wealth" and their Trojan Horse of "free trade" is the vehicle most prominently used to bring about their New World Order. Free trade is an oxymoron, a total impossibility unless all the citizens of all participating nations share the same basic incomes and benefits and all the laws of the individual nations are in compliance and are similar to each other. Free trade does not exist anyplace; what is instead the reality is government-controlled trade, which to be more exact is multi-national business-controlled trade, and the owners of these mega-corporations are the inheritors of Illuminism.

To prove my point is very simple. America has a population of about 280 million, the planned FTAA has 735 million; the average annual income in the 34 nations of the FTAA is about $857, while America's is about $24,000. This variance in annual income is 27 times, which means that an equalization of incomes between North and South America must result in a reduction of average income in North America to about $3,360 per year. If you do not believe that this is already taking place you must be delusional. Just since the enactment of NAFTA, America has lost over 7 million manufacturing jobs, over 2500 manufacturing plants, and our trade deficit is growing at a rate of over $40 billion per month. How long can we possibly spend more than we take in? With just three items, the 2004 war in Afghanistan and Iraq, the trade deficit, and the interest payments to the Illuminati, we are $1.4 trillion in the hole every year. Unemployment numbers rise every month – soon we will have as many unemployed as they do in Europe – and inflation is eating our lunch at a rate of close to 30% when compared to the Euro.

There are many ways by which your income can be reduced, while it appears that the opposite is true. All Americans have suffered loss of income for a steady 50 years. The consummate government and media propaganda, that Americans are better off than ever before, is an out-and-out lie.

Taxes consume 49.2% of the average American's income. This is and has been the fastest-growing increased expense over the last 50 years. Most citizens are unaware of this fact because taxes, fees, licenses, etc. have been so fragmented between federal, state, county and city that no one adds all the taxes together. At this point I should warn you that no government in the history of the world survived a tax rate of over 50%. In order to delude you, government data are falsified in compiling inflation statistics, by eliminating certain segments of the economy from the database used to compile the statistic. Those left out are taxes, energy and housing, the exact three that demonstrate the greatest rate of increase. To claim, as does the U.S. Department of Commerce, that inflation was less than 2% all during the '90s is ridiculous. Gasoline went from $0.78 to over $1.00, milk went up 30%, cars and motorcycles, meat, paper products and wood all went up over 15%.

The Department of Labor issues unemployment statistics; they compile these by counting only those unemployed who are drawing unemployment checks. Omitted are the homeless, the hospitalized, those whose benefits have expired, and those who are unemployable. To make matters worse, the Labor Department statistic of employment is increased every month by what they call the "Plug Factor." 35,000 jobs are added to the employed statistic every month, which the Labor Department claims have found jobs off the books in the "underground economy." In fact, every single statistic issued by any and all government agencies is suspect of being a hoax used to seduce you into believing that you are better off than your parents were. That is an insult. My father, after we became established in America (1954,) supported my mother (housewife) and myself, including sending me to private school; my mother had occasional household help, and we had two cars and a very nice house. Later my father purchased the house where we lived in Larchmont, NY, for $38,000. It was re-sold in 1984 by the then owner for $345,000, and I have been told that it would sell today for over $800,000. If that's not inflation, what is?

What I am demonstrating is that the bankers, i.e. the Illuminists, are operating a huge scam on all of us, and in fact, to use a metaphor, "taking us to the cleaners!" Do not for an instant think that Americans are alone in this gigantic rip-off. Let us examine the state of Argentina in winter of 2002.

The IMF[49], along with BIS[50] and the World Bank, are the banker's banks. In other words, these three are controlled by bankers who are members of national banks' boards of directors, the Bank of England and the European Central Bank (ECB) per example. The assets of these banks are in the billions. The directors are Illuminists to a man, and in addition a very large percentage are either Bones or Bilderberger members.

The latest victim of these banks is Argentina. Argentina was the third largest economy in Latin America; it had become dependant upon loans from the IMF to keep the Peso afloat. Bear in mind that by this time the IMF had already destroyed the economies of Indonesia[51], Thailand, Russia, and scores of smaller financial systems. They forced the Argentineans to tie their currency one-to-one to the dollar, and to open trade; i.e. institute "free trade" on a worldwide basis. They forced Argentina to privatize every sector of the economy in order to increase funding for the importation of cheap goods and to increase the float for the Peso. Argentina was almost instantly flooded with cheap third-world goods from China, something with which Argentinean manufacturers were no better equipped to compete with than are those in North America. The cheap goods flowed in, the Pesos flowed out and, surprise, surprise the economy collapsed. The rape was monumental; a French company purchased the water supply system for Buenos Aires and upped the prices by 400% in the first year. Then, to cap it all, the IMF forced Argentina to sign the "Technical Memorandum of Understanding," which forced them to: reduce civil service sector pay by 15%, and all pensions and social security to citizens by 13%. In addition, the IMF demanded that they balance the budget by the end of 2002. This would have required a $7 billion budget cut and an increase of $4 billion in taxes. The impact of this draconian idea would be an increase of over $5,000 in taxes for every Argentine family. Then comes the *coup de grace*, an offer to loan them $26 billion if they pay off all their debts in dollars. Due to the Peso's meltdown, they have to pay a 16% premium in Pesos to get dollars, so one year's interest on their outstanding debt of $132 billion works out to $27 billion per year. Not one penny is destined to go to Argentina, no more than the loans to Panama or Mexico in previous years; every penny goes directly to the bankers (Illuminists) to service the interest payments on the debt. Bear in mind that this covers only interest, not principal, so the total debt, just like our national debt, never gets smaller, and the bankers just keep collecting forever. The people are turned into slaves of the bankers to service the debt incurred by the politicians, who are the puppets manipulated by the Illuminati. Seems almost like our national debt, now does it not? Thus a nation has been kept in default for years while the bankers prosper at its loss.

The proof of the pudding, as they say, for my arguments against Free Trade can be instantly found in the economies of Japan and Germany. Japan was the last nation in the world to come out of feudalism, and it is reasonably argued that Japan in fact traded an entire class of feudal lords for a new and different plutocrat class, consisting of no less than ten huge multi-national corporate giants. [South Korea followed that model almost exactly] That corporate Japan is run and managed for and by a small number of large corporate entities is indisputable. This system originated in the pre-war era of 1937-45 and worked well in the development of imperial Japan. Large corporations are the easiest for government to identify with, (both are huge bureaucracies) and proved to be the model of operation in all the Axis, Italy, Germany and Japan for the duration of W.W. II. Taking a lesson from this, we can rapidly relate our plan for the future. Like Japan, America and the entire Western world is finding itself in a crush for mergers, acquisitions, down-sizing, and consolidations to ever-larger corporate entities – the Japanese national wisdom being that "what's good for these corporations is good for Japan." Beginning in the early '90s, this as has proven not to be the case. Japan has been languishing in the economic doldrums for the last fifteen years. They are seeing, just as we and the Germans are, the destruction of the domestic manufacturing sector through the unrelenting movement of their national manufacturing base to any place that can provide labor at lower costs. For Japan, it's Indonesia, Thailand, and China; for Germany it's Portugal, Greece, and southern Europe; and for America it's Mexico, China, and the Pacific Rim. You must understand, very clearly. that these corporate entities have no allegiance to any nation, currency, or government. They are governments onto themselves, their god is Mammon, and their only allegiance is to the corporate structure and money.

Now the supporters of these New World Order concepts will tell you the wonderful benefits that they have succeeded in achieving in such backwaters as:

Country	GDP growth	poverty reduction
Uganda	3.8%	5.9%
India	4.4%	7.1%
		(Over 6 years)*
Vietnam	6.4%	7.5%
China	9.9%	8.4%

* 1993-99

Source: World Bank. David Dollar. Globalization Inequity and Poverty since 1980.

What is vigorously omitted is that, as a result of these policies of "free trade," Japan has sunk into a deep depression; Germany has an unemployment rate of over 20%, while America has lost over 7 million manufacturing jobs to Mexico. America also has rapidly rising unemployment, as of 2000. Paramount in this equation is that most new jobs created in the G7 nations' economies are service-sector jobs that pay about 40% less. So governments tout the new jobs created in the economy, but do not publish information as to the pay scale of the new jobs. One would assume by the rhetoric of the New World Order that this entire effort is a humanitarian effort on behalf of starving and suffering poor people around the world. In fact nothing could be further from the truth. The only reason for all of this is the cost of labor.

The minimum wage federally mandated in America is $5.15 per hrs. (2002).[52] It includes such items as the Fair Labor and Standards Act, required Social Security co-payment of the employer, Workmen's Compensation Act, and naturally all the various OSHA, EPA, etc., etc., laws. The average Mexican blue-collar worker (2002) is paid $1.47 per hr. without any benefits and no labor union, and no OSHA or EPA enforcement. If you were an American manufacturer producing widgets and had to compete against foreign manufacturers without the protection of any duty or customs protection—where would you locate your plant in order to remain a player in the market?

Now, without becoming laborious, I hope that you understand that there is a group of financial gangsters who get richer every year, while all the rest of us get poorer and work longer hours. We are rapidly traveling toward a feudalistic state in which the privilege of title rests not in a family but rather in a small group of incredibly wealthy plutocrats, whose ultimate goal is a pyramidal feudalistic society with themselves at the peak. These people all are either Illuminist, or else they support and succor the cause of the Illuminati. All of the original Illuminist package of 10 principles, which can be found repeated by the Marxists, are now law in every single G7 nation. They only seek expansion, which is taking place at breakneck speed through such devices as; free trade, gun control, cultural Marxism, judicial activism, political correctness, graduated income taxes, environmentalism, National Park and Monument creation, rivers initiatives, destruction of small business and family farms, glass-ceiling issues, and education. Go back and review again the ten principles of the Illuminists!

The weakest link
In our American
Constitutional
Republic
Is
The apathy of our people for their own and
their posterity's future.

IMMIGRATION AND CULTURE

To destroy a society you must first dissolve the cohesive bond that binds it together.

ON Jan. 1 2005 news came out that the Mexican Foreign Ministry has published a 32-page comic book called **The Guide for Mexican Migrants.** Among other things is informs on the best way to sneak across the border without getting caught, how to avoid the American border patrol, how to cross rivers, not to carry any valid ID, and Mexican illegal immigrants rights under U.S. law, and so forth. 1.5 million of these comics will be published and distributed in Mexico.

A country, nation, state or community, right down to a family, is bonded together through the experiences, culture, and religious similarities they share. To annihilate this is not a complicated process. There are three ways in which it can be done; first, by unrelenting immigration of people of differing culture and religion, second, through wars of empire in which large parts of the male population are removed from the society, and third through an unrelenting *Kulturkrieg*. That we are as a nation in the midst of a culture war is testified by the fact that we even have a magazine by that name. *Culture Wars* is an outstanding publication, which exposes these Illuminist plans, published by my friend and fellow author Dr. E. Michael Jones. That all these processes have become an integral part of American society in the twenty-first century cannot be disputed. We learn some very interesting facts from the census of 2000, information that was released in early 2002.

The latest in a long line of goofy cultural beliefs is Afro-centrism, which is a pseudo-history developed by blacks who felt that Caucasians and Mongoloid peoples occupied a larger role in history than did blacks, whom they believe to be equally important. The fact that no black culture in the world ever rose beyond the Bronze Age[53] – none developed a written language, the wheel, or a numbering system – does not seem to impeach this judgment.

The basic premise of this idea is that Egypt, as the source of Western civilization, was a Negroid culture. On its face this is ridiculous. What do Afro-centrists believe? All based on no scientific evidence whatsoever; ancient Egypt was a totally Negroid culture. That melanin[54] is a superconductor, which absorbs all frequencies of the electromagnetic spectrum, can convert sound and energy into light and *vice versa*, and that it functions as a microcomputer to process information. If that's the case, why are blacks disproportionately unable to pass the high school curriculum, by a margin of 50 to one over other races? Afro-centrism believes that: In accordance to Allah the earth separated from the moon in the year 65,999,999,998,062 BC by an explosion. The black race was then born. For the next 66 trillion years they lived in happiness and perfection, speaking Arabic, just as they do now in the jungles of the Congo (where in fact no one speaks Arabic: now, the AIDS- and Ebola- infested jungle, which yields a life expectancy of 48 years.) All this tranquility was upset when a scientist named Yakub created an inferior race in the year 4707 BC. He worked for 600 years and finally succeeded in producing the blue-eyed devils, Arian Caucasians. Allah allowed these devils to live, and they developed an evil thing called civilization. Allah then allowed the devils to rule the world, but that would be limited to only 6000 years. He also allowed the creation of an evil religion called Christianity (it seems that Christianity came into being in about 4000 BC.) Their time was up in 1914; the white devils have been given a few years of grace but the jig is up, and blacks will rebel, kill all the blue-eyed devils, and live happily ever after.

One of the proponents of Afro-centrism is the inventor of Kwanzaa, the Afro-centric replacement for Christianity, invented by a convict while incarcerated in prison in California, and now a professor in the California state education system. (Only in California . . .) Kwanzaa is no less racist than is Zionism.

Distressing is the only word I can find for the situation on the Mexican border. At a welcome center on the Rio Grande in the state of Texas, staffed by volunteers from the local Democrat Party, we see a huge picture of President Bush hugging Vicente Fox, the president of the world's largest narco-republic on the wall. They can sign up right there for public assistance, learn where to get jobs taken away from Americans, oh, and yes, they can also sign up for future voter's registration, and get their American driver's license, without as much as a how-do-you-do, or any proof of age, birth certificate, or picture ID. It seems that Mexicans have more rights and privileges than do Native Americans.

The INS determined in 2002 that the previous policies, which allowed immigrants Green Cards with refugee status, primarily based on nothing but a homemade ID and the word of the individual, were no longer tenable. The World Council of Churches, the organization that is the major conduit for legal and illegal immigration, launched immediate complaints. Pregnant females without husbands are accorded special privileges; after all, with our convoluted immigration laws they can no longer be deported after they give birth, because their offspring are citizens by fact of being born in America. Five years after the birth, the mothers become citizens who then immediately sponsor their husbands and other relatives. When I immigrated in 1952 you had to have a sponsor who could guarantee your financial independence, and had to sign a document saying that if you were unable to support yourself, he would. Senator Kennedy had those provisions removed, and influenced the enactment of legislation that resulted in the immigration of so many indigent, uneducated immigrants. In the meantime, in California, birthrate statistics indicate that over 50% of new births in the state are Hispanic and over half of them to non-citizens. Nationally as of 2000 Hispanics outnumber blacks by 1%. In five years the Hispanic population in CA, TX, AZ, and NM will outnumber Anglos. *Adios amigos!*

On a national basis our State Department lists many nations as supporters or harborers of terrorism. These include Libya, Afghanistan, Iran, Pakistan, Syria, Yemen, Sudan, and Saudi Arabia; one would think, after the numerous terrorist incidents of the previous ten years, that we would have some fairly serious immigration restrictions from those nations. Wrong again, the U.S. State Department from 2000 to 2001 granted over 500,000 visas to citizens of the afore-noted countries. The second World Trade Center attack, on Sept. 11/01, was one of the resulting acts of that Clintonesque policy. As I have so often said and will continue to say: The U.S. State Department is the greatest enemy we face, and if they were a foreign power Congress would have declared war on them eons ago.

Department of State and HUD statistics:

- There are now 31.1 million foreigners in America. That corresponds to over 10% of the total population.
- There are 19.8 million illegal immigrants in America.
- There are just over 380,000 illegal immigrants who have been convicted of felonies and ordered deported by the federal judiciary, whom the INS[55] (Homeland Security) claims they cannot locate.
- Total Hispanic population is now 35.3 million; they are now equal to blacks in numbers.
- Average home values soared to $120,162 from $79,000 in the ten years since the last census. (No inflation here!)
- 17.6% of Americans speak a language other than English at home, mostly Spanish.
- In California, 39.5% of the population does not speak English at home.
- The number of households of heterosexual couples has declined from 54.5% to 52%.
- 63% of child suicides are attributable to fatherless homes.
- 90% of child runways are from fatherless homes.
- By percentage:
- 211,460,626 Whites are 75.1%
- 35,303,818 Hispanics are 12.5%

- 34,558,190 Blacks are 12.3%
- Hispanics now officially outnumber blacks.

Now I want to make you aware of some statistics that were not covered by this census, even in the exhaustive over-70-page question-naire that they sent out.

- The homosexual population of America is now between 1.4 % and 1.7% of the total population. (American Psychiatric Association) This information differs sharply from the touted line of the gay community, which claims they are between 10-15%.
- 50.5% of all child molestations are committed by homosexuals, the largest percentage being lesbian schoolteachers. (American Psychiatric Assoc.)
- Almost all of the mass murderers have been homosexuals. (USDJ)
- 85% of all children who have been diagnosed with behavioral disorders come from fatherless homes. (Center for Disease Control)
- 80% of all rapists motivated by anger come from fatherless homes. (*Criminal Justice and Behavior*, Vol.14, pp. 403-426.78)
- 71% of all school dropouts come from fatherless homes. (Nat. Principals Assoc.)
- 70% of all child incarcerations are of children from fatherless homes. (US Dep. Justice Special Report .78)

- Almost half of convicted felons were not born in the United States.
- America now has 6.5 million men in prisons, the largest number in the world.
- Hispanic immigrants in the South- Western United States are refusing to learn English or to assimilate into our society.

Well, I strongly suspect that this gives you a somewhat different view of our immigration policies as they now stand. There are paradigms here that we as a society simply cannot overlook. The current wisdom spouted by our leaders is that immigration is a great benefit and that the one-parent home (mother only) is of little social consequence, the wave of the future. The social concept that everything is a different shade of gray, and that truth and honesty are relative, is toppled by the above statistics. Illuminists are systematically destroying our society through these actions, and their lap dogs, the media, continuously support their stupid and wrongful dialogue. Anyone who cannot understand that this is a concerted organized and long-performing program, orchestrated by a small select group of individuals, must not be paying attention to current events. What I want you to understand is that these actions will destroy our countries – America, Canada, Britain, Germany, France, Italy, Switzerland, all of them – utterly and completely, and that is exactly what the New World Order wants. Some people are waking up to this, and the cases in point are Austria, Switzerland, and France, where nationalists opposed to uncontrolled immigration are winning election after election.

The Austrian Freedom Party, as well as the Swiss, French and Danish ones, has been the most active in N.W.O. opposition. In Switzerland they have succeeded in keeping the confederation out of NATO, as well as the EU, and in 2004 elected by large majority a nationalist party which will turn the immigration policies of the left around. In Denmark they have blocked the introduction of the Euro, while in Austria, an EU member, they were actually censured by Brussels for opposing the diabolical EU immigration policies. These policies call for virtually open borders between member states, an extremely liberal policy for immigration from non-member states, and political-refugee laws that are super-liberal. What the Illuminists have done in the EU, as far as immigration policy; will become the *modus operandi* for FTAA. When that takes place, which will be very soon, it will mean that the United States and Canada will be swamped with millions of *émigrés* from South America and the Caribbean Basin. The first to arrive will be those who are pregnant, now a very common practice from Northern Mexico, those with AIDS, particularly from Haiti, and all those that are criminal, sick, unemployable, and useless. After all, we must remember that in most cases people immigrating to the United States in the latter half of the 20th century and thereafter did so because they were the waste of the society from which they came. Our state welfare apparatus will be totally shattered within two years of FTAA acceptance. Reversal is impossible, because there is no instrument for member withdrawal from NAFTA, and there will be none for FTAA, just as there is none for the EU or the newly construed Russian Federation. Just as in *1984*, that famous book by George Orwell, the world is planned to be separated into several huge constructs. The Illuminati plan is then to keep these groupings in unending conflict, and thus keep themselves in power perpetually. If you are hesitant in accepting this fact, you can look it up in UN, as well as U.S. State Department, documents that go into great detail outlining exactly how the United States, Mexico and Canada are to be separated into regions that will not be run by any elected official, no indeed, these regions are to be managed by appointed mandarins. Governance in fact is to be very similar to the way that China was run by the imperial court; thus the word *mandarin* is more appropriate than *bureaucrat.*

The general immigration policy of the United States, as amended by that odious bill pushed through by socialist Kennedy, is one of the causes of the present American decline. The changes brought about by it have almost totally stopped European, white, educated immigration in favor of the uneducated, indigent, and sick from every third-world state in existence. There can be, when we examine this issue in a rational manner, only one explanation for this. I do not mean to intimate that legislators were in actuality intelligent enough to concoct this – in fact I doubt that Kennedy ever read the immigration law his bill enacted, any more so than did any legislator read the NAFTA accord or the U. S. PATRIOT Act; all these laws were passed by Congress before they were published, and had not at the time of passage been read by anyone elected to Congress.

At this point I think we should digress to explain how laws are enacted and where they come from. The average naïve American thinks that laws are thought up by the legislators brought to the floor of legislative bodies, possibly at the recommendation of some group or individual constituent. Absolutely nothing could be further from fact. Laws as proposed come from two directions, first from the lobbyists who provide the bulk of the "soft money" to the politicians in their re-election bids – all these funds may be assumed to come in the end from the Illuminists, who have most of the money, or from organizations that they totally control – and secondly from the bureaucrats who are employed by legislators as their aides and helpers, who again do not actually work for the politicians but for the "System" which again is totally controlled by the same powers.

The fact that our Western civilization is in a serious state of decline is no secret. Ben Wattenberg wrote *The Birth Dearth* in 1987; he concludes in it that by 2020, with current Anglo birth rates below replacement level, which has been a fact of life for over 20 years now, with our continued replacement decline, we will be a fact of past history. It is my contention that we are the first racial grouping in history to have demonstrated a totally suicidal bent. Any competent demographic researcher can verify that contention. That we are our own worst enemy in letting these multi-cultural morons eliminate our way of life, our society and culture, from the face of the planet speaks volumes for our brain-dead populace. In fact, all that was predicted by Oswald Spengler (in German, later translated) *The Decline of the West* (1918). Like myself, Spengler calls this process racial suicide. This is one of the hallmarks of empire. There are stages through which a society travels; they are, from a republic to a democracy, to an empire, to a dictatorship. We are today in the last stages of empire, and are rapidly approaching the totalitarian state, which will be the feudalistic New World Order of the Illuminati. Rome took much the same path; all the hallmarks of our current malaise were features of Rome in its decline. All we really need do, if we desire a more recent set of circumstance is to look at England from 1850 to 2000.

The policies of our Department of Immigration and Naturalization (INS) (Homeland Security) and our Border Patrol are no more helpful than a cow clap in a punchbowl. The Department of Justice initiatives after 9-11 leave one breathless. The very first speech given by our Homeland Security *Oberschturmbahnfuehrer* was that we would have to accept some considerable curtailment of our freedoms in order to fight terrorism. Let us look at this issue with at least a modicum of common sense. Every single terrorist act can be proven to have been committed either by foreigners – the majority Middle Easterners– or by people in league with one of our federal police agencies. These include the FBI, BATF, U.S. Marshal's office and the Department of Justice. Why do the freedoms of the people have to be infringed when none of the "people" were at any point involved in any acts of terrorism?

Unfortunately, things never seem to get any better. I am in possession of a flier issued by the FBI's Phoenix, AZ, office. The flier implores the reader who encounters any of the following to contact the *Joint Terrorism Task Force* immediately.

Right-Wing Extremists

Super Patriots; "defenders of the US Constitution against the federal government and the UN."

Can any one demonstrate one single case of a patriot committing any act of violence against our government or, heaven forbid, against the horror that is the UN?

Common Law Movement Proponents

There are numerous items listed under this heading. The fact that some of these people may be misinformed on certain issues of current statutes does not make them a danger to other citizens – in fact, the only so-called opposition that they do commit, in the eyes of the Illuminist-run bureaucracy, is opposing their will. Well, good for them!

Some of the items in this listing are downright stupid:

-Refusal to identify yourself, making numerous references to the Constitution, claiming driving is a right, not a privilege, attempting to police the police.

I can only assume that the author of this diatribe of rubbish has not only never read the Constitution but does not have even a vague concept of it.

Single Issue Terrorists

From the silly to the stupid and on to the moronic!

-animal rights.

I totally disagree with animal-rights activists, but to consider them as terrorists against America is moronic.

Then there are numerous headings that, unfortunately, I do not understand, and some that have at times done terrorist-type things.

-lone individuals.

What does that mean? If I'm walking down the street by myself I'm now a terrorist?

To make a long issue short, the brochure, which was widely distributed in Arizona and sent to me by one of my fans there, is without doubt the most witless stupid moronic piece of government crap I have ever read. Its three authors (stooges), Investigator Al Shearer of the Maricopa County Attorney's office, Jodi Stanul, FBI, and Terry Chapman, an analyst at the Maricopa Sheriff's office, should best be sent to a re-education course on law, civil liberties, and constitutional law, with emphasis on the Bill of Rights.

Not one single agency of our government has the guts to oppose the PC[56] Cultural Marxist ideology that has been introduced by academia and widely distributed by government law-enforcement agencies. Everybody knows who is committing these acts of terrorism! Now, almost no one has any idea why, but rest assured by the time you have finished this book you will know exactly the who, what, when, why and where of it all. If over 100 people are involved in a terrorist act, all of them are of Middle East origin and three quarters of those caught or killed are Saudi citizens, why don't we have a directive to watch all foreigners, and especially Saudis who are not holding proper Saudi papers? What in God's name is the purpose of checking airline baggage against boarding cards, when we know perfectly well that these people love to kill themselves? Why are constitutional rights suspended[57] for citizens when we know with certainty that all the perpetrators are either foreigners or U.S. Government assets? Foreigners do not have constitutional protection, and government assets are never tried, regardless of what crime they commit.[58]

Ted Gunderson was a regional FBI director for Southern California under the real FBI run by J.E. Hoover, before the bureau succumbed to PC. He at one time had 75 agents under him. I also know several other retired FBI agents and regional directors, who all share several convictions in common with me. All of us agree on these basic issues: 1) No Islamic cleric living in a cave in Afghanistan managed the Sept 11, '01 attack. 2) The Bureau was involved in the first Twin Towers attack, and in fact was the fabricator of the bomb. 3) Hoover would not have allowed the Bureau to become involved in either the Ruby Ridge or the Waco events. 4) The obvious politicization, feminization, and PC of the Bureau have basically compromised their effectiveness. 5) Actions by the FBI, BATF, and U.S. Marshal's office, have used military assets illegally[59]. (6) Waco was reprehensible, and someone should be prosecuted for over 80 murders. My good friend Clayton Douglas, who was the publisher of *The Free American,* also, I assume, supports those contentions.

Another way to disrupt the cohesion of societal formation is through relentless military adventurism in foreign nations. Since the end of W.W. II America has seen its military forces spread around the world. While this policy had some credibility during the Cold War, that is no longer the case. No more credible is foreign aid.

Military postings, particularly in the Army and Navy, have increased in duration to over one year. For families to meet a few times a year for short durations does nothing for family unity, it fosters divorce and, in the case of troops in the field, the highest suicide rate in American military history. At least the Roman armies had their camp followers; our troops are subjected to ridiculous Puritan ethics, and are supposed to stay celibate for terms of up to 12 months if they are single. Only morons would have developed such convoluted polices. All this is predicated on the false assumption that a professional military is in the best interest of the republic, which it is not. In fact, this is the very same mistake made by Rome. They replaced their militias with a professional military, which then, over time, took over the government of Rome and turned it into an empire. We have arrived at that point without any military take-over, but nevertheless we have become an empire. This militarism, by which thousands of young men are removed from the society, causes drastic cultural changes, which, when combined with other Illuminist-inspired processes, result in societal transformation.

The wars in the Middle East are about the control of a commodity and the advancement of Zionist hegemony over the Middle East, and not about America or American interests. If it were our true desire to absolve ourselves of the oil problem once and for all, we would simply begin to build Sasol[60] type coal-to-oil reduction plants. America has the largest supply of anthracite coal in the world, and the original technology dates back to the 1930s. At this time we have over 250,000 regular army troops stationed overseas, and unreported numbers, but exceeding 80,000, of Air Force, National Guard and Navy personnel. Any society that removes 25% of military-capable males from the community causes foundational alteration of that society.

The *Kulturkrieg* has been in full swing for well over half a century. The means used in its implementation is "Political Correctness," more aptly called "Cultural Marxism" or CM for short. CM is the insidious process by which language is altered from the norm in order to bring about a desired change in the society. The process is laborious and takes a long time to become a medium of change, but in modern America it has been at work for over thirty years. Derivations in meanings of words are a way of accomplishing this. Sodomite to homosexual, to homo, to Gay. Gun to rifle to weapon to assault weapon. Bum to hobo to homeless. There are literally hundreds of words that have been altered from a good to a bad, or a bad to a good, meaning, all depending on what the desired outcome was to be. The next and simple step is to enforce language by social pressure or, in the case of academics, punishment for violation of set codes. This results in the removal of free expression, and thereby free thought. This has now reached the point where college graduates are so strenuously brainwashed that they are unable even to defend their own race, in the case of Caucasian males. In the case of Aryans, they have been so extensively maligned by the Zionist-controlled media that any racial slur against them is perfectly acceptable. In the case of Jews, the exact opposite is the case, whereby anyone daring to say anything in opposition to Zionism or Judaism is immediately labeled a Nazi, and worse. All this meets the goals of the Illuminati well; it divides the entire social structure, whose individual elements then are easier to attack. All this leads to the inevitable group rights *vs.* individual rights, which is nothing less than just another Illuminist means of societal division in order for them to gain supremacy.

All the while the Bush administration is reporting about the phenomenal job growth rate; what they don't tell us is significant. In March, 2004, the administration reported a record new job-creation number of 277,000. They don't tell us, however, how many of those jobs are military recruitment, because HS graduates are unable to find jobs. They don't tell us that almost all new jobs are low-paying service-sector jobs. They don't tell us that none of these jobs are in manufacturing. Let's look at the numbers: 71,000 jobs in construction, how much of that are government-funded highway jobs? 47,000 health care, how many at VA and military hospitals to take care of the thousands of crippled vets returning from the Gulf? 39,000 restaurants, great jobs waiting on tables. 27,000 technical service jobs, fixing all that junk we import from China. 17,000 repair and maintenance, fixing more Chinese junk. 12,000 wholesale, moving the Chinese junk out of the warehouses. 7,000 logging and mining, so that we can ship our raw lumber to Chinese factory ships off the Pacific coast to make plywood. The list goes on; not one manufacturing job has bee n created. In fact, job losses in primary metals, -1,000, transportation equipment -1,000, electrical equipment -3,000, machine tools (the backbone of any economy without which you produce nothing) -1,500. The worst statistic may be found in foreign investment in America: 92% of all foreign investment from 1999 to 2002 (the last four years for which statistics are available) demonstrates that the funds were used to purchase existing American facilities. In other words, we are financing our import craze by raising money through the sale of our production capacity.

The white race is the cancer of human history, it is the white race, and it alone—its ideologies and inventions -which eradicates autonomous civilizations wherever it spreads, which has upset the ecological balance of the planet, which threatens the very existence of life itself.

–Susan Sontag (PBS)
Partisan Review 1967
Died Dec. 2004

No "Sunday" this bitch! And a commentator on PBS to boot!
How a total ass like this was able to maintain her position as a journalist at PBS, a taxpayer-funded institution, is incomprehensible Conceivably ZBS would be more in keeping with current employment levels at the network - Z for Zionist.

EDUCATION IN AMERICA

The major purpose of our association (Labor Union) is not the education of children. It is, or ought to be, the extension and/or preservation of our members' rights.

–NEA Union UniServe Bulletin
October 1991

"The NEA is a terrorist organization."

–Sec. Of Ed. Rod Paige
Monday 23rd. Feb. '04 at the White House
Addressing the Nation's Governors.

"I do not need your support, I already have your children's."

–Adolph Hitler,
when heckled by a protester,
in 1934.

THE AFT (American Federation of Teachers) and the NEA (National Education Association) are the most powerful and largest unions in North America. They are, and have been from their inception date, managed and run by a perverted group of leftists, who have an agenda that coincides with that of the Illuminati.

A.H.K.

Academia adverso flumine!

American teachers' unions, and there are two of them, operate on a social and political agenda that is totally contrary to the interests of the public, the children, and the republic (that was). The reader should also understand that the management of education, and by that I mean the superintendents, business managers, etc., shares the same goals, as do the teachers' unions.

Greek traveling professional teachers called themselves sophists; the word derives from *sophos* and *Sophia,* meaning wise and wisdom. They did not suffer from any form of modesty. For that matter, neither do our American edu-crats, who appear to be cut from the same cloth. The meaning of the word *sophist* gradually changed in ancient Greece to become; the itinerant traveling teacher who teaches for money.

Our modern American educators, like their Greek counterparts, give and leave little of value to our society, being much more concerned with financial rewards for their services rather than the goal of educating their pupils. Think, when was the last time you heard anything from the sophist society but fees, salaries, class size, workload, benefits or accommodations for them? American schoolteachers have the most generous benefit packages of any employment sector in the nation. Average teachers' benefit packages cost between $6,000 and $10,000 per teacher per year. On an hourly basis, they are paid over 80% more than private-sector occupations, and in work time they are occupied in their pursuit of teaching over 54 days less than the average American worker. The general public, which has been taught to have a greater interest in sports than in the education of their offspring, goes to compound the problem. We would all do well to remember that education is for the purpose of creating a responsible individual who will be able to reason soundly and to support himself, and not to play football, however much we might enjoy that endeavor.

The best-known opponent of the sophists was Plato. He particularly disliked sophists for three important reasons: they claimed to be wise, they claimed the ability to impart their wisdom to others, and they thought themselves justified in charging fees to impart their wisdom upon paying students. I don't know how you feel about Plato, but I'm surely impressed. The great philosophic debate between Plato and the sophists was rooted in the Athenian philosophy, which concluded that wisdom and beauty were not simply academic concepts, but were in fact rooted in the cultural and ethnic heritage of the Athenian civilization. Sophists, on the other hand, were of the opinion that any concept could be imparted to any individual, regardless of their cultural heritage. We certainly should by this time, over 2000 years later, have realized that the sophists were wrong. Contrary to this, the sophist beliefs of 2000 years ago have been heartily endorsed and promulgated by our own sophist academicians. Plato was right, and modern edu-crats are wrong. Any contrary statement may be drowned out by the noise we call rap.

Today, at the forefront of our raging *Kulturkrieg*, we find our sophist educators industriously indoctrinating our children with Illuminist "Cultural Marxist" (CM) rubbish. In fact, our entire civilization is paralyzed by CM. CM by its very nature is diametrically opposed to everything for which America stands; it violates our constitutional republican precepts, and runs counter to our national conscience. It destroys civil discourse between citizens, our governmental functions, our educational institutions; it is foreign, evil and Illuminist. The process of browbeating your fellow citizens into compliance with a dogmatic Communist philosophy is an affront to every citizen of every Western nation. It is not Christian in nature; it stems from Middle Eastern Judaist concepts. As such it violates every consideration of Western Culture, and the societies that have come to epitomize our civilization.

CM is the primary propaganda tool used in an effort to change our society, and destroy our common cultural heritage and unity. In this endeavor we find numerous means employed; pornography, radical feminism, the acceptance of homosexuality as normality, the suppression of reliance on constitutional law, the alteration of government from a republic to a democracy, and the vilification of anyone daring to oppose the plan, to the extent of making laws for the prosecution of violators of CM. Hate laws are an example, as is the concept of group rights. Words have meanings, and changing the meanings of words is another trick used by the Illuminists. This process, developed by the Tavistock Institute of England, has been rapidly growing in the last 30 years. All the phrases and words in truth express a concept contradictory to reality; cop-killer bullet, jacketed ammunition such as is used by every military in the world, assault rifle, in fact a semi-automatic rifle such as has been in common use since the 1890s, homeless, the anachronism that went from hobo to bum, hippy, how many can you think of?

At the outset of any discussion on education it is important to grasp that schools and education must be a local concept. Furthermore, that the crux of the Illuminati plan is to federalize and then internationalize education, so that they can control it. Regardless of the lip service provided by edu-crats, they do not want, and are wholly uninterested in, parental or local inputs to the educational process. These people are elitists, in whose opinion you are far too stupid to contribute anything. Their opinion on qualifications extends to school boards and anyone not a sophist with a PhD in reading and writing. The federalization of education is only in it's beginning phase, but has already resulted in disastrously lower student competency, test scores, and reasoning ability. One obvious cause for this is the reduction of parental involvement and local community participation in the subject. The federal government then begins to finance the local system, and naturally to mandate procedures, curriculum, class size, and what have you. None of these mandated programs are fully funded, and as we shall explore later, many are funded with less than 20% of the overall cost. This results in drastic shortfalls on the financial side, and the inevitable tax increases then required to meet the new federal guidelines. All these are then taken out of the local community, mostly through property taxes, requiring many retirees to sell their homes due to inability to pay the mounting taxes. Only with parental input in education can it be successful. All the driving force of the Illuminist plan of federalization of education rests with the AFT and the NEA, who are the principal proponents of it.

In verification of my précis of the issue I will make you privy to the resulting polling of their membership at the national NEA meeting in 2001. To grasp the enormity of this you must realize that the NEA has a national membership of 2.6 million members, and is the largest labor union in America. Together with the AFT, with whom it is closely affiliated, the two unions represent, due to closed-shop rules in many states, 95% of America's sophist edu-crats. During the convention numerous issues were brought to the floor and were voted on by the general membership, these included:

They Voted For: Reparations for slavery, the promotion of homosexuality, that 20% of the board must be minorities, to promote homo-sexuality as a positive social force, sustained support for the UN, and means testing for all Supreme Court Justice nominees. The last issue is particularly galling, because it is a violation of the Constitution.

They Voted Against: Abolition of death taxes, testing teachers' competency, merit pay, students' performance testing, attendance recording, advising union members of the *Beck* decision[61], charter schools, private schools, religious schools, prayer or a moment of silence, and any and all educational funding not under the direct control of the NEA or AFT.

A simple review of just the aforementioned issues illustrates with clarity that edu-crats are out of touch with reality as well as with the parents of their entrusted pupils. They do, however, seem to be in tune with the principles set forth by Weisshaupt. When examining the issues and teaching methodology espoused by the two unions, issues like Team, Goals 2000, OBE[62], you obtain quickly a clear understanding of the driving force behind these unions. In light of the fact that all teachers in Massachusetts were required to take competency tests and had a failure rate of 59%, that over 50% failed the second time around does not surprise one. Death taxes, merit pay, and competency testing – they voted the Illuminist line.

The disastrous state of our American public education system is in no small part the responsibility of the NEA and the AFT. They are the culprits directly responsible for the declining student aptitudes in public schools. In the international statistics of developed nations' education (1998), America managed a poor 19th in mathematics, 16th in science, and 35th in literacy. It is verified by statistical correlation that there is parallel between the unionization of education by the AFT and NEA and declining student proficiency. Just exactly how bad the situation is may be verified by the fact that

17% of all parents send their offspring to private schools, while 47% of public schoolteachers do the same. Not to be overlooked is the statistic that the largest by percentage of sexual child molestation, as reported by the child psychiatric association, is by lesbian schoolteachers. What a marvelous group of statistics for the endorsement of a profession. In an article in 1996 in the *Wall Street Journal* entitled "Lessons in Hypocrisy" we find:

Teachers and Choice

Teachers' Children vs. Other Children in Private Schools

City	Teachers'	Other	Difference
Baltimore	43.6%	18.1%	25.5%
Boston	48.9%	28.9%	20.0%
Cincinnati	42.0%	23.1%	18.9%
Cleveland	52.8%	25.5%	27.6%

In almost every instance and in almost all cities where an alternative to public education could be located, the average number of teachers opting to place their offspring in private education exceeded 18.9%. If that is not an indictment of the public schools I don't know what is.

The united front of these edu-crats can be characterized as totally in tune with the concepts of Francois Babeuf's *Nationalization of Children*, along with Marx and Engel's *Universal Public Education* theories, both of which were developed out of the Illuminist doctrine of Weisshaupt. In the 20th century we were to add Hillary Clinton's (ghost-written) *It Takes a Village,* which advances the same Illuminist theme that parents are far too stupid to see to the education of their own offspring. Such luminosity is then reinforced by OBE, introduced through Goals 2000 into all local school districts.

There exists in addition to all this a very well developed program that is actively pushed by industry and large business, and is in implementation stage by the education establishment, called "School to Work". This insidious program plans in the near future to do away with HS diplomas and replace them with a detailed school report for employers, and planned advancement in education. The record will include every detail of the student's performance during his entire time in school. It will be stored on an electronic data card utilizing RFID[63] technology which will allow any employer total access to the students performance and health record. You can forget about privacy, because employment without a card will prove impossible. This same program will do away with choice of advancement in education, and replace it with edu-crats mandating it, when and how your developmental education may or may not be allowed. They will pick your job, your college, your university, or if you are not in tune with their programs make you a garbage man. Parents and students are not to have any say in the process. The idea of the plan is to provide industry with single-issue employees, who are basically uneducated. They will not question authority, or instructions, they will not think, they will not reason, they are intended to do menial boring work in single-issue jobs. The subtle change away from the classics, reason, individual achieving, and self-reliance into an insect mentality more amenable to the multi-national megaliths that will employ them, is the plan. It is this group mentality that is fostered by another program called "Team". It is a debasement of Western Culture and education, in that Team requires five students to work jointly on any problems; thus the smartest one does the work and the rest coast. The fact that all great developments, inventions, art, literature, science, etc., have been made by individuals is strenuously avoided in this system. Once you understand that the educational department in universities and colleges has the lowest entrance standards, you begin to comprehend the cause that cultivates these programs.

To further obliterate education as it once was, we need only examine a present HS textbook on any subject. These texts have undergone, first, censorship by Cultural Marxists, and second, a process of dumbing down of all topics to levels far below what was taught in the past, as far back as 1800. In modern education as envisioned by edu-crats it is more important to feel good about oneself and be well adjusted with other students, and tuned in to multi-culturalism, than to learn anything. Above all, the most important subjects are no longer the three R's, but the three S's, Sex Ed, Sports, and Self-aggrandizement. History texts spend more time on the KKK than on Edison, Tesla, and Jefferson; Tesla, the greatest inventor of the 20th century, is not even mentioned, while any number of our founding fathers is omitted because they owned slaves. In fact, the names of past presidents have been removed from school names because it was determined that they had been slave-owners, as if that had any impact on their thought processes. Girls in grade schools are not taught abstinence, no indeed; they learn how to put condoms on bananas. Man-hole covers become people-hole covers, sodomites become gays, fat slobs become vertically challenged, cripples are disabled, morons are educationally challenged, and so on.

I have a reasonable number of friends who were college professors around the country, who quit their vocation for but one reason, the products made available to them as undergraduates lacked the ability to reason, to read and comprehend, or to write more than one paragraph in any rational manner. They did not desire to become grade-school instructors; it is not what they took their job to do. As a result of the revolution in education, we see the Harvard graduating class of 2000 containing over 75% honors graduates, thirty years ago the number was 5%. But as a result everyone felt good!

While it is difficult to determine where to begin examining American secondary education, I choose to start with the school board, which one would assume to be in charge of the running of public schools. The unnerving fact is that school boards are mostly impotent. Unless the entire school board is of one mind, something that rarely happens, the school superintendent of the district most usually gets his way. In addition, the board rarely has oversight of more than 5% of the budget, due to state and federal unfunded mandates. District school boards usually represent a cross-section of do-gooders and housewives, whose knowledge of education and management are vacuous. The superintendent and his usually able business manager thus manipulate the board like a troop of marionettes. The superintendent, who is well up on state and federal regulations. and is an education specialist, sets the agendas for the meetings, presents the budget through his business manager, and informs the board, often wrongly, of regulatory requirements, which necessitate actions recommended by him. He sets the curriculum, recommends which teachers to hire, and selects what facilities are to be expanded and why. It is the superintendent and his business manager who decide when, and how high, a bond issue is to be placed on the ballot. And so they run the district at their pleasure. When I was on a school board I took over the facilities committee, which in short order was able to cut the proposed budget by 15%; every year I was on the board, we determined that thousands upon thousands of dollars had been padded into the budget for unnecessary, wasteful and useless items. A resourceful super is more than involved in the election of board members; in my case he used, illegally, school funds and teachers to support my opponent's campaign. Why? A superintendent's pay is dependent upon the size of the district and facilities; the larger these are, the more he earns. The ultimate goal of every superintendent of schools is to: increase the size of the district, enlarge the facilities, hire more staff and teachers, falsely inflate student class-sizes, inflate student-to-teachers ratios, and work behind the scenes with the teachers' union to increase the teacher population. No matter what teachers and superintendents tell the public, they have one common goal, and the very same agenda, which has everything to do with their income and benefits, and nothing whatever to do with your children's education. Through all this they firmly support the Illuminist principles as found at the beginning of this book.

Special Education (SE) is a very serious problem in all public school districts. On average it is the quickest-growing portion of school budgets. SE was created by a federal mandate, which was to be funded by the federal Department of Education, but was not fully funded. The DE does contribute, but at a level covering only about 14% of the overall cost. This leaves school districts, children and the parents of them in a limbo world, where the government enforces a very bad and expensive law and then refuses to contribute any meaningful amount toward its maintenance. The average school district spends between 24% to 34% of the overall budget on SE. Parents whose children are CODED[64] as SE students, and who benefit mightily from the process, will vociferously attack anyone who criticizes, or attempts to curtail spending in, it. The program is pure socialism hiding under the guise of "The Children." I know this from personal experience, being dyslectic.[65] I never had any special help and seem to have come out OK after all. We must ask the question, where did the concept of SE come from? It stems out of the very often promulgated but mistaken idea that all children and indeed people are equal, and that society must therefore make every possible effort to insure intellectual equality. This is pure crap. Not only are we all intellectually different but also we are physically different, gender different, ability different, and don't look alike. The concept came from the distortion of the constitutional precept of equality before the law.

It was in the Illuminist French revolution that the false concept of equality between all became a paramount social hypothesis. The Illuminists perverted this into a rigid dogma, falsely taught to every child in America, that every human being is socially, intellectually, and physically and gender equal; this is the greatest perversion of equality before the law that could be made. We see clearly the motto of the French revolution, *liberté, égalité, fraternité*: the second of these words, *égalite,* does not mean equality, but rather egalitarian, the proper meaning of which is equality with those who are better. Marie Antoinette explained it by saying, "The violent egalitarian mood, which has now for a year and more driven the military fury of the Republic". Napoleon's disposition of the republic by making himself emperor of France after the murderous revolution's ending gives one a clear perspective of what Marie meant, and the difference between the false translation and the actual meaning of the words.

Equality, or equality between peoples of various abilities and races and genders, is a paramount issue in the 21st century. The fact that the basic constitutional notion of equality before the law has been perverted should escape no one. Equality before the law is a basic God-given right accepted by our forefathers as far back as the Celtic civilizations. The perversion of that to intellectual, physical and other than legal equality is an affront to the ability to reason. The falsification of this basic idea to something that is totally impossible is an Illuminist Trojan horse, which is destroying our youth's abilities. God made us all with our special talents; they are different between genders, and even different within genders. They differ in race, where it is more than obvious that blacks make better boxers, and Asians make better professors, and males make better mathematicians, while women are mothers, and men are fathers. These roles are written in nature by God's own hand and are unalterable. Any attempt to change this will meet with failure and is moronic. This is, however, exactly what is being done. Women assigned by the military as combat infantry, blacks portrayed as professors, Caucasian males as garbage men. On TV there is the continual representation of blacks as the good guys, when in fact they comprise 15% of the population and commit 87% of all crime. There are protests that too many blacks are in prison, on death row, and that this is racist, when in reality they commit most murders and are exactly where they belong. There is absurd opposition by certain groups to the police "profiling" criminals or terrorists. This is not meant as a racist or anti-black paragraph, it is simply the truth, and unless we begin to accept the truth we are in more trouble than you can imagine.

A common process in education is that of Social Promotion[66]. We live in a very competitive world, and if we mean to succeed and eventually triumph, then we had better begin to spend more on our best product instead of on our worst. This is naturally the problem with all this equality crap. In order to make everything equal we spend most of our money and effort on the worst product (Head Start[67]) with little or no result. If we instead spent our time and money on the best we would reap great benefits. The insidious part of this equation is that teachers and school superintendents love these programs because they invariably increase teacher population, thereby meeting the primary desire of both groups. When I was on a school board in NH, I proposed capping the cost attributable per coded student to double the cost of a normal student. This would have meant that we would spend about $10,000 per coded student; in an op-ed article in the local newspaper by a parent of a coded student I was called a Nazi. We had at that time students who were costing us over $30,000 per year. It was my contention that it is blatantly unfair, and in fact a violation of the Constitution, to tax unequally and then to apply collected taxes to benefiting one particular group over another. This then leads us to the fallacy of "Group Rights", which is a primary means by which the Illuminists divide and conquer society.

Social miscreants have also instituted a diabolical formula for the federal funding of local school districts. This formula is based on family income, and is based on the fallacious concept that many children's parents are unable to provide for their offspring's proper dietary needs. They have ingeniously tied this dietary idea to district funding by the federal government. The to-be-expected result is that local schools do their very best to code as many students as possible for free lunch programs, and thereby increase the funding of the entire district by the Fed. It is at this point wise to remember that all federal funds come from your individual taxes, so the illusion of something for nothing is shattered.

School superintendents are enthralled with building expansion and construction; after all, the larger the plant, the more pay for its managers. They forever suggest that there is a dire need for more classrooms, libraries, gymnasia, and office space. The district I served in had the superintendent tell the school board that we were in calamitous need of more classrooms and teachers because the average class size was 32 students per class. I refused to go along with this and suggested that we do a study on it, to which the board agreed. What we determined was that, in order to inflate class sizes, the superintendent had counted as a single class, the entire football team, the band, the baseball team, the track team, and even the school choir. Then they eliminated all very small classes by identifying them as SE. The actual average class size was 17. Our district had seven plants, most with multiple buildings, four of which were single-story. Our superintendent said that we were required to install elevators in the three multi-story schools to meet the federally mandated (ADA) accessibility standards. When I studied the law it was very clear that we could send any handicapped students to the single-story buildings and save the district well over one and a half million dollars. We did that, but the year I was voted off the board the elevator construction began. We had two students in wheelchairs, and thus spent $750,000 per student to give them access. The average school superintendent in NH earns about $100,000, plus a very comprehensive health care plan and a very good pension. Average overall cost for a superintendent in a NH School district is between $150,000 and $180,000. To make matters worse they are edu-crats, so they have no knowledge of operations or management, and therefore hire a business manager for an additional $100,000 to $150,000. After an exhaustive facilities study we determined that the district was growing at a rate of one percent per year, and had done so for the previous ten years. This did not stop our superintendent (from prior to my election) spending $850,000 for a new library in 1993, a proposal for a $5 million bond issue when I was gone (defeated) in 1994, a 6-classroom expansion in 1997, and then in '98 another attempted and failed bond issue. He finally got me off the board in '98; costs began to mushroom, and before he left the district for more fertile grounds in '99 he had succeeded in raising local property taxes by almost 20%.

Budgets proposed by the financial officer (business manager) of the district are always carefully worked out to reflect 20% to 25% inflation over actual anticipated needs. In all cases there is also built in 4% to 6%, which is necessitated by the teachers' employment contract's mandated increases. These contracts are negotiated between school board members (non-professionals, or elected volunteers) and professional NEA contract administrators and negotiators. No wonder the teachers always wind up on top. Teachers represent the most over-paid and under-worked segment of the economy. Before we even begin with pay and benefits, let us consider that the school districts pay for; teachers', principals', and superintendent's association fees, teachers' licenses, and even union dues. This may change from district to district, but it is the overall procedure. Let's cut to the quick: the average starting salary for teachers in our NH district was $ 23,000 with a benefit package that cost the district $7,800; combined, we come up with a whopping $30,800 as a starting salary. To this we must now add additional perks like teachers' licenses, paid sick days, personal days, and so forth, another $2,000.00 making the grand total $32,800. The average salary of a college graduate in NH at the time was $23,000 with an average benefit package of $3,000, thus making private sector employment $6,200 less. That unfortunately is, as they say, only the tip of the iceberg. Teachers work an average of 182 days per year, while private sector employees work 236 days. This represents a difference of 54 days of work. While teachers on average obtain a 34% benefit package, private sector employees average 24%, or 10% less. This can all be calculated into hourly costs and pay scales. Our teachers' contract clearly stipulated that teachers must be on hand 1/2 hrs before the first class and 1/2 hrs after closing. So they worked from 8:30 AM to 3 PM with 3/4 hrs off for lunch. Teachers usually have two study halls and some dead time, but we will be generous and say they work six hours a day, only two less than industry. So we can work it all out: 6 hrs x 180 days = 1080 hrs. 1080 hrs divided into $32,800 = $30.37 per hr. The starting private sector employee is in a different boat. 236 x 8 = 1888 hrs. 1888 divided into $26,000 = $13.77 per hr. or just under what the starting teacher earns. This is certainly not the picture that the NEA, in their bulletins and press releases to the public and the media, reports. We had a teacher in our district who retired, at age 58, from the district after 20 years (full pension) at $65,000 with the usual $7,800 benefit package, the benefit package is continued, as is a pay scale just about double that of the starting salary of a private sector employee with the same qualifications. Often you read in the paper of some wonderful teachers volunteering to help students with the yearbook or some other project. Don't you kid yourself; every single motion by any teacher for sports, yearbook or what-have-you is by contract paid for. The teacher who volunteered for the yearbook while I was on the board was paid $2,000 for the effort. Sports coaches are the greatest recipients of such benefits. Sabbaticals are paid vacations of one year to tenured teachers[68]. These concepts concocted by academia are an affront to working people. Needless to say, no one was tenured and no one was granted a sabbatical while I was on the school board.

In the spring of 1998 the state of Massachusetts, for the second year, tested teachers seeking employment in MA schools for competency. 59% of those taking the exam failed it. Lest you think the exam was difficult, it contained questions like; what is a preposition? define a noun, define the word abolish. Teachers were allowed to take the very same exam over again in October of that year, about the same percentage failed.

If money were the cure for the educational woes that we suffer, our problems would have been solved years ago. To the contrary, in my opinion too much money is the problem. Schools, which are as a whole grossly over-funded, thus find the time to expand the nuclear curriculum to include numerous courses that dilute core subjects. The process of then offering students easier subject matter for required graduation credit produces less educated and less competent graduates. It is possible in almost all states to graduate from HS without having taken, algebra, geometry, botany, biology, chemistry, economics, world history, comparative religions, US government, or any higher mathematics. This was impossible when I graduated HS in NH in the '50s. According to the *National Center for Education Statistics,* the United States spent over $274 billion on public education in 1997. Average per-student outlays, in constant dollars, rose from $2,153 in 1960 to $6,123 in 1995. With this horrendous increase, which far outpaces inflation or the CPI, student performance went down every single year, while teachers' pay went up every single year. No wonder teachers don't want to hear anything about salaries tied to results. Private schools in the same time frame (1994) cost an average of $3,116 and produced better-educated students and higher competency, as tested through SAT exams. Furthermore, Roman Catholic parochial schools, at an average cost of $2,178, also produced substantially better results.

A former U.S. ambassador, Walter Annenberg, a multi-billionaire, wanted to memorialize himself, and thus gave public schools a gift of $500 million. The funds were parceled out to a number of mediocre performing schools in major cities; these included Boston, Chicago, Detroit, LA, NYC, Philadelphia, and SF – not one single beneficiary of Mr. Annenberg's largess showed even one percentile increase in student competency.

Goals 2000 and OBE, Outcome Based Education, are more of the curriculum of foolishness to be foisted on an unsuspecting public by the educational establishment. Since its inception the NEA has palmed off one losing stupid program after another; all these failed teaching methods have resulted in lowering student aptitude every year since this union took charge of organizing teachers. Who can possibly remember all the hundreds of new innovative teaching systems that were to bring our students to the top of the world's educational ladder worldwide? Today, at the dawn of the 21st century, our HS graduates are at the bottom of the industrialized world in academic competence, in fact numerous third-world nations produce a better graduate.

The latest two solutions to this are OBE and TEAM[69]. Goals 2000 is the vehicle designed to bring OBE into the local districts. OBE was introduced into the Chicago public school district some years ago; it was scrapped after three years when the determination was made that the result of three years of OBE was a 15% lowering of students' aptitudes, bringing Chicago to almost 20% below the national average. OBE was tried in Sweden and Germany, both of which scrapped the program within two years. Every known place where this system was introduced it resulted in drastically lower student competency and was scrapped. That, however, did not impinge on the NEA or the AFT, who are vigorously pushing this program to this very day. The obvious benefit of TEAM is for teachers; by placing a good student in with every team of five students the teacher is assured of a higher average grade, thus coming out smelling like a rose, when in fact he lowered the competency of 80% of his students.

Yet another burden upon education is the Americans with Disabilities Act (ADA), it is unquestioningly the worst piece of legislation enacted in the 20th century, perhaps in world history. Again we are confronted with "group rights" and equality as the basis of this law. Group rights do not exist in constitutional law, only individual rights do. This law requires that students who have some handicap be MAINSTREAMED[70] into classrooms regardless of their disability. I have personally seen paraplegics with an attendant and on oxygen placed in a classroom. The child had no idea where he was or what was going on. I have seen students who start fights four and five times in one day mainstreamed into classrooms, causing continuous turmoil. I have seen poor school districts spending so much on making every classroom wheel chair accessible that they then lacked the funds to have a sports program or a science lab. This ridiculous law is based on the concept that we are all equal, and if not the State will make us so. Humans are not equal, and any exertion to equalize educational procedures to create something that is impossible is sheer Jacobin folly. All such circumstances do not edify the recipient of the benefit; instead it reduces the entire exposed group to declining to the lowest common denominator. This effort requires school districts to divert funds intended for education toward the construction of ramps, elevators, and physical aids, hiring attendants and special aides in a vain and pointless effort to equalize what can't be equal. Mainstreaming is simply an effort to integrate mentally and physically handicapped children into regular classrooms, a process that arguably does not help the handicapped children and diverts time, money as well as educational substance from the rest of the student body. This egalitarian process insures the hiring of lots of unnecessary personnel, and the national waste of well over $20 billion annually. To go from the ridiculous to the stupid all we have to do is examine 1993 EEOC regulations and rulings.

- In 1993 EEOC ruled that obesity was a protected disability. So being a fat slob and stuffing your face all day makes you disabled.
- A 410-pound NYC subway worker, who was not promoted because, according to the MTA, he could not fit into the subway driver's compartment, sued the city under EEOC. He Won!
- A 470-pound woman sued Lowe's cinema because she could not fit into any of the seats in the theater. She Won!
- A deaf woman sued Burger King because she was unable to hear the order-taker at the drive-by station. She Won!
- A Hartford CT schoolteacher sued the school system when he was fired for addiction to cocaine; he said it was a disability. He Won!

The national association of counties has estimated that conformity to ADA will cost counties $3 billion each to bring them into compliance. All this plays into the hands of the Illuminists who use these laws and acts to wreak havoc on the citizenry, small business and family farms that are financially unable to meet the requirements of this law. It is a great aid in the destruction of small business.

In an orgy of CM our children are herded into state-run and -managed compulsory schools, which are better called brain laundries, where their minds are mutilated by a troop of nihilistic morons. Caucasian males are subjected to the spearhead of this, being instructed that they represent an inherent evil displayed by all Caucasian males. The fact that most schoolteachers are females and represent the largest lesbian segment of any employment sector, does not escape notice. Neither does the vote by the NEA to promote homosexuality as a role model. Students are then subjected to the notion that all cultures are of equal value, an assumption so stupid that it requires no comment. They are allowed to venerate some third-world Stone Age feminist idol Gaia[71] that has no intrinsic value and absolutely no relevance in the 21st. century. The continuous stream of false information about Western Civilization, and the Caucasian and Aryan race, is never-ending. It is distressing to an intelligent formative mind, demoralizing the best and the brightest of our children. All schools continuously teach that black African cultures developed numbers, writing, the wheel, which they did not; only one single tribe on the African continent attained the Bronze Age[72] and that was in the 18th century, probably under the influence of Caucasian Arab traders. The Afro-centrist assumption that Egypt was a black culture, one that is fostered by numerous corporations and organizations[73], is silly.

While everything written of above is progressing, the NEA has been hard at work to see to the enactment of regulations so as to increase the teacher population. One of these is a square feet per student requirement dependent upon age. Another is a planned law mandating teachers' benefits; another is a requirement for teacher's aides in all classrooms. Certification of school districts based on plant size and classroom dimensions. Please do note that not one of these has anything to do with students, their competency, or students' abilities after graduation, the very things with which teachers should be concerned. All these NEA-sponsored programs drive up the cost of education (your taxes) without one iota of benefit to your children.

The NEA and AFT have been very busy for a long time in the development of modern methods by which any intrinsic value our public schools ever had, are destroyed. Among these we find: INCLUSION, this is the process whereby CODED students that have been identified as CHALLENGED, a) stupid, b) criminal, c) crippled, d) paraplegic, and any unable to learn, are merged into the general student population in the process called MAINSTREAMING. The result, obvious to anyone, is the lowering of all educational standards. MAINSTREAMING also indicates the doping (particularly of boys) with Ritalin[74] in order to make them docile and amenable to the dogmatic rubbish taught. DEVELOPMENTAL EDUCATION is a process whereby the teacher alters the subject matter with his own interpretation of events, thereby preventing parents from finding out what is being taught to their children. COOPERATIVE LEARNING is a real winner. In math, per example 2 x 2 = 4, well, not always; if the child comes up with 2 x 2 = 5 he may well get a passing mark, effort = 20%, attendance = 30%, attitude = 20%, so if the teacher likes you 2 x 2 = 5 gets you the passing mark of 70%.

While school financing varies by state, costs tend to be close to similar. The actual method utilized to raise revenue for schools is unimportant; the funds come out of the taxpayer's pocket one way or another. Dare you criticize the demanded amount of loot, or to suggest that a lesser amount would do, you are immediately labeled as a child hater, or person "unwilling to pay his fair share." Before we even get to this argument I want to be very clear, I and my father paid for my education, I and my sons paid for their education, and the notion that I must pay for others children's education angers me considerably. Furthermore, I am uninterested in arguments of affordability; the parents in question should have thought of that before they engaged in procreation. This, by the way, happens to be a constitutional issue, nowhere in the constitution does it say that I am responsible to pay for your brat's education, all it says is that we all have the right of education. It must also be strongly pointed out that the only relationship between educational expenditure and students' competency is that the less money spent the higher the competency. Arguments by teachers unions and edu-crats to the contrary are false, as can be proven in every instance in every public school system. Washington DC per example spends the highest amount of money per student[75] : it also has the highest dropout rate, the lowest competency, and the highest crime rate. In NH the funding was drastically increased, and beginning in the year of increase students' scores began to plummet downward. The cause is obvious; as more funds are pumped in the curriculum is expanded and the requirements for graduation are diluted, and the entire system is on a downward slide.

Solutions to the problems in education are in fact very simple. I would guarantee that if my suggestions were followed we would turn the entire educational system around within four year, and in ten have the highest school system in the world.

- Disband the NEA and AFT
- Require competency tests for all teachers.
- Eliminate all bi-lingual education
- Test all students at the end of Jr. HS and separate them by ability into two different and separate end-goal systems.

First System:

- Change the required curriculum in HS to the core subjects of: one foreign language (four years), three sciences, mathematics including geometry, calculus, and algebra II & I, world history, American history, geography, U.S. government, economics, English (four years), world literature. Four years of gym. Four years of computer skills.
- Require a state-issued exam on all courses, like the NY State Regents exams.
- Extend HS class time to 5 hrs per day with one hr. of homework.
- Alter the HS education into two separate systems. The above and the below given.

Second System

- Is related to work/school program:
- Curriculum concurrent with extensive ability testing of all students in this classification.
- Identified ability to be matched with education and an employer.
- Student goes to class in morning and apprentices in the afternoon in industry.
- Class curriculum is tailored to planned vocation.
- Requirements also include one foreign language and computer skills for four years.

No student is to be allowed to drop out. HS graduation, either in job-related or college-planned continuation, is mandated. In addition, all federal involvement in education must be eliminated. The most basic reason for this is that the DE wastes over 40% of collected taxes in their bureaucracy's management. This means that over one third of the collected taxes earmarked for education are wasted in government administration. In addition, the federal government has not been shown to improve, or in fact even contribute anything to the improvement of, education.

The assumption that economic freedom
And political justice are
Our inheritance and that of our
Offspring, is foolhardy and naïve.

The belief of many is that a professional
Military is the salvation of society
And that the militia is not necessary.
You need only examine history
To see what are the results of a
Professional military.

Wise and careful examination of our path
Is the best plan for the
Continuation of our freedoms.

GOLD WARS

Mammon, as it is said, is the substance that makes the world go around.

GOLD is, as it has always been, the ultimate medium of exchange worldwide. While fiat currency is still conven tional, in lieu of hard money, that situation will soon change. "Gold is always accepted" was a statement made by no less a guru on the issue than Alan Greenspan, chief of the board of governors of the FRS[76]. Many peoples, including those of Brazil, Panama, Columbia and Argentina, are painfully aware of the reality of fiat money value. With the drop of the U.S. dollar of almost 30% in the administration of Bush the Lesser, Americans are apt to become more familiar with government-created inflation sooner rather than later. The drastic drop in purchasing power of fiat currency which is always the result of speeded-up printing presses, often resulting in blocked access to banks, safety deposit boxes and hard assets, together with confiscation of such assets, would not be anything new here in America, either. The manipulation of currency for the profit and gain of the leading elite has been a fact of life since the inception of fiat money. In fact, the debasement of currency is as old as its history. Romans under various Caesars debased the currency in scores of ingenious ways, even to the plating (silver wash) of bronze coins.

In a fascinating new book entitled *Gold Conspiracy,* Ferdinand Lips, a retired Swiss banker, urges us to heed the printing presses and the lack of moral control displayed by national bankers worldwide. He was surely in position of knowledge, having managed the Rothschild bank in Zurich, and being the founder of the Lips Bank Ag. also of Zurich. He states quite plainly that it is the purview of the banker to see to the interests of his client, to the preservation of his assets and to the growth of that asset.

This is also the responsibility of the national banks in relationship to the nation's assets. What a ruse! How can one even consider the issue of national banks as protectors of national assets, in view of the fact that they are private corporations whose only and primary interest are not the nation and its well being, but the profits and growth of the banking monopoly? When Congress in 1913, after three arduous years of in fighting, finally enacted the Federal Reserve Act they transferred the management, control of, production of, and issuance of currency to a private monopoly of international bankers. What they in fact did was to follow the lead of the Bank of England that had already submitted the pound sterling to a similar monopoly. It is true to say that all of the international cartel banking houses that own the "National Banks" of so many nations are under the control of the very same people. While Mr. Lips hints at this, he does not say it outright. The fact is that the Rothschild banks are one of the primary proprietors of these banking monopolies. Anyone who actually believes that the FRS is an American bank had better wake up. All large banks are, by nature of the international trading of goods and services, international in scope. The amounts of money that transfers on a daily basis are in the hundreds of billions a day; the ownership of these institutions of trade must therefore be international. This makes the assumption that the FRS is an American institution fallacious.

The problem for America in particular, but in fact in all the developed economies, to some extent, is that in the 1930s all these nations bought into a Ponzi scheme which we call social security. What's much worse is that the political structure, wanting to increase their constituencies for re-election, has instituted all sorts of expensive welfare schemes that they piled into the social security benefit systems. It is not unreasonable to make the assumption that over 50% of the total benefits paid out of these systems is being provided to people who paid either nothing or very little into the system. This is resulting in the gradual bankruptcies of all these schemes. The fact that residual funds of social security have been looted, replaced with IOU's and funds placed into the "general fund," goes to compound the problem. It is only fair to say that in the American system there exists a shameless series of lies, which the administrators of it have perpetrated on the unsuspecting public. When an American recipient requests a statement of participation he is informed that he has contributed *xxx* amount of dollars to the system and that his resulting monthly benefit is to be *yyy* dollars. The facts that the employer contributed an equal amount, and that no interest for the entire duration of payment is attributed to the benefit total, makes it not only a lie but also a crime.

The fact of the matter is that Congress maintains responsibility over the social systems and costs, but after relinquishing their mandated responsibility over control of the currency,this becomes impossible. Congress opted out of the Social Security system for themselves a very long time ago and that includes congressional staff, health care, as well as pensions. They have a system, which is over ten times more generous than the maximum attained by the rest of us mortals, and it costs them nothing. All things being *correct*, the funds collected for social security should have been invested in bonds,

T-bills, and other interest bearing investments, and the payout should have been from interest earned, not principal, but then that would be the real world. It is a fact than any private corporation or partnership that managed funds as Congress has would see their management in jail in a heartbeat. This absolute irresponsibility is one of the fulcrums upon which our present economic problems rest. The most severe problem, however, is seated in the fiat money that is relentlessly inflated by the FRS.

Why, as a matter of course, do all these national banks inflate the currency so relentlessly? The answer to that is the progressive income tax that the Illuminists have succeeded in getting implemented in every industrialized economy. By having one of the principal tenets of Prof. Weishaupt's theorems adopted by Karl Marx, a graduated increasing income tax, instituted taxes for all rise automatically by proportional percentage as inflation rises. One of the primary results of inflation is rising prices, as prices rise so does income, and taxes based on higher percentages of income automatically rise at a greater rate. The man who was taxed at 32% gets a pay increase and his tax rises to 38%: his actual take-home pay has gone down, not up, in value. When one comes to realize that the bankers earn about 22% of their income on national debt interest payments, the understanding of their why and wherefore are easy enough to grasp.

The amount of money is astronomical. Consider that over 20% of the entire nationally collected taxes go to these bankers. Let's assume that to be about $600 billion per year. If you now bump 10% of the population into the next tax bracket, and assuming that is only two percent higher, it is over $30 million. You need not think you have any way of escaping this perilous nightmare.

Because all banking is international and most transactions on the international level are consummated in U.S. dollars, we are all in the same boat. Swiss bankers have invested the bulk of the Swiss treasury asset of gold into dollar- denominated investments, because of their greed. They wanted to earn interest consummate with the higher rates enjoyed in America. The Germans and British did the same: no currency is immune; the Illuminists all equally screw us. While the citizenry of every nation gets poorer, the rich get richer, and the Illuminists, who are the richest of the rich, gradually cast their net and create the new global economy. Then they call it the New World Order, or, as Bush Sr. said, The Thousand Points of Light, which by the way refers to the assumed 1000 Illuminists who will run and control everything. Don't disdain my statements: I have studied this issue for twenty years. Bush, Sr., is a member of The Order, as is Mr. Kerry (Kohn), as well as Bush the Lesser. The Order, also called 322, Bones, and the Order of Death, is the American Illuminist establishment.

The Order is located at Yale University in a windowless three-storey building called the Tombs; they have an annual meeting on Deer Island, in the Thousand Lakes region of NY, with about 900 members, 300 of whom are active in government, banking, law and the media. There are some organizations, which they control completely. The Harriman Brothers Bank, with assets of over one billion, is one of these.

As discussions of gold, its value, and the implications for our monetary system come up, the first thing we must realize is that gold and silver are political metals. What I mean to say is that both of these metals are subject to manipulation of their value. This is more the case for silver, but in any event is a prevailing issue to be considered. Because both metals are sold as commodities they are subject to short selling, as well as massive speculation. Often this has the effect of over- or under-valuing this hard asset. It must also be remembered that gold in particular is incompatible with fiat currency as we now use it, because that paper money has no relationship with any fixed hard asset whatever. Factually, the money you use every day is backed by debt. This obviously leads to the question, how can debt be valuable; the response to that is also obvious, debt is not valuable.

Let us start at the beginning; fiat money is created through the process of creating a debt instruments. The way this works is that Congress spends more money than they have, creating a deficit; then they go to the FRS and ask for money. The FRS, being honest, tells them, we have no money but we will gladly give you some. So the FRS instructs the Treasury to issue T-bills, Savings bonds, and other loan instruments in the amount that Congress requested, naturally at interest and profit, and sells those loan instruments. As these are sold, they issue new money based on DEBT.

This in fact is the way the entire banking system works; it is called fractional reserve banking. It is dishonest. The process is the development of Jewish bankers during the Babylonian captivity. The entire process of issuance of currency ceased to be a viable process when Congress in 1913 opted out of the responsibility of overseeing "Coinage" as written into the Constitution, Article1, and Section 8 Paragraph 5.

Until Aug. 15, 1971 a linkage between gold and fiat money existed. However, on that date Richard Nixon, the sitting president, unilaterally defaulted on the government's solemn obligation to pay $35.00 per ounce of gold. Then, in 1978, the other shoe dropped, when the IMF modified its articles of agreement (Section 4-2-b) stating that no member nation may link its currency to gold. In other words, the Illuminists had made a massive coup by forcing the only remaining gold-backed currency, the Swiss franc, to cut its linkage to gold, thereby forcing the entire industrialized world into the same reserve banking system based solely on debt. Ever since that event the Illuminists have manipulated all currencies for profit and political gain worldwide. George Soros has proven himself a master at currency manipulation, earning billions in looting numerous national economies. The value of this money depends on the fallacious belief that the debt upon which the currency is based will someday be repaid. The obvious problem with this faith is that the total outstanding debt of the United States far exceeds its gross national product and will therefore never be paid off.

The economic danger of blackmail by parties holding huge amounts of American debt instruments is very real. As an example of what I think took place; when the PRC[77] wanted MFNS[78] they called Governor Greenspan and told him they were holding about $300 billion in American loan instruments and would dump them on the market unless MFNS was immediately granted. It would, in such circumstances, take Greenspan about twenty minutes to explain the dilemma to Congress. With unprecedented speed Congress issued MFN within days of China's request for such status. No Communist nation had ever received such benefit before, nor has one since.

Commodities markets are subject to manipulation of value by very large investors, especially if they act in unison. Regardless of market manipulation, the value of no commodity can be manipulated in the long run. While central banks hate gold because it exposes their smoke-and-mirrors operation, even they are unable to manipulate gold in the long run. This is clearly demonstrated by the labors of the national (central) banks and bullion banks[79] efforts to suppress gold prices, which have been totally unsuccessful.

From April 2001 to Dec. 2004 the value of gold has risen from $255.95 U.S. dollars to just over $430. A probable real value for gold, without the interference of short selling commodities or attempted gold value manipulation, is well over $600, based on 2004-dollar value. Because of inflation, whose consummate fallout is falsely reported by corresponding governmental agencies, gold must continue to rise. As we inflate our fiat money it loses value, as its value drops the price of gold in relationship to fiat money rises.

When governmental agencies report inflation numbers and routinely leave out the very factors that have the highest rise in price those statistics become worthless. CPI[80] is the primary measure used to judge inflation. The CPI utilized for reporting that statistic does not consider the following factors: 1) fuel prices 2) housing and 3) taxation. These three happen to be the most rapidly growing items in the entire economy; they demonstrate the highest inflation index. This is more smoke-and-mirrors in that, by falsely reducing the inflation index and the CPI, the U.S. government is able to keep Social Security payments and government benefits, and government pensions, at an artificially lower level. The VA, per example, based on these convoluted statistics, gave their employees a 1.4% pay-rise in 2004, the first in two years: does anyone actually believe that the total inflation from Jan. 2002 to Jan. 2004 was 1.4%? They, in fact, cut everyone's salary. Social Security recipients fared no better. Congress, on the other hand, fully aware of the farce over which they preside, gave itself an increase of $3,400. in 2002 and a like one in 2003 and $4,000. in 2004, this is more in pay increases in three years than the average SS recipients average annul pension.

If we now consider our astronomical trade deficits in the overall equation, things become downright scary. China is running a $125 billion trade surplus with America annually, with which they continue to purchase Treasury notes. Japan is doing the same thing. Combined, they have accumulated just over $475 billion of our debt. The interest payments alone are staggering. It is conservatively estimated that foreign central banks will purchase another $400 billion of American debt by mid-summer of 2005. By instituting NAFTA with Mexico we have gone from a $5.7 billion annual surplus to a $37 billion annual deficit. When we add the falsely reported trade statistics with Mexico[81] we can add another $60 billion to the deficit – more smoke and mirrors. In the last 2 years the government has added $1.94 trillion in debt. This represents an average of about $44 billion per month, but in Nov., Dec., Jan., and Feb. '03-'04 this has risen to just over $50 billion per month.

How do we pay for this? Easy. The Fed prints more fiat money. To be exact, the M-3 money supply has been increased on Governor Greenspan's watch by over 290%. To be more precise, increases in February of 2004 were as follows: $34.1 billion in week one, and subsequent increases of $30 billion, then $37 billion, then $17 billion, for a grand total of $118 billion. This would indicate a planned total increase in the money supply of $1.5 trillion dollars for 2004. Anyone who does not understand that this will devalue the fiat paper that we all hold must be in *Alice in Wonderland* world. A resulting effect of these policies is a sinking dollar. The American dollar has fallen a total of 29.7%, while gold has risen substantially, in the last twelve months.

There is only one more item I want to impart on gold and the dollar. Many Middle East oil producers are now demanding payment in Euros, a factor that has dire consequences for the dollar. China is expected to be increasing its requirement for gold to about

3000 tones per year: this in part is due to the anticipated selling of American paper and converting it to gold. The Islamic gold dinar is gaining popularity for the payment for petroleum products. If the oil-producing nations were to become aggressive in accepting only gold as the means to pay for oil, it would drive the price up to over $2,000 per ounce.

Many people within and outside government have warned of an imminent financial collapse unless some rapid changes are made. The U.S. Comptroller General, David M. Walker, has stated that government accountants have hidden massive amounts of debt, sums in the amount of trillions of dollars being not reported. He stated "These additional amounts total tens of trillions of dollars in discounted present value terms." He later added, "These additional amounts are likely to exceed $100,000 in additional tax burden for every living American man, woman, and child." The available solutions to this are: (a) raise taxes, not really an option, as taxes are already 49.20% for every American[82] (b) Cutting federal spending; this would work and would be simple to do but will not happen. To continue along, and place our children and grandchildren in hock, is most probably what the idiots we elect will choose to do. Robert Rubin, a man who, as a board member of Goldman Sachs and past Treasury Secretary under Clinton, should know, has said "Federal government deficits are expected to total around $5 trillion over the next decade." In my opinion, that is the very least we might expect. Based on the aforementioned numbers, and our expansionist military adventures, my guess would be closer to double that amount. Even the IMF has warned that "the deficit is as far as the eye can see" and may be anticipated to cause great pressure on Social Security payments.

Greenspan then rubbed some salt into the wounds by telling Congress that they should – ASAP – cut Social Security payments, increase the age of participation, and consider other cash-saving options. The FRS has every possible interest in maintaining the *status quo*, which allows them unpredicted profits at the expense of America's middle-class taxpayers. What Congress should in fact do is to eliminate useless and unproductive government departments and agencies like the Department of Energy and the Department of Education, the FRS, and FDA etc., saving over $200 billion, and apply those funds to the reduction of the deficit. They should scrap NAFTA: that would save another $42 billion. They should withdraw all American troops on foreign soil, with the exception of South Korea: that would save over $170 billion. They should force all government departments to cut costs by 3% and eliminate all budget increases. They should cut all government staffing by 5% through retirement and not hiring replacements. They should freeze all purchasing of capital goods. Last but not least, all government employees, including those elected, should participate in the same Social Security we do, as well as paying for their own health care: that would surely save $ 10 billion annually. As a last but most important item, they should fire every employee of the Department of State and begin again from scratch. All these should continue until the outstanding debt is paid off – whereupon the FRS should be disbanded.

JUNK SCIENCE

Is the driving force behind the socialist environmental movement!
It supports an agenda of stealing private property, through scores of ways.

SCIENCE is the published and peer-reviewed product of dedi cated research. Junk science is the politicized product of groups and individuals, who seek, through lies and distortions, influence over society in order to achieve some nefarious ends. Junk science is most often propagated by politicians and is, in the latter half of the 20th century, the almost exclusive product of the political left. Junk science is never subject to publication prior to being announced and most certainly not peer- reviewed by anyone. The greatest advertisers of junk science are the media, whose members in almost every case lack the educational acumen to reach realistic decisions in the sciences.

The most prolific producers of junk science in the last 50 years have been the environmentalists. Surely we all remember, a few scant years ago, when they cried out that man's influence on the earth would bring a new ice age. Or perhaps the Club of Rome's pronouncement that we would deplete all the world's oil, uranium, tin, copper, food, and gas by the 1980s. They, of course echoed the Malthusians who, more than a century ago informed us that while our food supply production grew at an arithmetic rate, population grew at a geometric rate, and the world would run out of food and space by 1900. The really humorous one was in the 1840s, when the *New York Times*, ever the paragon of leftist thought, advised us that due to all the horses pulling the NYC trolleys, doom was in the wind owing to all the horse manure, in which the city might well drown. NYC's downfall, as we all know, was not horse manure, but rubbish issued by the premier fish-wrap, the *NY Times*. The latter half of the 20th century was not devoid of numerous prognostications by the same group of idiots. The most astounding fact in relation to junk science is that its salesmen seem incapable of understanding that the sciences are not static, and that one cannot attribute presently known science to future solutions. Like nature, science evolves; thus foresight is a prerequisite to solving current problems. The success of their environmental campaign can clearly be foreseen in Dr. Goebbels' pronouncement that people are more apt to accept a big lie than a small one, and that lies repeated often enough become accepted reality.

A prime consideration is why do they continuously do this? The reason is political power – power over land and people. One of the prime directives of Marxism, as plagiarized from Weisshaupt, is that the state should own all the means of production, and land is a primary production tool. The total failure of Communism, socialism, and Illuminism seems not to affect its supporters in any way whatever. This single fact is one of the most puzzling in all of history; why would anyone support a system that has seen no success, and has in fact failed in every single application of its tenets to governmental operation? The desire for control is not difficult to understand, but why utilize a failed system? The reply to that is obvious. The reason Illuminism uses socialism and Communism is because they know in advance that either of the two will fail in short order. It is out of the failure of the socialist and Communist systems, and the turmoil caused by their failure, that they intend to take over the reins of world government.

Environmentalism as it exists in the 21st century is not about the environment at all; it's about control. In order to glean an understanding of this issue one must of necessity examine the environmental movement from the 19th to the 21st century. Any serious study of this issue will lead one to the conclusion that socialists and Communists, due to their inability to sell those -isms to the greater public, overtook the entire movement. All of the environmentalist movements of Europe have affiliated with the socialists and now joined the coalitions that govern in Germany, France and Spain. So, in order to attain the prime directive of Illuminism, they are redirecting their efforts from socialism to environmentalism. Communism has failed so miserably in every one of its applications that, with the exception of some minor stupid third-world movements, it has died out. Cuba is an economic basket case, the Communist movements of Columbia and Peru are simply terrorist organizations, and the entire remnants of the Soviet empire repudiate Communism as unworkable.

In support of my contention one of the primary environmentalist organizations worldwide is Global Green and Green Cross International. They are two of the most pronounced environmentalist organizations. The man behind both of them is Mikhail S. Gorbachev the former dictator of the USSR. As other 'Green" organizations their principal slogan is; "Fostering a value shift toward a **sustainable** and secure future". Every time you see the word sustainable you can link it to the UN, Club of Rome, and all the various environmental clubs. Sustainable is indefinable as a process, what it actually refers to is that some international agency will tell you what you can do and what you can build on your property. What has Global Green accomplished?

- $4 billion for sustainable energy in California. [The California energy crisis]
- $550 million for environmentally correct housing in the USA. [Solar energy that costs more than it saves]
- $12 billion for California schools. [I don't believe it]
- Wants to collect $ 50 billion for solar energy development in the next ten years. [Solar energy does not work in our present industrial situation]
- Collecting $ 100 million (in the west) to destroy Soviet era chemical weapons. [Built under Gorbachev's rule]

The world's most prominent environmental movement in the 21st century is in Germany. The German Green Party is a coalition partner in the present government, and accounts for a substantial percentage of the German electorate. It is my belief that the growth of the environmental movement worldwide is the direct result of very poor education in the sciences everywhere. It is virtually impossible to sell stupid and wrong ideas to an educated public, so we see that the requirements for graduation from high school internationally have been continuously and conspicuously downgraded to the point where, in America, it is possible in most jurisdictions to graduate from HS with a single science credit called health – i.e. the process of placing a condom on a banana.

At the time of the rejoining of the two Germanys, East and West, the three factions remained mostly outside the central sphere of German politics. These were the East German *Buentniss 90*, which in fact was an arm of the E-German Communist party posing as environmentalists. This party's primary function was a Soviet KGB-driven effort to destabilize Western industry through the enactment of draconian environmental legislation, in the West, in order to impede Western industrial prominence that had so far outpaced Communist systems as to make the entire Soviet industry uncompetitive in all terms. The second was *Die Bunten*, which translates into the Gays of the West, and *Die Gruenen* that translates into the Greens. We see by this the first portion of the puzzle, the joining together of an arm of the Communist party with the homosexuals and the environmentalists of the West. In fact it is no secret that the Greens of Germany had been infiltrated by socialists two decades before, and were in fact carrying out directives of the KGB. Neither is the realization that the present foreign minister of Germany was part of a cell of dubious parentage.

It is important to understand that the 20th century growth of Western environmentalism is based in a KBG directive to destabilize Western industry, particularly the production of electric energy. In contemplating a means of accomplishing this, the Kremlin [Gorbachev] determined that the most economical means of producing electricity in the latter half of the 20th century was nuclear electric generation. They directed all their preliminary efforts at the destabilization of this means of making electricity. They were very successful in this endeavor. This, in the long term, has resulted in draconian safety regulations that boosted the cost of building nuclear generation plants by a factor of over ten. In fact they succeeded not only in shutting down almost-completed plants, (Long Island, NY) but in creating a huge scare scenario out of Three Mile Island in Pittsburgh that in fact did not harm even a single blade of grass.[83] They created a totally unrealistic and silly fear of nuclear waste, and succeeded in blocking the construction of proven safe dumps for nuclear waste. Once the KGB had succeeded in the nuclear option, they went on to greenhouse gases, acid rain, etc. The Greens, whose direction and information stems from the old Soviet KGB system, have actively supported all these actions. It is ironic that nuclear technology is the cleanest means of making electricity that we know of, with the least impact on our environment. And this is a further proof that the issue is not the environment, but rather the control of land.

How did the KGB produce their false global warming model? Simple: they produced a computer model of the world without any oceans. How did they produce their imminent- ice-age scenario? Simple! They produced another computer program with a world as round as a billiard ball, containing no hills, mountains or oceans, nor even tides. Outcome goal, junk science, is all that they produced.

A review of actions of the Green so-called political parties of the world indicates a uniform and common purpose, only superficially related to any environmental outcome goal. Examining these objectives reveals the following in all of the parties, wherever located: a total agnosticism or even atheism of the membership (this may be assumed to be based in their belief that they are more knowing and far cleverer than God or the rest of society), and the false idea that the state is a better guardian of the environment than are individual property owners. The fact that almost all environmental catastrophes have been the result of governments is overlooked, as is the fact those individuals who own land have a vested interest in maintaining its value, whereas government has none. The Greens advocate universal confiscation of land, or its control away from private ownership, for the benefit of "society." These lead to socialist control of all land, one of the prime directives of Illuminism, as well as socialism and Communism. The conclusion that the entire direction, as well as management, of the Green political structure rests in Illuminist hands is therefore sustained. The response countering this is, how will Illuminism gain if the state in fact winds up with all the real estate? The very simple reply is that the Illuminists, who through their NGOs control every aspect of governance, also control the state.

"The Ozone Hole over the Polar Regions represents a disaster of epic proportions" has been one of the recent environmental pronouncements made by their bureaucrat ally NASA, as well as former VP Ozone Al. Let us subject this statement to some scrutiny. The timing of the announcement by NASA, that they had located this catastrophe, was just two weeks before congressional hearings to reduce NASA's budget. It was intended to prove the scientific worth of NASA, and to ensure further funding, so as to keep thousands of bureaucrats living in the style to which they had become accustomed. I should insert at this point that NASA employees are very well paid, and that as a past NASA consultant I am qualified to make that statement. It is not at all unusual for the environmentalist/socialists to ally themselves with one of the alphabet soup of federal agencies, as those are forever seeking self-aggrandizement to increase their slop from the public trough.

Real science reveals that the earth rotates as it circumvents the sun; it does so at an angle because the axis of rotation is tilted. This tilt creates polar winters, in which a winter of darkness continues for about half the year, whereupon the six-month summer of light occurs. This procedure is swapped every six months from the South Polar Region to the North Polar Region. Ozone is a gas comprised of three (instead of the usual two) oxygen atoms combined to form one molecule. There are two ways that ozone is created in nature; first, by lightning, and second, by exposure to solar radiation. Now if you have six months of darkness there is no solar radiation, and thus no ozone is made. As if by a miracle, according to NASA, we have a hole in the ozone layer. Rubbish; the hole is promptly fixed in the six months of ensuing summer. This process has taken place throughout eternity, or at least since the earth tilted on its axis. It represents no danger to anything or anyone.

"CO_2 is produced by man in the creation of energy (electric generation) and by automobiles, CO_2 is a greenhouse gas and is responsible for Global Warming". Wrong on both counts. The Soviet KGB concocted the entire global-warming scenario in the late 1950s. It was based on a computer model that ignored the oceans, which cover three quarters of the planet. The nuclear-winter scenario, another bit of junk science, was based on a planet as smooth as a billiard ball, no hills, no mountains; more junk. It was the KGB's idea to reduce Western industrial progress. American industrial production was the cause of this non-existent idea. The KGB was in fact so active in this field that they infiltrated numerous environmental groups, directing some of them. The Clam Shell Alliance (CSA) of New England, per example, was so thoroughly infiltrated by the KGB that FBI investigations of protests at nuclear generating sites in Massachusetts located KGB documentation in the hands of the CSA, listing guard positioning, defense strategies, and the methods best used to disrupt generating capacity. [Gorbachev was head of the KBG at this time] The most interesting part of this particular action is that nuclear power plants are one of the lowest producers of environmental harm of all large generating systems. Thus the uneducated fools carried their protests against the only environmentally safe and sound means of electric generation.

Real science teaches us that American industry and America's population is responsible for from 4.2% to 4.7% of total world production of CO_2. That Yellowstone National Park is the single largest producer of CO_2 in this hemisphere, producing over 40 thousand tons per year, and that termites, together with swamps (that's wet-lands to you environmental geeks) are responsible for 1000 times more CO_2 production than is man. This in effect means that if we shut down our entire industrial production, closed every single utility, and turned off every single car in America, the results would be barely noticeable. Global warming is in fact an unproven theory; there is not one single atmospheric scientist who will clearly state that this is in fact taking place. All these statements come from politicians who flunked HS science and bureaucrats whose employ is subject to this false theory. Global climate functions on a sine wave; this wave spans many hundreds of thousands of years, and results in alternating ice ages and tropical ages. Man has not been on earth long enough [recorded history] to know if we are on the way to another ice age, or a tropical age.

What environmentalists are unable to enact as land grabs, via parks, national monuments, national rivers initiatives, and confiscation of private property through eminent domain or other means, they steal through estate taxation and subsequent purchase. In Florida it is not uncommon for these Greens to *subpoena* elected officials to place Green legislation on ballots. In the Manatee County March 2004 Democratic primary, which posted a participation of less than 15% of the electorate, they proposed a 1.5 percentage increase of the sales tax, claiming falsely that it was for parks and the purchase of land for recreation. In fact, almost none of the proposed tax, which was anticipated to raise $18 million annually, was earmarked for any environmental purpose. Fortunately, it failed, even though the Greens had spent well over $50,000 to propagate it, while the opposition did not spend one cent.

So it is that, with the educational organizations of America and the world actively involved in reducing rather than improving education, we wind up with a population unable to cope with or to understand the ramifications of junk science. When I went to HS, I was required to take botany, biology, chemistry, and physics; in college I took one required science course, geology. Today it is possible, in some jurisdictions, to graduate from HS without a single science class, without economics, without government or comparative religion, all of which were demanded prior to the 1960s. The reason that junk science has become the mainstay of the political left is that most people, unfortunately including many college graduates, are unable, due to the lack of education on the topic, to dispute their garbage.

NAFTA–FTAA AND BEYOND

HORRESCO REFERENS
– I SHUDDER TO RELATE IT –

> *To compel a man to furnish funds for the propagation of ideas*
> *He disbelieves and abhors is sinful and tyrannical*
> –Thomas Jefferson

IN 1620 the Crown appointed Governor Radford to establish what was the first socialist community in the world in America. Within two years the experiment proved to be a total failure. The colonists were decimated, starving wretches. When, in the third year, facing annihilation, they threw out all the socialist ideas and began to operate in a libertarian free-market mode the colony thrived.

Opposition to the Illuminist plans for world conquest has grown every year of the past two decades. The first major opposition was the meeting in Seattle, Washington, which produced about 14,000 protestors, at least 13,000 more than participants. This accelerated to the meeting of the elites in Quebec, where 34,000 demonstrated under the cruelest military, police, fire department, and RCMP opposition that Canada could muster. Then came Genoa, Italy, where over 120,000 protesters brought the city to its knees. Shortly thereafter the Bilderberger meeting in Gothenburg, Sweden, saw a meeting held on an island with the bridge to it held by the Swedish army, concertina wire, tanks and all blocking access. This has reached the point where the location for the coming Bilderberger meeting scheduled for May of 2004 remains a secret two weeks before the meeting. Even the members of the organization have not been told the exact dates or the location.

The growing use of ski-masked hoodlum police officers to secure unpopular meetings, opposed by the people, is now a standard practice. I point out that in a free and open society there is no plausible reason for police officers to hide their identity. It is only when the realization comes that unpopular and often illegal law is being enforced that the state finds it necessary to hide their enforcers' faces. The meeting in Miami held in 2004 demonstrated police brutality, lack of understanding of republican governance that was simply unbelievable. In a free and open society police powers are very strictly limited to public safety, this is no longer the case in America. The Illuminists have turned the police forces of the world into an enforcement constabulary for their own needs. The average citizen who pays for police services no longer counts. Para-military trained pit bulls attack the very people who pay their salaries, and whom they are sworn to protect and serve.

It is ironic that the socialist and communist alliances are the only true visible opponents of "Free Trade" while the middle class who has most to loose is docile and indigent. This demonstrates another failure in that the communist system used to bring free trade about has lost control of its cadre.

Trade, we are informed, is free. The establishment at every opportunity ceaselessly informs all that we are pursuing a policy of Free Trade. This is in fact a lie. It is the Trojan horse with which societies and economies are destroyed. Free Trade is a fallacy, because no such thing can exist in a world ruled by international treaties foisted upon society by NGOs[84] and implemented by governments. GATT (General Agreement on Trade and Tariffs) and WTO (World Trade Organization) and NAFTA (North American Free Trade Area), and EC (European Community), and scores of other treaties and agreements dictating to governments and multi-national corporations control all trade. There is only one reason for these odious large-business entitlements. Large business operators have always disliked family-owned and small-business entities, because they beat them in the marketplace in every instance. Small business is more innovative, faster to react to market forces, more productive, better managed, and far more flexible. This is why all large corporations are perpetually gobbling up smaller business, so that they can reap the benefit of their superior product. The establishment of the SBA (Small Business Administration) was nothing more than another wealth distribution scheme benefiting minorities. Anti-trust laws are nothing but a farce in that they are not applied honestly and never will be.

When I was in business, my company, with a scant 60 employees, produced more innovations, new patents, and new manufacturing methods from 1963 to 1986 than Black and Decker, Skill, IR, CP, and Milwaukee, Bosch and AEG, all competitors combined.

Alas, the entire American machine-tool industry has been systematically destroyed through two processes. First was the buy-out of individual- (and always) family-owned companies by large firms, which were unable to innovate in what is the most demanding and complicated industry in the world. And secondly, by the international drive of the multi-nationals to produce at lower cost and therefore to transfer the manufacturing technology to third-world nations. I should point out that without a viable machine tool industry an industrial economy becomes non-performing. Without machine tools you produce nothing. Jefferson's quote at the beginning of this chapter more than just applies.

I cannot overemphasize the disaster that is about to befall America through the free- trade fallacy. My good friend Gus Stelzer, a retired GM executive, wrote a book called *The Nightmare of Camelot: An Exposé of the Free Trade Trojan Horse*, in which he outlines in great detail for 373 pages the eventual result of this fiasco.

[What is most astounding] as I write this portion of the book, we are at the beginning of our presidential campaign for the 2004 election, a few short months away. Both Bush and Kerry, the front-runners of the Republocrat party, claim to champion American labor. The idiotic unions have almost to a man endorsed Kerry (Kohn), who informs us at every opportunity how he will create jobs, while Bush tells us that he is the champion job-creator, because the economy has lots of new jobs. Well, they are both liars. Both support NAFTA, both supports expanding NAFTA into FTAA. Both are incapable of producing jobs, which Bush and Kerry claim to be doing. Government does not produce jobs, it consumes taxes.

On trade, we must examine NAFTA, because it is the most important agreement of American history.

NAFTA is illegal. NAFTA was instituted by an Executive Order by then sitting president Clinton. The U.S. Constitution clearly and precisely forbids the executive branch of government from making law. The enactment of a treaty whatever you call it is the enactment of law. The Constitution, Article 1, Section 1, states: *All legislative Power herein granted shall be vested in a Congress of the United States, which shall consist of a Senate and a House of Representatives.* Article I, Section 8, concludes: *[The Congress shall have Power]*

To make all Laws which shall be necessary and proper for carrying into Execution the foregoing Powers, and all other Powers vested by this Constitution in the Government of the United States, or any Department or Officer thereof. Even if a provision is both necessary and proper, even if it affects only one U. S. officer, only State officers still can enact it.

Article II of the constitution deals with the power of the president. The words "executive order" do not appear anywhere. Article II, Section 2, Paragraph 2, deals with treaties. *He [the president] shall have Power, by* ***and with the Advice and Consent of the Senate,*** *to make Treaties,* ***provided two thirds of the Senators present concur... Then*** **in Article** VI, Paragraph 2, *This Constitution, and the Laws of the United States which shall be made in Pursuance thereof;* ***and all Treaties made, or which shall be made, under the Authority of the United States, shall be the supreme Law of the Land...*** We see by this that NAFTA was enacted outside proper channels, through a process called Executive Order.

Every president starting with George Washington used Executive Orders. However, during the term of FDR this procedure changed radically. Until FDR's presidency, executive orders were used to requisition supplies for the executive branch, to make repairs on the White House, and never once to make law. With FDR, our first socialist – or more correctly Illuminist – president, executive orders began to be used to make law, in violation of the Constitution. The Supreme Court has consistently refused to hear cases relating to this, claiming it to be a legislative matter. The presidency has now become so powerful that neither the Senate nor the House has the guts to challenge this illegal practice, the Supreme Dupes having already demonstrated their supreme cowardice. In the most recent case before the Federal District Court in Birmingham, Alabama, the Steelworkers confronted the validity of EO's in the NAFTA matter. The Birmingham appellate court ruled for the president and the case was brought to the Supreme Court, which ruled that it was a legislative matter and they would not hear the case. With the change in the election of senators from one of appointment by the legislative bodies of the various state legislatures to one of popular election, the act of impeachment, or enforcement of law, by the federal legislature against a sitting president has become highly unlikely.

Not only Clinton but also the entire media, and now Bush, have chimed in to tell us that NAFA will have no effect on our domestic laws. If you read the Constitution, at least up to the end of the Bill of Rights, it is more than abundantly clear that they are engaging in the propagation of a lie.

It behooves us now to examine who some of the prime supporters of NAFTA were, and how it came to be so popularly supported by the media, in view of the fact that it was opposed by an overwhelming majority, 86% of the population. At the time I first became aware of NAFTA I was an advisor on trade to the U.S. Department of Commerce in what are called DECs (District Export Councils). These DECs had on average 15 to 20 members from each state; because ours covered CT and RI we had about 17 members. The way this worked was that the Department of Commerce, before issuing any new policies on trade, would put this before the councils, who would then debate this policy and report on their findings through the secretary, who was usually a USDC employee. Having lived in Mexico for a year, I had a good idea what NAFTA would result in, so I was opposed to it from day one. If I recall correctly, I was greatly outnumbered on the Council, most of whose members thought that we would gain export sales to Mexico due to the agreement. I opposed this majority opinion, sitting more with the later-to-be-called "great sucking sound" attitude.

As the time for a vote by a post-election Congress approached, the USDC pulled out all the stops in an effort to get popular support for NAFTA. They, together with their Mexican counterparts, developed a strategy to win over the media to their position. In order to accomplish this, they decided on a 14-city tour in which they would present their case to the media in each of the planned stops. The first city was NYC; all members of the DECs of NY, NJ, and CT/RI were invited. I in turn invited my good friend the Swiss Consular commercial attaché, who was in his late 50s and had been around the world, as they say. We both had never before seen such a circus. The USDC front team that had flown in the day before numbered over 100. At least 50 Mexican payola masters were in attendance. We later learned that USDC had allocated $14 million for the blitz, and that the Mexicans had thrown in untold millions for payola. Members of the media were treated to free theater tickets, free dinners, yes, and even free massage-parlor visits, while the presentation was void of any redeeming value or even a factual statement on the issue; any media member from camera-man to reporter would, I am sure, have found it impossible to spend any of his own money for the balance of the week. So successful was the meeting that every evening-news source in NY touted the great benefits that would be reaped by all if NAFTA were enacted.

So now, nine years later, we are able to discern just exactly what those touted benefits were. For starters we had a Mexican trade surplus amounting to $5.7 billion annually, NAFTA turned this into an annual $34 to $44 billion deficit. In the first nine years of the agreement we lost just over 2500 manufacturing plants, my plant among them, and 3 million blue-collar jobs. In addition, European and Pacific Rim nations built plants exclusively for export to America, employing about 4 million Mexicans. So directly and indirectly we lost 7 million jobs. Furthermore American manufacturers rather than building plants in the States built them in Mexico, they allocated $2 billion to this in the nine years of the law. Unfortunately, that is not all; the Mexican Maquiladoro system assembles products that are 50% of American origin for re-importation to the States. When those parts are sent to Mexico, Commerce counts them as exports, when in turn they are re-imported they are not counted at all, and that includes the 50% made outside of the United States. In addition, the assembly labor lost on our market is also unreported. Altogether this amounts to about $12 billion per year. While total losses have not been computed, due to the nefarious way in which government tracks trade issues, a logical estimate of losses is $62 billion per year, while job losses are in the neighborhood of 7.4 million.

It behooves us now to examine the factual consequences of expanding NAFTA to FTAA, which both political parties desire to do. Mexico has a population of approximately 68 million. FTAA, we are informed, will consist of 34 nations of South and Central America and the Caribbean Basin, not including Cuba, but including Singapore. The total population of this planned region is just over 865 million, but the more telling factor is the average income of this region, which is substantially lower than the income of Mexicans. Annual incomes average: El Salvador, $1,020, Guatemala, $1,250, Columbia, $1,110, Peru, $880, Nicaragua, $470, Honduras, $890, Haiti, $380; the average income of the entire region is about $850 per year. Using these numbers of population and income, we are able to determine that in a level playing field scenario the median income of the region would be about $3,400 per year. This is a truly great deal for the aforementioned third-world nations, but a decided catastrophe for Americans and Canadians. The only beneficiaries of FTAA are large banking consortia and multinational corporations, in fact exactly the people who continuously push this on society. The specious argument that this will elevate the income of the third world is repudiated by the fact that, since the inception of NAFTA, incomes in Mexico have risen no faster than in the previous ten years: from an average of $1.44 per hr. to an average of $1.53 in nine years is no big deal. The statement that Americans and Canadian benefit from lower prices is likewise a lie, because average prices over the nine years of NAFTA have not gone down, they have gone up. The claim that Mexicans would use their income gain to purchase American made goods also proved to be a lie.

Now, having an understanding of the NAFTA agreement and the FTAA proposal, let us examine some remarkable similarities of all these trade block agreements and treaties – not just trade but all the various international accords made in the last fifty years. Let's also remember the definitive statement made by Professor Quigley of Georgetown University in his monumental work *Tragedy & Hope*, published in 1966, "*Our aim is nothing less than to create a world system of financial control in private hands to dominate the political system of each country, and the world economy as a whole. Freedom and choice will be controlled within very narrow alternatives.*" Naturally, this is all part of a much larger picture, but the chilling statement of Prof. Quigley expresses the goals of Illuminism exactly. The creation of trade blocks like the EU, NAFTA and the planned FTAA through the "free trade" scenario is the work of NGOs which, through their nefarious secret and semi-secret organizations, implement the treaties that allow them to control trade, banking and societies. These organizations are: CFR. TC, Club of Rome, Bilderbergers, RIIA, The Round Table, and Bones (The Order), all of them are either run by or managed by Illuminists. Every one of these treaties has the following similarities:

- The public elects no member of the ruling stratum of the pact.
- None of the operating organizations are responsible to any constituency of citizens, national or international.
- All office-holders are appointed bureaucrats, whose power exceeds that of nationally elected officials.
- There is no legally constituted means by which any member can withdraw from the pact.
- All of the agreements or treaties are dictatorial against the populace and enforced by bureaucrats.
- All supersede nationals in individual interests.
- All are expansionistic, and enlarge by economic intimidation or war.

With just some thought it is easy to see how these factors play into the hands of the Illuminati and their plans. It's as if one hand were washing another, a perfect fit as it were. An examination of the EU reveals that over the last decades power has been concentrating in Brussels, which in most cases exhibits a strong tendency to lord it over member states' elected officials. In fact, the Parliament in Britain is beginning to give the appearance of window dressing when it comes to most domestic issues. This is the beginning of the New World Order, in which governance will be changed drastically. The prime change is outlined in various EU, as well as UN, documents, all of which are in accord about the new and different way things will be run.

Electoral processes are to be changed, whereby people elect a political apparatus. What I mean to say is that you will vote, not for an individual but for a political party. That party will then appoint a representative on your behalf, as your agent to the ruling clique. Representative government, always a bother to Illuminism, will be eliminated, as will be your ability to influence your representative in any way or manner. This is exactly how the EU works in Brussels. It is how NAFTA works, it will be how FTAA works, and it is the model for government of the 21st century. If you think about this some more you will see that this is the way the Soviet empire was ruled, which as we know was an Illuminist construct; it is also how France was run after the French revolution, also Illuminist.

If we now examine the prime supporters of NAFTA we see support from the entire political spectrum, the left, the right, the center, the Heritage Foundation; all of them supported WTO, GATT, NAFTA, and are ardent supporters of FTAA and the EU. It gives one pause to consider the breadth of Illuminist control. No lesser person than Paul Gigot of the Heritage Foundation informed us in the *Wall Street Journal* that WTO and GATT would have no effect on American law. It would have been nice if Mr. Gigot and the Heritage Foundation had bothered to read the Constitution before they made their incorrect assertion. How can we blame them? Our own President Clinton, obviously not a constitutional scholar, made that very same statement.

Since 1998 I have been trying to get a copy of the FTAA proposals under the Freedom of Information act. I have been stymied, sidetracked and snowed half to death. My latest round of correspondence with the State Department, # 200400121, makes some astounding excuses for not providing the information in a timely manner.[85] The excuses are nothing short of ridiculous. a) We are very busy and simply can't keep up with the work. b) We cannot determine exactly what it is you want. c) All other requesters pay search time after 2 hours/ duplication costs after the first 100 pages. All these rubbishy excuses come from Katrina M. Wood [Requester Communications Branch.] I remember that during the Second World War the Germans had a wonderful way of criticizing the Nazi bureaucracy: they said, "*Sieg Heil Die Kreisleitung.*" An approximate translation would be "Hail the circumvention-department." What I asked for, and they, in violation of law, refuse to give me, is the proposal that was first made by Secretary of State Warren Christopher in 1966 in Asuncion, Buenos Aires, and Brasilia, and which he said would be enacted by 2005. This is hardly 100 pages; it was a proposal that outlined what the FTAA treaty would look like.

Am I being unreasonable in asking my government to let me and the rest of America know what it is they plan to do? In view of the NAFTA fiasco, should we not have a public discussion about the planned expansion of NAFTA? Well, I am disposed to tell you exactly why they insist on withholding the information from everyone. Almost one year after enactment of NAFTA, I was able to obtain a copy of the diabolical agreement. It consists of two books: Volume I is 8" x 11" and 1 1/4" thick: Volume II is 8" x 11" and 1" thick. The pages are not consecutively numbered, and frankly I don't have the time or inclination to count them all, certainly over 1000 pages. Now think about it! What is the purpose of NAFTA? NAFTA is to reduce all duties and tariffs between member states[86] to zero over a ten-year time-span, at the rate of ten per cent per year. That's it! Why the hell would anyone need over a thousand pages to say that? I do understand that politicians and bureaucrats are a devious lot, but this is ridiculous, or is it? What if the entire intent of the structured agreement had a great deal more to do with the establishment of a new governmental structure that regionalized the participating member states into geographic constructs? What if a Secretariat was to be built in San Antonio, Texas, to administer it all? What if the United States, in this plan, was to be separated into ten administrative units? What if that plan was previously announced in UN documents?

I should at this point make you aware that when NAFTA was enacted by executive order and submitted to the Senate, not one single senator had read the agreement; I am absolutely certain on that issue, because it was not printed until one year after it was enacted, and was backdated to 1992.

Our friends the Illuminati are taking us on a little ride. They are the drivers, vehicle operators, vehicle owners, and destination aspirants. We are the fools who ride along to be fleeced at the end of the trip. Fleeced of our freedom, our economic rights, our Constitution, our freedom of speech, our Bill of Rights. By the time they are through with us, the peasants of the dark ages will look great in comparison.

The Constitution and all its provisions, and the Bill of Rights, serve the people only as long as they vigilantly protect those documents from the politicians whom they elect and their serving bureaucrat stooges.

A vigilant citizenry is the bane of politicians.

It is not the prerogative of the Department of Justice, nor of the Congress, and certainly not of the executive
To defend the founding documents.

That is the responsibility solely of the Citizens.

When the people fail to uphold their bargain
In a republic they will suffer
Democracy!

THE MAIN-STREAM MEDIA

If you control the media you control the subjects under consideration by society.
If you control the subjects, you control the discourse.
And if you control the discourse you control the society.

America's media is completely under the control of Zionist/Illuminists.

THE aforementioned statements are indisputable. No mat ter how the subject is approached, America's main-stream media, and by that I include cinema, newspapers, magazines, recordings, TV, radio, pornography and book publishing, as well as distribution, are under the absolute control of the aforementioned people, exactly like the Bolsheviks of the old Soviet empire. For every Christian you can name in the media, I can name ten Zionist/Illuminists. For every Muslim – who by the way outnumber Zionists by large percentage in America – in the media I can name 100 Zionists. We will not even mention blacks, which are not under-represented, they are un-represented, appearing only on the screen but omitted form the decision making process. I want it to be perfectly clear that I am not speaking of the faces we see in the cinema or that read the news; they are, on the issue of content, irrelevant. What I speak of here are the movers and the shakers, the opinion makers, the bosses, the news editors, writers, and producers, those who direct content.

Seven of these people are in direct control of 85% of America's media. When one considers that Zionists account for about 1% of America's population, that percentage becomes fascinating. Could it be that the predictions in the *Protocols* are on target? They certainly seem to be, in that the takeover of the means of information technology dissemination is a key feature.

- Gerald Levin:

  CEO and director, AOL Time Warner

- Michael Eisner:

  President (former CEO and chair) Walt Disney Co.

- Edgar Bronfman, Sr.:

  Chairman, Seagram Co. Ltd.

- Edgar Bronfman Jr.:

  Pres. and CEO, Seagram and Universal Studios

- Sumner Redstone:

  CEO and Chairman, Viacom Inc.

- Peter Chernin:

  Pres. COO News Corp. Ltd.

What do these men severally control? ABC, NBC, CBS, CNN, MTV, HBO, AOL, FCNN, CNN Europe, Turner Broadcasting. But that's only the tip of the iceberg; Zionists own *Time*, *Newsweek* and *US News and World Report*, which account for almost 90% of magazine news-reportage in America. *Time* Magazine is a Time Warner subsidiary, Gerald Levin; *Newsweek* is Katharine Graham of the leftist *Washington Post*, and *U.S. News and World Report* is Mortimer Zuckerman, who also owns the NY *Daily News*.

Recently the retiring Malaysian premier said that Jews controlled the media of the world; the "never again" hyena cry could be heard in the Zionist-controlled media from London to New York. After reading this chapter, someone will please explain to me what part of the media do they do not control?

Let's take a short look at one of these, AOL-Time Warner. This conglomerate consists of: Time Warner Co., HBO East. HBO West, Warner Music, Interscope Records, Warner Brothers, Warner Brothers Stores, CBS (20%), Turner Broadcasting, CNN, FCNN, CNN Europe, Time Warner Publishing, *Time*, *Life*, *Sports Illustrated*, *People*, and *Fortune*.

What kind of entertainment do these companies visit upon society? I will not inflict the lyrics of the music on you; the titles are sufficient. *Kill d'White People, Sweating Bullets, A Fight, Lick Dem Mothaphuckas, What the Fuck, The Day the Niggaz Took Over.* Every title of these rap lyrics incites the listener to wreak havoc on Caucasians; not only can these morons not spell, they are incapable of rational thought. Lyrics suggest, among other things, that one murder, rape, rob, and bludgeon to death any white findable. Time Warner is the largest producer and distributor of racist hate propaganda.

Could you imagine the furor, lawsuits, and pandemonium if a white Christian company began producing records admonishing Caucasians to go out and kill, maim, murder, rape and sodomize Zionists and blacks? The Wiesenthal Center, the ADL, the Jewish Defense League, and The World Jewish Congress, along with the SPLC (Southern Poverty Law Center) ACLU, NAACP would be litigating and attacking everyone involved, while the government would be implementing hate-crime prosecution against them. Never mind that over 80% of the crime committed by blacks is against whites; in the eyes of our government and the FBI those are racist statistics.

If these people were Jews all this would not be a problem; however, they are Zionists and, as we have learned, they are motivated to take over the world, at least that's their plan. This then is the problem, a biased, un-informed, group of companies run by a monolithic racist set of individuals with a shared goal, which conflicts with a free society. This, as any intelligent individual will understand, does not bode well for a republican America. The general influence of the management of a corporation over its executive, editorial and functioning day-to-day operation is absolute. In other words, management, particularly in news reporting and editorial oversight, institutes general policies. Rarely are we privy to coverage of the IDF[87] shooting boys throwing rocks at tanks, beating up women, bulldozing homes and businesses, destroying orchards, stealing water supplies, killing innocent by-standers, and humiliating the general Christian and Muslim population.

Statistically we can see that the overall behavior of media personnel leans to the left. The political left is the side used by Communist/Zionists in the effort to implement their plans. Thus we see that in the Gore-Bush election 87% of the media workers polled voted for Gore. This is simply astounding; with all due consideration, Gore is stupid. His collegiate record is one of continual failure; he graduated with a C average, he entered both divinity and law schools and failed to finish either. But the real clincher is his ghostwritten *Earth in the Balance,* a book so full of errors, omissions, false assumptions, and just plain stupidity that any HS senior would flunk science if he turned it in as a term paper. When queried as to their political affiliation, a full 92% claimed adherence to the Democrat Party. When the question of political direction was asked, 85% said they were more attuned with the political left.

Considering that all wars and most insurgencies of the 20th century were seated in the political left (socialism, Communism, Nazism) this last persuasion is most unnerving. It goes without saying that if you are an ardent adherent to a political party or philosophy you cannot under any circumstances be impartial. The result of this is a from of historic and news revisionism (a Stalinist procedure) whereby all news and indeed everything related by media is distorted, tortured, and revised to meet the outcome goal of the reporting agency. They utilize all propaganda means, omission, invention, linkage, and distortion. It must be clearly understood that this process is not limited to news. All media – cinema, radio, TV, entertainment, music, and available literature – are parts of it.

The most difficult case to prove is literature and the printed text of books. I have had three 20th century politically incorrect books published in the last ten years. My first book, labeled a best seller by Amazon.com, sold three thousand books in the first year. But because I exposed the actions of the CFR, TC, Bilderbergers and Bones[88], I could not get a book review in any mainstream publication. When I approached the book review editor of the Tampa (FL) *Tribune* she promptly informed me that they would review my book directly after it made the *NY Times* best-sellers list. It is an interesting fact that the publishers and editors of the *NY Times*, *Washington Post*, *Time*, *Newsweek*, etc., are all CFR members. Print media offers a prize much coveted by writers; it is called the Pulitzer Prize. The choice made in awarding the prize comes from establishment officers in the mainstream news media field, most of whom are either CFR, TC, or Bilderberger members: thereby not the best article or the best exposé, or the truth, is the prime consideration for winning, no indeed – adherence to the established doctrine is the prime consideration. The simplest proof of that is the number of Pulitzers granted to journalists whom, it turned out, had fabricated their entire stories. This has not only been the case in newspapers but also in magazines, on the radio, as well as on TV.

Why, in any event, is the media so very important? It was not the case 45 years ago, what has changed in society to give the media such pre-eminence in information technology? Television is the answer. TV slowly became a prominent American means of news in the mid- 50s. Americans began with the idolization of such left-wingers as Walter Cronkite, who, in the opinion of the majority, was elevated to sainthood and could do no wrong. With the rapid growth of TV, print media became a mere second fiddle. In the 50s, 80% of households were supplied with morning papers; today that figure is down to less than 25%. Well, what can we expect; we live in a nation with 35% illiteracy in the 21st century.

Coupled with the merging and consolidation in the newsprint industry, which has shrunk from over 4000 papers to less than 230 in 50 years, we see the means used for control. The fact is that with TV more people can be reached in less time and with fewer words. Thus we have the development of sound bites, by which important and complex issues are reduced to inconsequential rubbish. In the mean-time, all media sources are being consolidated under the very same group of Zionists, many of whose companies own papers, radio and TV stations, magazines, as well as publishing houses and even book distribution networks.

Consider the Newhouse conglomerate. Si Newhouse through this company owns over 25 newspapers, and the Sunday leftist *Parade* magazine, which is delivered with almost every newspaper in the nation, the Conde Nast collection of magazines, including *Vogue,*

The New Yorker, Vanity Fair, Allure, and *GQ*. Well over one million subscribers overall! What I am trying to tell you is that your local paper is in all probability not local at all. When I lived in NH my local paper was affiliated with the Baltimore *Sun*. Now I live in Bradenton, FL, and my local fish-wrap is owned, lock stock and barrel, by the *NY Times* syndicate.

This however is not the real problem. The difficulty with newspapers is the three P's, Paper cost, Print cost, and Postage cost. The three P's are driving most smaller newspapers and magazines, with distributions under 10,000, out of business. Postage is one of the most insidious means of doing this, in that large-distribution papers are given postal breaks that are simply unavailable to smaller publications. My friend Paul Hall, who had published *Media Bypass*, has had to change to Internet publication, my friend Clayton Douglas, publisher of the *Free American*, is finding profits so low that he also is considering changes. All this is part of the overall plan; the total control of all media sources is in the hands of a very small group of control freaks.

Radio, once the most free and open means of news, is now in the middle of a consolidation cycle brought on by Bill Clinton's Communications Act of America. Instituted in the mid- 90s, at the request of Hillary to "stem the rising tide of the great right-wing conspiracy," it has more than accomplished its intended goal. Over 800 AM and FM radio stations have been consolidated into huge mega-conglomerates. Programming is no longer diverse, or local; programs that come from one of the radio hub centers are a canned bore, and espouse the same valueless drivel nationally. Where in the mid- '80s and early '90s I could line up 20 talk shows a month, in the 21st century I am lucky to line up two a week. Of the over 50 radio talk show hosts whom I know, 30 are unemployed. If programming in the station where they previously worked is now produced in Chicago and fed to the station transmitter via telephone line, they are no longer needed.

Book distribution, which in the past was one of the freest and most open venues, has degenerated to the point where a few large booksellers control over 90% of the market. This is a literal catastrophe for independent small publishers and authors. It does not bode well for the reading public, which winds up having good and interesting texts censored through omission. The deck is so stacked in favor of the large publishing houses, some of which also own distribution networks, that getting a book into the local Dalton's, or Barnes & Noble, is almost impossible. All purchasing is centralized in these corporate conglomerates, so that local managers have no input on the purchase of titles. I have had personal experience with Barnes & Noble, where you must run the gauntlet of the Small Publishers department. I had sold over 200 of my first title out of B&N stores in a short time span. I wanted B&N to stock three books in all of their stores. The person in charge told me that they could not do this because my book would not sell; when I told him that they had sold over 200 in two months, all on special order, he remained uninterested. Sales of books have nothing to do with the popularity of the subject, sales volume, or even redeeming value; no, as things now work the success of a book is based on the size of the publishing house and their insane distribution and sales strategies. Wining and dining of major news outlet book reviewers is also a factor of some considerable significance. Having been involved in the sales and distribution of industrial and hardware products, I can only say that book publishers have created a marketing nightmare due to policies that are not only stupid but also unprofitable. First off, unless you are a big-time publisher with lots of clout, the chance of getting a book review in any mainstream medium is non-existent. Large publishing houses have reps who wine and dine book reviewers continually; in fact, I have considered becoming a reviewer for a major magazine, as it would absolve me from purchasing food for the span of my career.

By the time my second book was published, my titles had sold over 4000 copies, and one year later the number was up to over 8000. After a serious disagreement on payment of my royalties[89] I was forced to dump my original publisher and begin looking for a new one. The only way to be a successful author is to acquire an agent for a percentage of your royalties, who will then try to find a large publishing house to carry your works. I decided to go POD[90] with Elderberry Press, a small house in Oregon, for my third book, *Our Political Systems*. Because authors get only a very small percentage of the take in book sales I hesitated to retain an agent, the only way to approach large publishing houses. As the author I have done 90% of the work, but I get only about 10% of the list price as a royalty. Booksellers, dependent on volume, get between 40 and 55%, wholesalers obtain a take, and the publisher, printer, and binder also get something. Considering that a non-fiction book takes about two years to write, plus about $1,000 in editing costs on a book that sells 10,000 in the first year, the author makes a measly $9,500 per year on a book selling for $20. You can only guess at what group of invertebrates controls book publishing, sales and distribution.

If, on the other hand, you are well-connected, particularly politically, all these problems evaporate – witness Hillary Clinton's ghost-written *It Takes a Village*, Al Gore's ghost-written *Earth in the Bal-*

ance, or William Bennett's ghost-written *The Book of Virtues,* which in fact was nothing but a compilation of other people's writings. All these books were published by large publishing houses, had disappointing sales, and, in the case of Ozone Al's book, could be characterized only as infantile. Then we have the Clintons getting between them an advance of over $20 million, which as far as I'm concerned is nothing but a political pay-off.

Cultural diversity is without question one of the main issues to promote Illuminism. The fact that the entire media, along with the academic establishment, are the principal culprits in selling this rubbish to an uneducated and malleable public is undeniable. PC, or as I prefer, CM – Cultural Marxism – is at the forefront of every media effort. Be it cinema, news, theater, publication, radio or TV, it is the dominant process found in all, and equally applied in all. The academic wonders are right behind, trying to outdo their media friends.

In 1972 then-President Richard Nixon, in a conversation with Billy Graham,[91] spoke at length of the stranglehold Zionists had over the media. While he mildly qualified the statement under pressure, he never once recanted it, much to his credit.

Among the glaring supporters of everything Zionist are the born-again idiots who have been led by their radio preachers into this unrelenting Zionist cabal. Hoping against hope for the instant Armageddon, so that they can immediately achieve heaven through rapture[92], they blindly follow any preacher who endorses this fatalistic nonsense. Unfortunately for the rest of us, there are no less than 40 million such believers in America, whom the Zionists groom and encourage in support for their "Greater Israel", both parties knowing full well that the expansion of Israel into Syria, Iran, Lebanon, Palestine, and part of Egypt, will most certainly result in W.

W. III. The actual crux of this lies in media control of the radio and TV stations. The Zionists control virtually the entire radio and TV industry, and they will not allow any criticism of Israel, or Zionism, but will actively support anyone who is in tune with their goal. These Christian preachers know on what side their bread is buttered; they have a very lucrative business whose ability to raise Mammon is seated in the media.

The most unlikely culprit in this entire situation is none other than the entertainment industry. The continuous stream of distortion of Western civilization, the adoration of third- world cultures, and the unending glorification of anything Zionist are relentless. Consider now the sensitive homosexual fine artist who is denied his rightful place in society due to a cruel and clueless Arian male, or the TV screenplay with the black scientist and his Hispanic assistant and the Caucasian janitor, or the great black enterpriser who has uncovered the evil white businessman who is raping society. Well, I have news for you: How about Michael Milken and Ivan Boesky and Ron (well, actually Aaron) Sommers who milked Deutsche Telekom of 300 billion Euros, or WorldCom, Qwest, Global Crossing, Tyco, Enron and Jack Gruberman, Andrew Fastow – these companies and people screwed society out of well over two trillion dollars, and every one of them is Zionist. Does the media ever report the fact that almost every case of corporate theft was and is committed by Zionists? Or how about the Rosenberg's, Pollard, Klaus Fuchs, Bruno Pontecorvo, Emanuel Bloch, Harry Gould, David Greenglass, William Perle, Abraham Brothman, John Vag-Weiszefeld, Edwin David, and all the host of Zionist spies against America and the West – are we ever apprised of that? No indeed, what these people do is to create hatred between blacks and whites, in order that they might have time to take over. By creating enmity between all their potential rivals for power, they unbalance the opposition. Every single movie produced by a major studio is directed at that issue. And then we have the pornography industry, which is 100% Zionist. Ron Braverman, Colin Bone, Wesley Emerson, Paul Fishbein, Herbert Feinberg, Hank Weinstein, Lenny Freelander, Bobby Hollander, Rubin Guttesman, Fred Hirsch, Marci Hirsch, Paul Apstein, Steve Crenstein, Jack Richmond, Theodore Rothstein, Rubin Struman, David Sturman, Ross Sullivan, Jerome Tanner, Armand Weston – sounds more like the membership of the Supreme Soviet, but then they also were Zionists to a man. The Hollywood-produced films of *Amistad* and *Pocahontas* are two fine examples of Hollywood historical revisionism, as are most produced movies. The diabolical nature of this beast is the direction taken in diverting a large portion of the effort to children.

Managing Diversity is a newsletter published by one Dr. Harris Sussman. The main line of this newsletter is to see to the replacement of Anglos in the workplace by minorities. In it Sussman, whose doctorate must be in one of the soft sciences, poses the question, "What are white people's values?" Well, since he asked, how about Plato, Socrates, Beethoven, Bach, Mozart, Rafael, Michelangelo, Shakespeare, Goethe, Schiller, Mann, Dante, Jefferson, Washington, Franklin, but I digress. Perhaps brain-dead Harris has a doctorate in crap, as this is what is probably in his head. In fact Sussman belongs right in with numerous Zionists like Morris Dees, the Bronfman's and others, they are all like peas in a pod.

News reportage, or the way in which news is presented, reported, and shown, has become a branch of the entertainment industry. In an ever-expanding fight for ratings, all the major TV networks appear to be solely an attempt to co-opt their competitors' viewers. News, as reported by ABC, NBC, CBS, CNN, PBS, FOX, hardly ever differs. While FOX at least attempts to be more even-handed, all news content comes from the same sources. As these networks all have only limited foreign correspondents, they must, due to financial restraints, depend on the large wire services to provide most of the content of international as well as national news. In the reporting of the Fallujah standoff in Iraq during April 2004, all the American news agencies pooled their resources and had only one team in that city. As a consequence, all reports from Fallujah came from only one reporter, how very convenient for them all. Unless they have an affiliate on location, speed and finance almost dictates that. International news services are Reuters, AP, and UPI, and some smaller ones like the *NY Times*, *LA Times*, and *Washington Post* syndicates. In any event, the entire news information network consists of a very small and select group of companies who are all controlled by...? You guessed it. I am always astounded if I switch channels, or record the news on one station while listening to another, that the net result is that all the stations report all the same news every evening. Just by the sheer number of events occurring worldwide that would appear to be impossible. Someone someplace is making a decision, and that decision is what will be in the news that evening. One of my friends calls TV Talmudvision. Neither Dr. Goebbels nor Uncle Joe Stalin could institute an improvement on the propagandistic means of media control exercised by the Illuminists who run our media enterprises.

The plain fact is that 85% of all media in the United State is in the hands of just five companies – when we add the other but smaller two, it's about 90%. This is unhealthy and wrong. If we look at Disney, Viacom, Time Warner, Universal/Seagrams and Rupert

Murdoch we have most bases covered. In the newsprint we can examine the *NY Times* syndicate, reasonably accepted as the most influential newspaper in America. The publisher is Arthur Ochs Sulzberger, Jr., executive editor, Bill Keller, managing editor, Jill Abramson. The syndicate owns 33 newspapers, 12 magazines, a wire service that has over 500 newspapers as subscribers, and some radio stations. *The NY Times* publishes America's largest-circulation international newspaper, the *International Herald Tribune* that is printed in Europe, America and Asia. Katharine Graham owns the *Washington Post* and her son Donald is its publisher; they also own one of the three largest news magazines, *Newsweek*, The Dow Jones Company owns *The Wall Street Journal* and is run by Peter R. Kann. Just three publishers account for 90% of all newsmagazines in America: these are:

Time	4.1 million	Time-Warner, Gerald Levin.
Newsweek	3.2 million	Katharine Graham.
US News and World Report		
	2.3 million	Mortimer Zuckerman.

Did anyone at all notice the name of even one Christian, Black, Hispanic, or Oriental in this paragraph?

It has come to my attention that all these Illuminists, who often claim to be American patriots, are in fact something quite different. It also does not escape notice that all of them seem to have either similar or identical outlooks, and without question share the same set of values. They slavishly support ideas and philosophies that are not American, counter to our entire Christian value system. Let me expand on that. The issues most commonly upheld by Illuminist philosophy have come in the 20th and 21st centuries to mean:

- Racial integration and race mixing is of benefit to everyone except the Chosen People.
- A woman's right to abortion, if she is anything but a Jew, is constitutionally guarded in any trimester.
- Hate crimes (thought crimes) can only be committed by white Anglo-Saxon males; all Jews are exempt from such crimes.
- Israel is the only democracy (actually a socialist theocracy) in the Middle East, and must be supported financially and militarily regardless of her positions or actions.
- Israel is our only friend in the Middle East—before Israel we had no enemies in the Middle East.
- It is a responsibility in all cases to vote for higher taxes and socialism.
- God is to be removed from every place, including coinage, prayer, public places, and from the public eye.
- Israel can do no wrong.
- The Nazis killed six million Jews in W.W. II, even though the entire German-occupied area, after counting survivors, did not contain six million Jews.
- All newscasts and all entertainment will place Judaism, Zionism, and Communism in the best possible light.

It would probably not be very difficult to add to the above list. But then, what's the point? If, by this time, you still don't understand the direction, or who is in control, words would be wasted.

There is but one more company that must not be missed when discussing the media. Walt Disney was a very great man; he was inventive, had a set of morals, produced great children's entertainment, and ran and managed an ethical company. Eisner has single-handedly dragged the Disney Empire into a quagmire of revulsion, Cultural Marxism, pornography, and films espousing hatred of Christianity, Catholicism, America and all for which it stands. One of the first companies to recognize gay partners, whose theme parks have a gay month and gay parades – one can be only revolted by a company that exposes children to such depravity. As the Baptists so aptly put it, Boycott Disney!

There is another matter not commonly known; Shamrock Holdings is a very large holder of Disney stock, the Roy Disney family is listed as the principal client. Shamrock has over two billion in assets, a large portion of which is Disney stock. Shamrock is a nebulous organization whose two principals are Michael Geiger and Robert G. Moskowitz, and which reports that 24% of its holdings are in media and 26% in communications. Outside the fact that they also have a stake in Netina Holdings, Koor Industry, Shamrock Broadcasting and a few others, we know very little of this company. In fact, I have never seen a firm that has assets of over $2 billion on which so little information is available.

Disney has 71 subsidiaries, but some of these, like ABC Radio, have 3400 affiliates, while the TV arm has 225. Among other things Disney operates theme parks, cruise lines, radio and TV stations, newspapers, industrial news magazine syndicates, publishing companies, movie theaters and movie theater production companies, art companies, education companies, software firms, sports and entertainment companies, recording studios, consumer stores, travel companies, sports networks, and Disney networks, just to name a few.

Other big media players are:

- VIACOM – Murray Rothstein (Sumner Redstone, né Rothstein, CEO):
- 12 TV stations, 12 radio stations, Paramount Studios, Showtime, MTV, Nickelodeon.
- Major accomplishment: "Beavis and Butthead."
- TIME WARNER – Gerald Levin, CEO:
- HBO East & West, Warner Music, Interscope Records, Warner Bros., Warner Bros. Stores, CBS (20%), Turner Broadcasting (100%), CNN, FCNN, CNN Europe, Time Warner Publishing, *Time*, *Life*, *Sports Illustrated*, *People*, *Fortune*.
- Major accomplishment: Gangsta Rap.
- NEWS CORP. – Rupert Murdoch (Edgar Bronfman, Pres. of World Jewish Congress, CEO:)
- Fox TV, 20th Century Fox, Universal, Seagrams Bronfman as head of the World Jewish Congress is more than involved in actions not befitting the owner of a media empire.

In world-recorded history, no nation or party or organization has ever had anything near the power of the 21st century media. The prime reason for that is the rapid change in the way information is made available in this century. TV and radio now account for well over 70% of available information. In addition to this is the fact that the entire mainstream media walks as if in lock step and is completely Illuminist, resulting in a propaganda machine controlling the entire society. As I stated above, if you can control the words, and the dissemination of information, then through control of the dialogue you control the society. Those who decide what *is* the news make the news. If you control the news, you control the issues addressed by society.

Nowhere is this more glaring than in Middle East news reportage. I have never read of a good Palestinian, never mind Arab, and conversely not once about a bad Jew. I remember when some sick Israeli reservist entered the Dome of the Rock Mosque and machine-gunned over 25 worshippers; my paper made it appear as if the Arabs in the mosque were at fault. Likewise, when an Israeli soldier shot an unarmed British newsman in the head, it took the entire international community protesting to get the soldier charged. The bull-dozer driver who ran over a peace activist protesting the destruction of yet another Arab home was written up in the *NY Times* as if she had been a trespasser. Conversely, every Arab who opposes Israeli illegal occupation of over 30 years is written up as a terrorist. Let's think about this. Thirty-four years of military occupation, over three million residents driven off their property and not allowed to return, an unemployment rate of over 70%, continuous and relentless humiliation, children throwing rocks at tanks gunned down, water rights denied, not allowed to have an airport or seaport, not allowed to marry an Israeli, over one million living in refugee camps for over 30 years, businesses that compete with Israeli ones destroyed, leaders targeted and assassinated, land continually stolen to build alien settlements, and the resisters of those action are called terrorists? As an impartial observer without an ax to grind on the issue, it seems to me that the entire media has it backward. No, of course, they don't; they are simply following the Illuminist ideology and the Zionist control of the media.

Reporting on the wall being built by the Sharon government is simply astounding. Let me apprise you of some facts that seem to have slipped away. The entire wall is being built on Palestinian land. Much of the wall is miles inside the Palestinian West Bank. Some of the Wall places entire Palestinian villages inside Israel. Over sixty Israeli kibbutzim[93], which before wall construction were in Palestine, will after construction be located in Israel. The West Bank will still have over 150 kibbutzim inside Palestinian land. The wall is purposely being placed in such a way as to be built across the path of the Stations of the Cross, so that Christians will no longer be able to worship there at Easter. The IDF is building roads to connect the kibbutzim together; these roads also contain barriers and thus make movement within the West Bank very difficult for Palestinians. Have you heard any of this reported in the media? I should say not. Quite to the contrary, we are informed that the wall needed to be built to protect Israeli citizens from terrorism. Well then, how about ending the occupation, removing the kibbutzim, which are under UN sanctions, leaving your neighbors alone and minding your own business? Oh, but I digress, how would you then get all the cheap labor that you employ, without social benefits or any rights? As I said before the Palestinians, of whom by the way almost one-third are Christians, are treated far worse than blacks were ever treated in South Africa under apartheid. America's and the world's media are so thoroughly controlled by Zionists/Illuminists that we will never get the truth in "news" from the Middle East.

The next Pontifex Maximus *to occupy*
the White fortress on Pennsylvania Avenue
will again be a Bones-man!

The Order (Bones) is the American
branch of the Illuminati.

Bush and Kerry are both members.

The danger when men stop believing in God
Is not that they believe in nothing,
But that they will believe in anything.
–G. K. Chesterton

THE WAR ON: TERRORISM, DRUGS, POVERTY,

AND SO ON *AD INFINITUM*.

All these things are constructs to keep
Your eyes off the ball!

Acceptance Speech:
We Americans today are nearer to the triumph over poverty than ever before in the history of any land. The poorhouse is vanished from among us. We have not yet reached our goal, but given a chance to go forward with the policies of the last eight years, we shall soon, with the help of God, be in sight of the day when poverty will be banished form our nation.

–Herbert Hoover RNC convention 1930

I SUSPECT you have noticed all the wars we are engaged in as a nation. In fact, there seems no end in sight; every time you think there might be *PAX* another one is begun. When we are not fighting a foreign entity, we are engaged fighting ourselves, or some perceived or imagined social evil. When all else fails, we appear to have wars just for the sake of having them. Unfortunately, it is more than obvious that we are a total failure in our relentless prosecution of wars. Well, I mean, just look on the war on poverty begun by LBJ; what a total flop, three trillion dollars spent and what have we to show for it? By percentage of population we have the very same number below the poverty line as on the day the

Democrats began throwing money at it. Then the Republicans joined in, so now it's the Republocrat national slopping at the troughs of government largess, all for the collection of a few votes.

This venture proved unsatisfactory, so we began the war on drugs, just when I thought that the FDA had been fighting this war all alone for decades. After all, the FDA has a viable war against the American consumer, having succeeded in raising the cost of medicines to the highest and most over-regulated status in the entire world. While drugs are from 30 to 50% cheaper in Canada, they are from 40 to 70% cheaper in Europe, and to add to it you don't have to go visit some charlatan quack and pay $40 for the prescription for a drug, which you knew you needed. But have no fear; on March 25, 2004 Tommy Thompson introduced the Health and Human Services discount card. It will get you a whopping 10 to 25% discount on some prescription drugs, if you are old and poor enough. Private independent corporations not in any way concerted to the government issue the cards.

The FDA is a growing bludgeoning bureaucracy that is inflating their payroll at astounding rates. Drugs that have been proven safe for use in the entire world, in some cases for decades, remain unavailable here because the FDA has not had the benefit of American testing, which for the average drug exceeds $14 million. Well, we know those stupid foreigners are incapable of carrying out such controlled tests with 40% placebo use. And then there is the obvious (perhaps) anatomical difference between Americans and the rest of the world. But I digress. The war on drugs is a war on illicit drugs, you know, deadly dangerous marijuana, well of course I jest, we all know that marijuana has some considerable medical benefits as well as preventing hangovers, but then the liquor lobby is well aware of that handicap. Anyhow, we all know that there are drugs that we should not generally use because, like excessive drinking, they are unhealthy. The war on these has been an unmitigated fiasco. Opium is produced in Afghanistan; well, actually, not during the rule of the Taliban, but now that we have eliminated them and replaced them with a free and just government that controls about half of Kabul, they're back to being number one in opium production. Then we have Columbia; now there is a case of wanton war. Our boys in Sodom on the Potomac have been shoveling Mammon into that revolutionary state for over 30 years, and cocaine production and distribution seems to have swelled to being the largest single American domestic industry. We actually have a ground war in Columbia now, with our own troops, helicopters and advisors. The possibility that the problem does not rest with the production of coca, but rather in the demand of consumers, has not yet struck any of the bright lights in DC. In any event, all the drugs are imported through Mexico, because we have more troops in each of Germany, S. Korea, Iraq, Kuwait, Afghanistan and Columbia than on our own Mexican border. I want to tell you this has been a very interesting little war, costing only $75 billion over the last five years.

So, that brings us to reconsider the war on booze, you-all remember prohibition, don't you? That was another marvel brought on by the Women's Christian Temperance Association. This bunch of busybody fembats was responsible for the largest criminal expansion in world history. Prohibition established organized crime firmly in America and expanded it in Sicily. The XVIIIth. Amendment was short-lived, being nullified by the XXIst. 14 years later, the damage had already been done. We still today have remnants of various crime organizations that have now diversified into gambling, prostitution, illicit drug distribution and manufacture. The Israeli Mafia is now one of the prime suppliers of chemically produced hallucinates, but those are not WMD unless you consider that those addicted usually die an early death.

The war against gambling is relentless, and pointless. Like all social legislation, it does not work. Opposition to gaming seems to emanate from certain right-wing Protestant Christian circles; we all recognize these same people who never seem to tire of saving society from itself and imposing their own convoluted ideas on the rest of us. While I am certainly no biblical scholar, I have yet to find a passage in the Bible that prohibits gambling. In virtually all matters the Bible teaches tolerance and reason, not prohibition. Gambling, like drinking, eating and sex, in moderation and reason, causes no harm to the participant or anyone else. We also note with great interest that the largest gaming operations carried out nationally are those of state governments, and that these lotteries run into the billions. So, what's bad for you is conversely good for the state.

Another war is against sex. America has always in my mind represented a strange Puritan view on this topic. When I was in the U.S. Army, they forbade our canteen from selling *Playboy*. While I am no fan of Hugh Heffner's, I found this prohibition ridiculous; after all we are not talking of a troop of Boy Scouts here. Sex was virtually outlawed in the Army; some silly old maids in Washington had decided that American men were to be celibate for their term in service to society. Obviously this policy was a total failure, but due to the basic policy venereal diseases was rampant. While in Europe, Mexico, Nevada, and most nations prostitution is an accepted outlet, Americans would prefer to have their daughters raped by perverts rather than to offer them an outlet. There was a funny story recently in the German *Frankfurter Algemeine*. Helmut H. Klang is married to a Thai lady. She went back to visit her relatives and due to her lack of funds was unable to return to Germany. Helmut felt the urge but had no wife; he applied to Social Services for help, as he lacked the funds to visit a brothel. Good old Helmut spent 24,642 Euros on porno flicks and at the local brothel, which were paid for by Social Services. Social Services then came to the conclusion that it would be cheaper to fly the wife back to Germany, which they did, saving lots of Mammon. As we see, Europeans have a somewhat more open-minded view of sex than do Americans.

The war on guns, or more correctly the ownership of guns by citizens of the state, has been relentless. Proponents of this Illuminist idea claim that guns cause violent crime. Years ago, in a debate, I confronted a leading supporter of this theory by placing a loaded gun on the table before us. She asked what I thought I was doing, placing a hated object of terror before her; I replied that I was waiting for the inanimate object to jump up and shoot someone. My point was not lost on the audience, which burst out laughing. America now has over 80,000 gun control laws, 99% of which are un-enforced. A close examination of fact is helpful. Crime, particularly violent crime, is rampant in all counties in America that have restrictive gun laws. It is a statistical fact that the more restrictive gun laws are, the higher the crime rate is. This statistical correlation is true worldwide. In England, a nation that has instituted the most diabolical gun laws, crime has virtually skyrocketed since enactment. In Australia, where guns were confiscated wholesale, crime has increased at exponential rates. Violent crime in America is most pronounced in Washington DC, NYC, and Boston, cities that have diabolical gun laws. Needless to say, the bodyguards of visible politicians who support gun confiscation in NY, Senators Schumer and Clinton, in MA Kennedy, have in the past been armed even with sub-machine guns.

Let me point out that all of us are very aware that none of these social laws work. But it is important to understand that these laws are used to bring changes to society that are not in its best interest. All these wars have an ominous debilitating effect on society. What they do is, take normal human actions and criminalize them so that they can be selectively enforced against any of those citizens who have the gumption to oppose the state. In other instances they use their "terrible power of the purse[94]" to force one group, usually the middle class, to support members of society who refuse to work. Social legislation throughout history demonstrates a total failure.

Our latest and greatest war is the one against terrorism. Am I the only person in America who perceives that something is badly amiss with this war? Is this the construction of another bogeyman for some other hidden and nefarious purpose? Do people really understand that this is the first war in American history in which we are the aggressor on a foreign nation, and that it was begun on felonious grounds? Have we found anyone in Afghanistan or Iraq who is or was connected with 9-11? Seems to me that there were no Afghans or Iraqis among the accused hijackers. Has anyone made any connection, even remote, between any terrorist organization and Iraq? I should say not!

No intelligence service or nation has to date provided any actual proof of our and the British government's pronouncements of this war. Not one bit of actual evidence supported the re-proving made by Tony Blair and George Bush or their advisors. Some of the assertions made are simply ludicrous. Consider the prospect of a group of Arabs living in caves on the Afghan-Pakistan border region coordinating over 100 men, in two continents, into what was the most complex multiple aircraft hijacking in history. We are over a year after the 9-11 attack, and frankly I have seen not one shred of evidence as to who committed this atrocity. All of Blair's and Bush's assertions have proven to be lies. Yellowcake from Niger, the gassing of Iraq's own citizens by Hussein, nuclear weapons production in its last stage, chemical weapons production facilities, bacteriological weapons stockpiles, mobile weapons labs, continental ballistic missiles, links to international terrorists, and all of these assertions were lies. To understand what is in fact taking place here, we need to look for the individuals who, behind the scenes, are orchestrating the policy of war against Iraq.

They refer to themselves as Neo-cons. What they try to imply is that they are new conservatives. Baloney! They are Zionist/Illuminists to a man. They are centered in our nation's capital, which may best now be called New Tel Aviv. Many work in the executive branch of government, some are columnists like Krauthammer, many are employed in the media. They under no circumstance can be considered American patriots, whom conservatives tend toward; they in fact are patriotic *Israeli* supporters and cheerleaders.

So first off we should ask some questions. Of these the most poignant is; who benefits from a war in the Middle East against Israel's most apparent adversary? The answer is more than just obvious. To say so, however, gets you into a lot of hot water, as a certain northern Virginia congressman found out. He has been labeled as an anti-Semite by the racist JDL just for suggesting that Israel is the only beneficiary of our present Middle East policies.

The term anti-Semite is a construct of Zionists. It is intended to place a social slur on anyone who in any way opposes Zionism. The word Semitic is derived from the patriarch Shem, and pertains to descendants of Shem. Jews are not Semitic; they are Canaanites, and the Khazars, their ancestors, were not descendants of Shem. True Illuminism seeks to make black appear white and vice versa;

this is reflected in Communism as well as Zionism, the three being part of the very same exclusionary movement of world conquest.

I am outraged that a bunch of extortionists like the JDL and WJC are able to malign a congressman simply for telling the truth. But nothing surprises me anymore. I just learned that presidential aspirant John Kerry's grandfather's name was Fritz Kohn, and he was a Jewish immigrant from what was then Czechoslovakia. Kerry's father Richard was active in the State Department, and had his name changed. A little phony Catholicism certainly helps in Massachusetts' politics. On this issue we must be very clear; the American domicile of Illuminism is the Yale University Senior Society called Bones, or The Order, or the Order of Death, or 322. George Bush, Sr. and George W. Bush, as well as John [Kohn] Kerry, are members of it.

All we have to do is to investigate who are the primary protagonists for the war against Iraq. We find documents to support this search readily available. These are primarily all members of the Diaspora, and are Zionist/Illuminist to a man. All other considerations aside, the total New Zionist Captivity of American foreign policy is now in effect. Any American who for one minute thinks that our foreign policy supports America is delusional. The Diaspora[95], which was, before the Inquisition, based in Spain, then moved to Amsterdam, Holland, at the height of the Inquisition, and from Amsterdam then to London, and then to New York City, is the organization, which makes American foreign policy. Zionists constitute a tiny minority of the Jewish community, which is neither American nor Jewish in makeup.

The world Jewish community is ruled over by an amalgamation of rabbinical[96] tyrants, their communities are called Kahals[97]. NYC is the Grand Kahal of the Diaspora of the world. That's why they installed the UN in NYC instead of Geneva: the Grand Kahal is always located in the major trading center of the world. The Rockefeller's provided facilities to the UN for their HQ for profit as well as being in tune with the Zionist community. As Herzel so aptly put it, "we thrive on the terrible power of the purse". It is for this reason that Jews universally have little allegiance to the nation in which they live; all their allegiance is to the Diaspora and the state of Israel. In other words, their sole loyalty is to world Jewry. The Talmud is very clear and specific in allowing Jews to lie, cheat, rape, or even murder any gentiles at will, because according to the Talmud only Jews have souls, all the rest of us are animals. Verification of this is quickly gained if one examines the people who have betrayed America in the last fifty years, or since the Diaspora has been centered in NY. Klaus Fuchs, Bruno Pontecorvo, Harry Gold, David Greenglass, Julius Rosenberg, Ethel Rosenberg, Emmanuel Bloch, William Perle, John Vag-Weiszfeld, David Boehm, Edwin David, and last, but far from least, Pollard. Every one of the aforementioned Zionists betrayed the nation that made it possible for Israel to become a state and then guaranteed its survival. These were not small betrayals either: nuclear weapons for Stalin, missile targeting technology for the PRC, air-to-air missiles for the PRC, ICBM technology for the Soviets, 21st century fighter aircraft technology to the PRC, American documented deterrence capabilities and all systems of deterrence to the Russians in the 90s. And then, to demonstrate the American electorate's total stupidity, the Democrats ran two Jews for the primaries in the 2004 campaign, their candidates John Kerry, a Zionist whose grandfather's name was Fritz Cohn, and Sen. Lieberman (D-CT).

The long and tortured process of Illuminist's take-over of American foreign policy is centered in the NYC-located CFR[98] which began to dominate American politics in the first term of FDR, whose Vice President Wallace was a hard-line Communist who was replaced by Truman in the second term. Since that time, all American foreign policy has come from 68th St. and the Pratt House in NYC, the same city that houses the UN and the Diaspora. CFR rule is so absolute that if you want to know what American foreign policy will be in the coming decade all you need to do is subscribe to the quarterly called *Foreign Affairs*, the lead publication of the CFR.

Many will say that the CFR is not a Zionist organization, and they are quite correct. However, the leadership of the CFR is either Zionist or in complete concord with Zionist goals, and as everyone knows it is not necessary to hold more than the leadership and about ten percent of the membership to control any organization. The Rockefellers have controlled the Chase Manhattan Bank for decades and own only about 10% of it; they also were the founders of the CFR as well as the Trilateral Commission, an adjunct agency of the CFR, and are affiliated to the RIIA (Royal Institute on International Affairs) an organization upon which the CFR was patterned. As a note, the RIIA was founded in London when the Diaspora was located there. The CFR has held every cabinet seat and all the Joint Chief of Staff positions since the FDR administration with perhaps three exceptions, which in view of a membership of only 3400 is astounding. Major CFR generals were Eisenhower, Hague, Clark, and numerous others, all promoted not on battlefield ability but rather on political expediency. One might consider the reason why the Bilderbergers are centered in Holland, a past Grand Diaspora, the RIIA is located in London, another past Grand Diaspora, and the CFR in NYC, the present Grand Diaspora.

It is obvious that there exists an over-riding controlling organizational structure that oversees international politics. For one thing we observe the single unifying posture is an unrelenting opposition against Western civilization and Caucasians. Let me cite some facts; as of summer 2000, Caucasians became a minority in California, representing only 49.8% of the overall population – as they say, California leads the nation. In London, the white segment of the overall population has shrunk to 60%; the currently used demographic model will make Caucasians a British minority by 2010. The U.S. Bureau of Census informs us that by 2050 Caucasians will account for no more than 7% of the overall European population. This sounds to me like a planned genocide of the Caucasian race. That in fact is exactly what it is. Infanticide, abortion, popularized homosexuality, feminization, Black Pride organizations, all of these are stratagems of the Zionist Illuminist cabal running our society. You disagree? Well, simply read the names of the individuals who either began or are still running any of the organizations that promote these insidious projects. You will find that they are almost all Zionists. From the creation of concentration camps in the Boer wars, by Lord Kitchner to the relentless bombings in W. W. II of civilian targets, to the bombings of the Balkans, we see a brutality and un-Christian behavior that clearly demonstrates a Zionist un-Western and Illuminist influence.

Before anyone begins with the anti-Semitic charge, let us look at some other facts that relate to my charge. Christianity or the teachings of Christ are not an eye for an eye – that is Old Testament – Christ taught to turn the other cheek, to love your neighbor, to help anyone in trouble. This is completely contradicted by the most evil religious text ever produced, one more evil even than the Thuggish Hindu worship of Kali. The Babylonian Talmud is the vilest religious document produced in the history of humanity.

In Christianity, the two most holy days are Christmas, the birthday of Christ the redeemer and the savior of all mankind, and Easter is the promise of resurrection and eternal life through the resurrection of our Lord Jesus Christ. In order to diminish these holydays the Jews celebrate Hanukkah at Christmastime; not only is it a minor holyday, but also it is a celebration of the massacre in 165 BC of the Jews over their enemy King Antiochus IV of Syria. This victory is celebrated with a long-burning oil lamp representing the re-capture of their temple. Christmas vacation has been replaced by Winter Break. At Easter, Christians celebrate the offer of salvation, beginning with Good Friday. Good Friday has been relegated to obscurity because it is a "Religious Holiday;" but Jews celebrate Passover. This most evil celebration is for the night in which the "spirit" God supposedly descended into the homes of all non-Jews in Egypt, killing the first-born male child, but passing over the homes of the Jews. Easter vacation has been replaced by Spring Break. Purim, which just by chance (maybe) was the day on which Gulf War II was begun, is the celebration of the betrayal by Esther, the wife of the Persian king, of the prime minister of Persia, allowing the Jews to massacre tens of thousands of Persians. One of the Purim items is a cookie called *hamantaschen*; Haman was the name of the Persian prime minister and *taschen* means pockets – it represents eating the ears of the murdered prime minister and of his ten sons. These, as all Jewish holydays, are celebrations of carnage, murder and betrayal – what a sick religion!

That, however, is only the very tip of an overwhelming iceberg of evil. Reading the Talmud, if you can find an uncensored version of it, is truly horrifying. Unlike the scriptures of every other religion, the Talmud remains obscure and hidden away from the prying eyes of non-Jews. They have gone so far as to produce dry-cleaned versions in which all the epithets against Muslims, Christians, blacks and non-Jews have been removed: these are what are made generally available, but they are not true texts as used in rabbinical schools or in teaching of Judaism to boys. Let me just give you a few quotes and where they originated from; but to place that into perspective:

Babha Metsia, fol. 33a

"Those who devote themselves to reading the Bible exercise a certain virtue, but not very much; those who study the Mischnah† exercise virtue for which they will be rewarded; Those, however, who take upon themselves to study the Gomorrah‡ exercise the highest virtue."*

Sanhedrin 105a *Balaam* (Jesus Christ) *fornicated with his jackass.*

Gittin 57a *Jewish priests raised Balaam (*Jesus Christ*) [*This in reference to the resurrection*] from the dead and punished him by boiling him in hot semen.*

Choschen Ham (34,19) a Goi [slanderous name for Gentile] *or servant is not capable of acting as a witness* [in court of law.]

Sanhedrin (43a) *On the eve of Passover they* [the rabbis] *hung Jesus.*

Book of Zohar III (282) Jesus died like a beast and was buried in a dung heap... where they throw the bodies of dogs [considered unclean animals] *and Asses, and where the sons of Esau* [Christians] *and Ismael* [Muslims], *also uncircumcised are buried.*

Abhodrah Zarah (22a) & Iore Dea (153,2) Jews must not associate with Christians because they are given to shedding of blood.

Why do Jews wear yamakhs? *Iore Dea, 3, Hagah: A Jew is not permitted to remove his hat to greet or to bow to a Christian wearing a cross.*

Yebamoth 98a All Cuthean [Christian] *children are animals*

Zohar (1,25b) Those who do good to the Akum [Christians] *will not rise from the dead.*

Baba Mezia (114a-114b) Only Jews are human, Goi are animals.

Baba Kamma (113a) Jews may use lies to circumvent a Goi.

Moed Kattan (17a) If a Jew is tempted to do evil he should go to a city where he is not known and do evil there.

Then finally, just to prove the point that this is the real Jewish law and what they believe in: *Rosh Hashanah 17a Those who reject the Talmud will go to hell and be punished for generations.*

I have taken only a very small number of quotations from the Babylonian Talmud, but I think it will impart to the reader an understanding of what these Zionists believe and how they came to be a "people apart". The relationship between Zionism, Communism and Illuminism is seated in their almost identical philosophies, and the indisputable fact that the original Communist principles, as espoused by Karl Marx, were plagiarized from Adam Weisshaupt, Illuminist name Spartacus, and have been wholly adopted by Zionists. Denial of this is impossible when one considers that the entire Russian revolution was led, run, managed and orchestrated by Zionists.

Illuminist's success may be demonstrated in the enactment of laws that are based in Illuminist philosophy. Regulation of banking, the Federal Reserve System, the graduated and progressive Income Tax, the erection of a governmental collection agency, the IRS, the federalization and centralization of education in the hands of the state, the gradual elimination of private property, all of these and other legislation are within the purview of Illuminism. All this while the Democrats fielded Lieberman, a Zionist, as a candidate in 2000, and then a hidden Zionist, John Kerry (Kohn). Proof of the pudding, as they say, is Kerry's ardent support of abortion – infanticide – of homosexual marriage, and masses of anti-Christian and violently anti-Roman Catholic dogma.

The fact that America had a foreign agent as head of the Defense Policy Board is undeniable. Richard Perle is an Israeli agent, if not in deed, then in persuasion. Perle presented a paper entitled *A Clean Break* on the future of the United States at the Institute for Advanced and Strategic Studies, which is a Jerusalem-based think tank with offices in Washington. It is one of the myriads of influential Israeli organizations that are adjuncts to the IDF (Israeli Defense Force). Another blueprint was produced in 1998 by one more think tank likewise connected. *Project for the New American Century* was written by Lewis Libby (VP Cheney's chief of staff), Paul Wolfowitz and Donald Rumsfeld for VP Cheney. The only short way to expose these documents is to call them exactly what they are. They are a plan for total hegemony over the entire Middle East by Israel, with America and Britain providing the material and personnel to accomplish that goal. These documents clearly demonstrate that their authors have little or no interest in Western civilization, America, Britain, or Western Europe and NATO; their only interest is the expansion of Israel at any cost to our allies and us. If we review American foreign policy in the Bush administration there can be no doubt in anyone's mind that this is the exact plan. No less a pundit than Charles Krauthammer singled out Baghdad as the planned target in his column in *Time* of Sept 11, 2001. Everyone in the world except the neo-cons now admits that Iraq had nothing whatever to do with the 9-11 incident. All this is part and parcel of a greater plan, of that there is no doubt.

In any event, attempts to take over the American government were unsuccessful through the 1940s. But with the bribe of the DNC and Harry Truman to recognize the creation of Israel (America was first) things began to change. By the time of the election of Jimmy Carter, Zionists were so proficient that they began to control foreign policy. During the Clinton administration they were able to finalize the take-over to the point where in the second Bush (the Lesser) administration they totally control all matters of foreign and domestic policy within the American government. Neocons control the CFR, TC, and are at one with The Order. They manipulate the American electorate like marionette masters.

It seems that wars have an ulterior motive not related to the supposed issues, as presented to the general populace. All these wars are to further the goals of Illuminism in its relentless efforts to become the masters of the world. Both Bushes are members of The Order, the Illuminist organization's American establishment. George Bush, Sr., aptly cited "the thousand points of light:" this phrase refers to the thousand Illuminists who will control the world government once it is installed. The phrase is a re-translation of one of the sayings written on the wall of the Tombs in New Haven, CT: "*Mit tausend lichter werden wir leiten,*" with a thousand lights we shall rule.

THE INTENDED PRODUCT

Let us review the 10 principles that Adam Weishaupt and his Illuminati developed, and then in each point examine where we have been since 1776 and to what we have come. Karl Marx in his Komunistisches Manifest published in England a century later adopted these exact same principles. It is the principle philosophy espoused by world Zionists.

– 1 –

The Abolition of Private Property Ownership.

Individual land ownership has eroded drastically ever since the revolutionary war. At that time over 90% of the population were involved in agrarian pursuits, and were landowners. At the turn of the last century, 2000, the number of landowners in America had shrunk to under 30% of the population, while family farming was down to about 4%. This is an important part of the plan because people who own land or who farm it have close relationships with community; it is exactly these relationships that are intended to be disrupted. The opponents of my argument will say that this is nothing more than the natural outcome of the industrial revolution and the gradual urbanization of populations worldwide. They have a valid argument in that industrialization requires centralization of labor assets, the inevitable outcome of which is urbanization. I, however, point out that this is far from the only reason for the drastic reduction in individual land farm and business ownership. More pronounced are inheritance taxes that strip ownership of businesses, as well as farms, from families, in the socialist cause of wealth redistribution. Death duties, as they are often called, are a totally illegitimate tax; it is the taxation of asset that has already been taxed and is also subject to annual property taxes. (These taxes are particularly debilitating for small business and family farms.) Additionally laws as promulgated by government in regulating and controlling all agrarian matters are so structured as to benefit large farm corporations and deny those benefits to smaller farms. When I farmed I found it impossible to obtain a farm bank credits crop credits or government help, which services were readily available to all the large farms located in the same county.

The greatest enemy of the N.W.O. is without doubt the family-centered business. The collection of taxes on interest on savings accounts held by individuals, and companies, is a second tax on moneys that have already been taxed once. America is the only industrialized nation that taxes interest income on savings. In fact, all sorts of taxes have been foisted upon the citizens in the name of fairness and compassion. Consider, per example, capital gains taxes. This odious tax is to be paid by the citizen if the value of his property has increased, either through his direct efforts or through inflation, which of course is nothing else but another tax. The argument that this is a tax break for the wealthy is ridiculous and not founded in any fact whatsoever. Not to be overlooked is the detail that taxes have already been collected once on these funds, and that capital gains taxes are therefore double taxation on the same asset. The usual case is that the capital value of the property or business has risen in price due to various factors, one of which in every single case is inflation, the direct result of Illuminist money-expansion policies. On the business side, legislation invariably not only favors large business but also is often written with the express purpose of eliminating small business competition. I have over 35 years of experience with this as a small business owner. When OSHA, per example, issued their voluminous new regulations, we were constructing a new plant; we requested a review of our construction plans and blueprints by OSHA to see all our plans were in compliance. They refused, and told us they would check out the plant after it was built and then fine us on any violations. This type of stupid government action is typical of all agencies.

I believe that all this is backward. Government should give incentives to comply with law and help people to do so, not fine them after the fact for violations. Another detail of these policies is the fining of large municipal suppliers for violation of some environmental law. This in effect shifts the cost not to the violator, its management or its stockholders, but instead to the consumer. This is again backward. First, it accomplishes nothing; second, there is no incentive not to do it again. The people to be fined should be the executives who allowed the violation. All these factors and many more are adjuncts to the reduction of land ownership and centralization of assets under the stewardship of plutocrats. This is an ongoing effort to which I am more than sure you can add even more volumes. I could write a book on the unfair treatment small business gets from big government. The greatest of these is the fact that small business and family farmers are financially unable to employ the required personnel to oversee the enormous burden of federal regulations enforced by a vociferous bunch of often-uneducated bureaucrats. It is through the selective enforcement of this vast compilation of federal and state regulatory acts that the Illuminists, through their bureaucratic allies, destroy small business. Not only is it frustrating to deal with all these agencies, but also a waste of time for people who fight every day to keep their heads above water. The plan is simply to convert all people privately employed in small businesses to being employed by government or multinational corporations.

– 2–

Progressive Taxation

For the first 150 years, with the exception of reconstruction, America prospered under a political system that was liberal in the classic sense. Taxes were collected on imports only, and the general environment was one of states' rights superseding those of any federal authority. America was closer to a classic confederation than a Constitutional Republic, but a Republic is what it in reality was. It is imperative to understand the difference between a republic and a democracy. Most people think them to be the same. In a republic such as we had, a constitutional republic, law rested in the constitution. Relationships and government both were overseen by a written document that provided an absolutely fixed rule that was the arbiter over actions of all. The Tenth Amendment to the Constitution affirmed this federal *vs.* state relationship, insuring the continuation of the republic. With the blatant violation of the Tenth Amendment, and the judicial branch's refusal to act against the violations, America turned into a democracy, which is exactly what the Illuminists wanted in the first place. In a democracy there is no absolute rule of law, law is subject to the whims of the majority, and the majority can change the law (rules governing the society) at any point. Thus in a democracy there is no absolute right or wrong;

everything turns another shade of gray, thus the state uses selective enforcement to achieve totalitarianism, the impending result of all democracies. One of the instruments of this *Road to Serfdom*, as Hayek called it, is progressive taxation.

U.S. Internal Revenue statutes contain over 2 million words, more than the King James Version of the Bible. Every single year Congress votes more rubbish onto this antiquated foolish law. The Clinton administration expanded the IRS statues by 850 pages, and then claimed it was simplifying them by doing so. The fact that the entire cabal was not ever legally congressionally ratified, and that the then (1913) Secretary of State perjured himself, claiming it to have been ratified, has never been addressed. Neither has the fact that the tax was promised to the public to be a temporary measure. The tax, as proposed by the Illuminati, is progressive. What exactly does that mean? Certainly not progressive in any sense of the word, but rather that the tax percentage is increased as the income rises. This word, [progressive] like Gay, Cop-killer, bullet, and assault rifle, are propagandistic conversion of words to attain a pre-planned outcome. There are several matters in relation to this that people may not really understand. The first of these is inflation. This allows a built-in perpetual tax increase, which does not have to be enacted by the legislature. Your salary is increased periodically, and for many the basis of the increase is related to the cost of living. E.g. many labor contracts contain a provision tying pay to government cost-of-living index figures. With a graduated income tax you cannot win, because as you obtain a pay increase your tax rate changes and the percentage becomes higher. The real irony of this system, however, rests with the fact that it punishes incentive, hard work, and self-reliance. The harder you work, the more you earn, the more you are punished. This is not just wrong, it's stupid. Consider now the argument of the supporters of this odious system: "It's only fair to make those who earn more pay more". Only a movie star could come up with such convoluted arguments. If I earn $10,000 and my tax is 10% I pay $1,000, and conversely if you earn $100,000 and pay 10% you pay $10,000. That is fair. If on the other hand I earn $10,000 and pay 5% ($500) and you earn $100,000 and pay 35% ($35,000) that's not only unfair, its criminal. Progressive tax structures are constructs of the Illuminati and one of the means specifically designed to equalize incomes of the producing class. It is creative in sponsoring class warfare, one of the primary ways that you are kept off-balance. Rather than seeking accommodations you are goaded into conflict with your neighbor, and thus away from examining who is doing what to you, where and how.

Now I want you to be fully aware that this system is not only unfair, it is criminal. Wealthy individuals (the Illuminists) who introduced this law in 1913 made absolutely sure that they would not themselves have to pay it. Through numerous vehicles like trusts, family trusts, dummy corporations, holding companies, foundations, etc., they created loopholes within the structure that allow them to be exempt from payment of the progressive income tax. In fact, I once saw a tax return of one of the Rockefeller family who had a tax liability for one year of less than $500. In America today 10% of the people pay 90% of the taxes, these are by no means the billionaires Illuminists; they are simply those who represent the upper portion of the middle class. The real billionaires by percentage are less than 1/10 of one percent of the population, and pay virtually no taxes.

– 3–

The Abolition of Inheritance.

When America was founded there were no inheritance taxes. The socialist concept of stealing a family's wealth did not rear its ugly head until the 19th century, after Karl Marx had published his plagiarized copy of the Illuminist dogma as *Das Komunistische Manifest.* This tax, above most others, is a tax of greed, intolerance, and a wealth redistribution scheme from those who worked to make something of themselves and their families to those who glean to live off the labor of others.

Inheritance taxes or, as they are often called, death duties are a crime against humanity. It is the convoluted concept of a tortured, sick mind, which is that after you die those you loved and cared for all your life long, should be cut adrift without assets. This type of idea can only be classified as Communist. We should always remember Winston Churchill's statement that: *"socialism is the philosophy of failure, the creed of ignorance, and the gospel of envy, its inherent virtue is the equal sharing of misery".* Every nation in the Western World has inheritance taxes. The worst, I am informed, are in Britain. America runs a close second. Every single penny accumulated in any estate was already taxed as income. Thus inheritance taxes are again a double tax on earned income. It is interesting to note that the very wealthy are well able to avoid this tax by placing their estates into trusts and foundations, which are subsequently tax-exempt. As in every issue relating to the Illuminist plan, they provided themselves a way out before they even brought the issue to legislation. Every single tax they have instituted was provided with loopholes, even before enactment, which have allowed them to avoid the payment of same.

– 4–

Confiscation of Private Property.

The entire basis of Western Civilization rests upon the concept of the ownership of private property. It is a proven fact that no civilization in recorded history has established success until it adopted concepts of private property ownership. All the nomadic cultures never really developed until they settled down and enacted private property concepts. All the great civilizations, East, West, Middle East, from Egypt, to Babylon, to Greece, to Rome, to Central America and China, came to growth and development only after they instituted private property ownership conception. Those who had no such concepts, such as the cultures in North America, Africa and Australia, came to nothing, and only one ever reached the Bronze Age. Thus the very concept of the ownership of land and property by the individual is central to the healthy development of a society. It is also clear to see how the Illuminist concepts are all related to attacking that very conception of property ownership. Inheritance taxes, progressive taxes, and all attacks on property rights, are in concert with their basic plan. They mean to make all mankind dependent upon them, their money, and their gracious allowances to all of us working for them. In this goal, they are instituting a four-tier society that is a classic feudal pyramid. The top are the Illuminati, then come their mandarins that administer all, and then the police/military to control all, and then the rest of the population that consists of 90% of humanity. I am far from the first person to understand this there are well over 100 books that attest to these concepts, which are not theories but are fact. The "thousand points of light" spoken of by then sitting President Bush (Sr.) are the thousand Illuminists who will run the world. An interesting fact is that the Illuminist Bones organization now has between 800 and 900 members.

The most active and virulent attack against private property ownership is vested in the environmental lobby. These socialist- influenced miss-conceived environmentalists are the cadre of the government-run war against all property-owners. The foolishness of their actions is best demonstrated by the fact that all environmental organizations manage their affairs in a very similar manner. In every case that I have investigated, funds collected from hapless volunteer donors are over 85% consumed in management payroll. In other words, 85 cents of every dollar contributed is payroll and benefits for those at the top of the organizations.

Contributions by corporations are often paid as bribes, no different from those paid out to various black and Jewish organizations to prevent harassment. This is, of course, simply extortion. In other cases large petro-chemical companies contribute in order to obtain a justification for yet another price rise of their products.

– 5 –

Centralization of Banking.

The year is 1913; it was the worst year in history for the American republic, and it was the year that it was changed from a republic to a democracy. 1913 was the year that several items passed in a Congress that must have been either asleep, staffed by a bunch of morons, or more likely came under the sway of the Illuminist movement. In fact, with few exceptions, all the amendments after the Tenth proved to be mistakes.

Notable is the XVIth. Amendment, the alteration of a Constitution that required equal apportionment of taxation among the states and citizens thereof: "*The Congress shall have power to lay and collect taxes on incomes, from whatever source derived, without apportionment among the several States, and without regard to any census or enumeration".* This of course is the odious law that has been used to implement a progressive unequal taxation of the people, as well as being the basis for the IRS. This is the law that was illegally implemented, not having been ratified, with the Secretary of State perjuring himself in claiming it to have been ratified. Official sources claim it to have been ratified on Feb. 3, 1913. That is the date the Secretary of State said he had counted all the state legislatures' votes and proclaimed that the 16th Amendment was ratified. It was a lie. The two thirds of states required by the Constitution had not ratified it, and two states had rescinded their vote for it. The 16th Amendment completely changed the entire structure of the republic by, firstly, changing the entire tax structure of the nation and, secondly, federalizing taxation in the hands of what was to become an oppressive bloated bureaucracy managed for and by the Illuminati. It is important to understand that these statues written over the last 91 years have with every legislative session become more confusing. This confusion allows selective enforcement and political mayhem. This was typified by the Clinton administration and their use of the IRS to harass anyone who had the courage to criticize the troop of liars, swindlers and traitors in it. It has been used by many administrations to silence the opposition. Just so you understand how obtuse these statutes are, consider the following: In the last ten years *Money Magazine* has created a mythical tax liability individual every year, and provided the information to ten IRS auditors and ten CPAs. No two have ever come up with the same tax liability. How's that for a stupid law?

The very same Congress struck again with the XVIIth. Amendment, in all, just as bad as the other one. It changed the republic to a democracy by making senators directly elected, rather than appointed by state legislative bodies. The consequences of that act made Senators puppets of the moneyed interests (Illuminati) by making them dependent upon financial support for re-election from the interest that has the money to make that possible. Independent action by senators was over, impeachment of a president became impossible, and the true "System" of political corruption was inaugurated. These two acts combined served to alter everything within America; and it was not for the better.

The new tax structure required a new tax law, and that was what developed into the IRS statutes. It required an agency to oversee the collection of taxes that were previously by law overseen by the Congress, and it led to the laws that established the private monopoly that is the FRS (Federal Reserve System), which is not federal but private, not a reserve, because the reserve is the Treasury, and most certainly not a system but a corporation. The owners of this private, congressionally established, monopoly are American and foreign bankers. A substantial portion of the ownership rests with banking conglomerates outside the United States, and all these banking conglomerates have interlocking directorships. They are the Illuminati. Over 20% of all the taxes paid by citizens of the industrialized world goes to this consortium of bankers. Want to know exactly how much it is in your country? All you have to do is to look up the interest payment on the national debt—that's it. So when you learn that 22+% of taxes go to service the national debt, all you have to do is find what 22%+ of your taxes were and divide it by 12, and you will then know how much the Illuminati earn from you each and every month.

Let me elucidate this a bit. In order for you to oppose Illuminism and all its evil you must understand where most of the Illuminist income is derived from; you. Constitutionally Congress is the only agency that has authority over the coinage of money, and coin is the only legal means by which taxes may be paid. All that went down the drain with the Federal Reserve Act and the 16th amendment. In that set of laws Congress illegally abdicated their responsibility for the issuance of currency and handed that authority over to the FRS. When Congress spends more than it collects in taxes (all the time) it must go to the FRS and ask it to print more money. The FRS, which is the creator of that fiat money[99], then prints the amount requested. Both parties look upon this action as a loan from the FRS to the U.S. Government to be repaid by the taxpayers, you. The total amount of this debt is called the National Debt or, as I prefer, your children's mortgage. This debt has accumulated to an amount of $5.9 trillion as of 2002; the interest on it is over $100 billion per year. Unfortunately it all gets worse, because of the totally dishonest accounting methods used in the national budget and federal bookkeeping systems. That aforementioned debt does not include IOUs, which have been issued to the Social Security system, Highway Trust Fund, U.S. Patent Office, and scores of other agencies, which operate in the black and have had their money taken away and placed in the general fund. The estimated national debt, when all amounts are included, exceeds $ 24 trillion. And that, my friends, is more than you could count in $50 bills in your entire life.

– 6 –

Centralization of all Communication in the Hands of the State.

If you believe that America has an independent media; then I have a bridge that I want to sell you in Brooklyn, NY. That very same group of Illuminists owns America's mainstream media, lock, stock and barrel. Before you say anything about the diversity of companies that can be called the mainstream media you had better investigate just exactly how many independent companies there are. I will not hold it back; the entire mainstream media consists of no more than nine companies. In Europe this problem was solved a long time ago, when socialists in government opened state-owned radio and later television stations and refused to issue licenses for private companies to compete. The very concept of government issuing a license to broadcast a signal is repugnant; it is akin to metering air and charging for its use. In America the process was complicated because government had developed a licensing structure in the broadcast media. To make a long story short, the matter was easily settled when the Illuminists simply, over the years, took over all the mainstream sources of news and entertainment, from print to broadcast, movies to theater. You doubt me – look at the symbol for CBS, compare it with the All-Seeing Eye on the Great Seal of the United States, and then read the Latin inscription at the bottom of the seal; if that does not convince you, how about the Hebrew script on the Yale University seal? American news is a practical joke; it consists of sound-bite info-mertials that cannot even be considered good propaganda. News in America is Zionist from word one. That's why they call it Talmudvision.

Last week I watched a PBS program on TV. It was a debate about mainstream media. The primary insider Marvin Kalb (CFR), acted as the chief apologist for them. His argument on behalf of them was pathetic. When confronted with the proven fact that 89% of the media voted for Clinton and 92% were proud to be called liberal, he argued that this had no effect on the reportage of the news. When it was pointed out that Sen. Bob Smith and Rep. Dr. Ron Paul were always referred to as "conservatives" but that Dianne Feinstein and Tom Lantos were never referred to as liberal, but as main-stream Americans, he could see no prejudice. After some very convincing arguments for media bias, he resorted to mumbling unrecognizable platitudes of inconsequential rubbish.

I want now to explain exactly what Zionism is, and I want to do this because of the very comfortable relationship in the media and banking industries between the Illuminati and the Zionists. Zionism is a socio-political movement related to Communism. This fact is absolutely indisputable. Zionism uses Judaism as a cover and means of protection for the practice of extortion from all non-Jewish societies, businesses and nations. A kibbutz is a communist cooperative farm or industrial community. Palestine is littered with hundreds of illegal kibbutzim. The Communist revolution in Russia was completely run, managed, and operated by Zionists. The entire Soviet central committee in the founding years of the Evil Empire consisted of Zionists. The entire Soviet field cadre was Zionists. They relentlessly persecuted all Russian Orthodox Christians, killing over 66 million of them and destroying over 900 churches and monasteries. Not one Jewish synagogue was damaged during this same period in Russia. Zionists ran all Communist parties in Europe and America in the 30s! Zionists work hand in glove with the Illuminati, and in numerous cases have overlapping responsibility.

The primary sources of Illuminists in America are certain senior societies, most notably the one at Yale called Bones, The Order of Death, or 322; their headquarters is at the Tombs, a two-story window-less structure on the Yale campus. Yale is run by and managed by Bonesmen, where they control an endowment of over one billion dollars. Communism and socialism are vehicles used by the Illuminati to change society, to bring terror and confusion, and eventually to bring civil strife to the point where people will accept Illuminist rule over the continuous terror and civil strife, which will have been instituted. If you don't believe that, then read the *Protocols of the Learned Elders of Zion*, the bible of Zionism. This is exactly what took place in Germany in the '30s but failed because the Nazis were faster in development of their power than the Communists. It is what took place in the French and Russian revolutions.

All media report news emanate from the dispatches of news services. These are Reuters, UPI, API, *The New York Times, LA Times,* syndicates and a very small number of insignificant agencies. These sources, upon which every newspaper, radio station and TV station depend, are all totally under the control of the aforementioned clique. Their blatant propaganda has reached the point where it is impossible to turn on the TV or go to a movie and not be assaulted by Zionist propaganda. The latest assault is the movie *Shreck* and *Shreck II*, (Yiddish, a German dialect: the proper word is *Schreck*) meaning fright. News in America is so censored and propagandized, that it is sickening. Every propaganda venue is used, omission, conversion, addition, linkage, falsification, and on and on. Dr. Goebbels, the Nazi Minister of Information would have been proud to have such total control.

Think about the reporting on issues from the Middle East. Every single day, rock-throwing Palestinian children are gunned down by Israeli military. It is a war of attrition of Palestinian children against Israelis in American-made tanks, helicopters and jet fighters. Weekly, Palestinian homes are bulldozed and another kibbutz sprouts up. In December 2001 and January 2002 over 30 Palestinian leaders were assassinated by Israeli hit squads. Every single international body, the UN, The Human Rights Commission, Unaligned Nations, has condemned Israel. Israel occupies most of Palestine in violation of UN mandates. Israel, whose present government is run by Zionists, not Jews, treats Palestinians ten times worse than the South Africans treated Blacks. I should know, having visited both places often.

How about the news of the second Iraq war? In the week of April 5, 2004, 60 American soldiers were killed and 84 American hired mercenaries (defense contractors) met the same end. Not one single word of this was reported by a single mainstream news-source as of the 14th of that month. The media keeps calling hired guns (mercenaries in our employment) defense contractors, when everyone in the know realizes them to be the people doing the dirty work that the military disdains from performing.

America's political leaders (cowards all) are so frightened of the power of the Zionist-controlled media, together with their enormous soft money contributions from Zionist/Illuminist sources, that they will not vote their conscience on this issue. So powerful are these people that they have placed all presidents in the Oval Office since FDR, with the exception of Kennedy, whom they assassinated, and Nixon, whom they forced from office. If a president steps out of line he is given a warning (assassination attempt on Reagan). If a representative or senator steps out of line he will lose the next election. In the last presidential cycle they even had an outspoken Zionist candidate for the position of VP, Joe Lieberman, who then ran as presidential material. Kerry, whose family name is not Kerry but Kohn, is nothing but a Zionist in disguise. George Bush (the Lesser) has so many Zionist advisors that they could move the Oval Office to Tel Aviv and there would be no noticeable difference. These people call themselves neo-cons, New Conservatives; they are in fact old Zionists. They call Lieberman, who supports infanticide, and went along with Gore's lies on the Florida election, the conscience of the senate. No religious or proper Jew would ever support such acts as are condoned by Lieberman. A massive step was taken in the mid '90s by the Clinton administration toward this goal: the Communications Act that was passed by Congress allowed the consolidation of radio communications by certain huge conglomerates like Clear Channel, Newhouse, and some others. This act has resulted, in a short nine years, in the elimination of over 800 privately owned and operated radio stations. Most of these were talk radio, which tends to be "conservative" or nationalistic. It was Bill Clinton's act to comply with his wife Hillary's request to eliminate the "Vast Right Wing Conspiracy".

– 7 –

Communization of Farming and Centralization of Production.

A kibbutz is a communal farm or industrial village in which the members jointly own everything and equally share in the profit; none in a kibbutz have any personal property, it is totally communist.

The very first organized community of Europeans in America was a socialist construct. The poor Puritans suffered and died *en masse*. The colony was a total failure. Then, in the third year, they opted for an open community, practiced libertarian economics, and created a successful and thriving community. Illuminists use Communism and socialism for the exact reason that it does not work. They know it will not work because in all of man's history there is not one single socialist model that was ever successful. None. Not the Nazi, not the Soviet, not Mao, not the Brown-shirts, not the Swedes, and not the British Labor attempt, not the Israeli models – every one of them utterly and totally failed. Socialism, however, is useful to the Illuminists because they know the end product of it to be dissatisfaction, hatred, rebellion, class warfare, and revolution.

There is one other and important feature of socialism, its ability to convince the masses that they may obtain something from government for nothing. It is that particular feature that politicians use to garnish votes for the promise of welfare, food stamps, housing, heating subsidies, utility subsidies, free schooling, police protection, and any number of other freebies. Soon the promised delivery begins, and shortly thereafter government increases fees, taxes, licenses, permits, duties, sales taxes, property taxes, etc. Always, always remember that government is unable to give you anything they do not have to take away from you and your neighbors first; government is not a producer, it is a consumer. When you hear of a government grant to your school, community, police department, or whatever, it is not a grant, it is money they collected from you to begin with, and because governments are the very worst administrators in existence, you can count on the fact that you are lucky if the return on your tax is 40%, the rest is consumed in the bureaucracy. Consider now how much better off you would have been if those funds had been collected in your community for distribution locally.

It is the desire of the Illuminists to create a climate of social strife such as has never before been, and then to use that strife (revolution) to seize power for themselves by offering their solution. This solution will in part consist of expanded police functions to "make our citizens safe". This is a repeat of Rome, Berlin, Paris, Moscow, and so forth. The ultimate end of all socialist states is an increase of police and law enforcement, just exactly as we are experiencing today. America has seen a rise in gun-toting federal officers of about 250,000 over the last two decades. It is imperative to understand that the enforcement of law in America is not a federal prerogative, but is at the sole discretion of the several states. To the best of my knowledge, there are only three legitimate and legally enacted exclusions to this federal prohibition and they are bank robbery, banknote forgery, and kidnapping.

The destruction of family farming and small business is a fact. It is an ongoing government policy that is demonstrable in thousands of laws, acts and actions. The super-rich have always mistrusted, perhaps it is better to say feared, the middle class. The middle class, whom grew out of the medieval trade guilds, forever represented an anathema to the ruling elites. This stems from the serf–noble relationship that these guilds interrupted and disturbed. Today's wealthy are no different, just like the nobles of the Renaissance, they want it all. Their motivation is power and their drive is greed.

Environmentalism and government actions are the two fronts of assault against family farming. Consider the actions taken by government in the eleven Western states, confiscation of lands, through the creation of national monuments, national parks, endangered species laws, suppression of water rights, closing of irrigation systems, uncontrolled forest fires, the American Rivers initiative, and various stupid (swamp) wetland laws. And just so you understand, the largest producer in the world of CO_2 in order of volume (green-house gases) are swamps, termites, and Yellowstone National Park, at 40 thousand tons per year.

The assault on family farms and forestry by environmentalists is unprecedented. Just one example is the "spotted owl" fiasco in the Pacific N.W. Thousands of people had their livelihood canceled, scores of lumber mills were closed, school districts went bankrupt, villages turned into ghost towns – all for an endangered, we were told, owl. These owls, we were informed, would only nest in Old Growth Forest. Honestly I'm over 65 and have lived in the country for most of my life, and can tell you I don't know any bird intelligent enough to discriminate on the age of a tree it nests in. Well, in 2001 we learned it was all a huge lie. Hundreds of spotted owls were found to be nesting around the San Francisco Bay; one of the places was the urban Golden Gate Park at the South end of the Golden Gate Bridge.

On the business side we see the relentless mergers, acquisitions, downsizing, and the radical changes all this has brought to America. We shop at Wal-Mart, not at our local store, we purchase foreign goods, not domestic, the local hardware store, five and dime, grocer, and cobbler are all gone, along with their American- made goods. Your neighbors are no longer storeowners or small-business owners; they work for huge corporations, multi-nationals, or government bureaucracies. The resulting effect on our society is measurable in the falling quality of life, the ever-downward spiraling culture, loss of independence of our individual freedoms, loss in self-esteem, and endlessly growing crime rates. We have become a society of self-indulgent materialistic grubby collectors of useless junk, and we accomplish this not on our earnings, no indeed, we do it on credit. Gone is the independent, self-reliant American; a new model that relies on government, expects free services, spends other people's money, and is generally lazy to boot has replaced him.

– 8 –

Equalization of Labor.

It is not necessary to go much further than "Glass Ceiling". This is the ludicrous contention in feminist circles that somehow women are paid less than men and are at the same time prevented from advancement up the corporate ladder. All this of course fits right in with Affirmative Action, class warfare, and the consistent and unrelenting whining of people unable to succeed, who then claim this is due to race or gender. Last week I cut down a large pine tree that was dead on my property; I cut it up into 24" logs and piled it up, with the branches also cut to 24" lengths, at the edge of the road for pickup by the sanitation department. The truck came and went; they did not pick the stuff up. I called, they sent out a truck with a female driver and no helper: I loaded the truck. The stupidity of Cultural Marxism in the employment field by government is simply unbelievable. You can rest assured that she is paid the same as the men, who also fluffed off on their jobs. I subscribe to an old saying, "you can't keep a good man down;" it obviously includes women. I ran businesses in retail, import-export, and manufacturing for most of my adult life, and want to make it very plain; there is discrimination of all sorts, but there is very little of it in jobs. If a man is a good mechanic, or a woman is a good administrator, and they use their God-given gifts in an intelligent and aggressive way, they will go up the ladder. There are no if's or butt's about this, my only advice is that if you are employed by or work for some moron whom you believe is not allowing you to advance because of sex or race, quit and go elsewhere. In the present market you will see him out of business shortly. The fact of the matter is that an employer cannot afford to practice racism or sexism in today's market place and stay in business. There are obvious exceptions to this. Females are not on average able to perform many jobs, infantry combat, artillery, Seals, Rangers, trash men, steel fabrication, and such jobs that involve heavy lifting and danger; feminists who disagree should demonstrate their personal ability in those fields.

There is, however, a course that was begun in the late '60s based on all sorts of ridiculous arguments. The primary instruments of this are "Set-asides," "Affirmative Action," "Hiring Quotas," and naturally the wholesale discrimination by such organizations as the SBA (Small Business Administration). On the last issue I want you to listen to a personal experience I had. Sometime in the '70s I had obtained a 50% interest in a manufacturing company whose principal was a black man. We became partners. Machine manufacturing, even on a small scale, is very capital-intensive, due to the extremely high cost of the required machinery. While our business was doing well, producing mostly products for one of my other enterprises, we really wanted to expand, but realized we would need several hundred thousand dollars. My partner approached the SBA, who promptly sent a representative to visit us. The woman they sent was Hispanic, knew nothing about manufacturing, and spoke very broken English. When she informed my black partner that we did not qualify because he had a Caucasian business partner he went ballistic. As he threw her out of the plant he bitterly vocalized the fact that she was obviously not even an American. In the '70s and through the '80s SBA had a strict racial policy, 'if you're not black don't bother to apply".

The only other thing they did, and probably still do today, is making the owner of the business personally guarantee any loan that SBA co-signs. The funds actually come from a local bank, the only thing the SBA does is to be the guarantor of last resort. What that means is that after they have sold the business, your car, house, furniture and TV, and all you're left with is your family, they will make good on the balance due the bank. Hey, those Illuminists at the local bank are not going to put their capital at risk unless it's for one of their own. The best two examples of that are Panama, and the sale of the Panama Canal by Jimmy the Twit Carter, which in actuality was a bailout of the Marine Midland Bank of NY, one of the owners of the FRS. And secondly the multi-billion Mexican bail-out, which again had payment (loan re-payments) go not to Mexico but to NY banks, also owners of the FRS, who were over-extended when Mexico defaulted on re-payment of principal as well as interest.

All these matters deal with the equalization of labor. It is an odious concept that completely circumvents logic and common sense. If I place my assets at risk by investing in a business, how does that allow one of my employees to claim he should be compensated comparably to me? If I hire a man to do a dirty and physically difficult job, how does that require a secretary to be paid the same amount? Conversely, if I hire a secretary who is more nearly a personal aide, how does a production worker claim equal pay to her? All these concepts are again socialist in nature and stupid to boot. Labor functions cannot be equalized: they are different in physical demand, intellectual demand, and those abilities are not equally distributed in man. Interesting how we seem to have come full circle, we are back on the equality issue that we saw so prominently miss-applied in education.

All these issues are related because all stem from the same Illuminist source. I want once more to make it absolutely clear. We are not equal! We are decidedly different. Our abilities differ both physically as well as intellectually. We are by nature equal before the law, which, however, has noting whatever to do with equality of ability. Equality is used by the agents of the Illuminati to induce racial, and gender, conflict through socialist/Communist doctrine to keep you from following their gradual takeover of society.

– 9 –

Reduction of Population by Force

The primary agents of population reduction are; the environmentalists, The Club of Rome, located in Paris, France, The Bilderbergers (Europe), The Royal Institute of International Affairs, London, England, The Council on Foreign Relations, New York City, and The Trilateral Commission – NY, Tokyo, and Geneva. The world population goal as demanded by these groups is one billion humans. They can be seen weekly on TV, heard on radio, and reviewed in the print media, as making that ridiculous demand. Consider that by best estimates this will reduce world population by more than two-thirds. Don't bet that the ranks of the organizations proposing this are to be trimmed by that number, it's not them; it's you, who are to be eliminated.

Population control is and has been a very active occurrence for a very long time. There are many ways to reduce population. Wars have proven very successful, and are a very active and on-going enterprise, with over 100 at the present time. Abortion and infanticide have become effective instruments of the Illuminist population-reduction formula. Unfortunately Caucasians seem to be the only racial group stupid enough to fall for it, having produced a negative growth rate in most European nations, as well as in much of America. Famine has also been more than just successful, through socialist and Communist manipulation of society's farm production methods. The Communist takeover of producing nations brought Rhodesia, now called Zimbabwe, from being the largest food exporter in Africa to a net food importer. And then we have South Africa, which will undoubtedly go the same way. Pestilence, the introductions of man-made virus such as Ebola, AIDS, and the newly expanding TB, has also taken their toll. Anthrax of a variety now known to have originated in an American weapons lab has made numerous appearances in the United States. On the food side, we have seen the introduction of hoof and mouth disease in England (2000) and now Germany, (2002) both strains proven to have originated in a British weapons lab. In fact, all the Four Horsemen of the Apocalypse have been loosed upon mankind. Into this toxic mix have been added social issues, such as the acceptance of homosexuality as a means of birth control, handing out of condoms to six-year-olds, birth control pills, and the gradual acceptance of euthanasia, already legalized in Holland.

Of all the most successful has been the communization of numerous previously productive nations. The only problem faced by the elites is that they do not control the situation in China and have limited input in Russia. The rest of the world is "their oyster," as the saying goes. In Africa they have total control, to the extent that it can be estimated that the population of Africa will be halved by 2010, and will continue declining at exponential speed. The AIDS epidemic has now expanded to over 70% of the population in numerous regions. Ebola, which to date has been isolated in Africa, may be anticipated to keep re-appearing. And it is reasonable to anticipate widespread famine in Zimbabwe, Botswana, Angola, as well as South Africa, at a somewhat later date. Politically, the rest of Africa is such a basket case that I can say with certainty that the native population would be ten times better off under colonial rule, such as they had before.

Population reduction has, however, seen its most successful endeavors in white European communities. Birthrates, particularly in the Anglo Saxon Northern populations, have been below replacement levels for a very long time. Countries like Switzerland, Sweden, and the United Kingdom are importing foreigners for labor, because they do not produce enough children to replace those retiring from the workplace to meet societal need. This is now also the case in America's West and Southwest, where Latinos now represent the major population growth. In fact, white Caucasians seem to be the only group of idiots who have bought into this population reduction plan. I find it ironic that the civilization that has brought the most to modern man, the civilization responsible for all of mankind's phenomenal achievements, is committing mass suicide by listening to a bunch of defectives whose only goal is to become the dictators of us all. While China is not under the influence or control of the Illuminati, it is worthwhile to note that they have succeeded in reducing their birthrate to one child per family.

– 10–

Centralization of Education

Adolph Hitler expressed his sentiments on the state of education in Germany in the 1930s when addressing a large audience at a university in Frankfurt A/M. A heckler during his speech stated, "you and your National Socialists will never get my support," to which Hitler replied, "I don't need or even want your support; I already have your children." That happens to be where we are today. The Illuminists, through all their nefarious programs and implemented actions, have our children; that is, if they attend public schools, or watch TV. The diabolical evil that these schools and the mainstream media promulgate to their students and listeners cannot be under-estimated. What we know as Western civilization, a sense of values, understanding of moral behavior and ethical action, are gone. Classics are gone; science, and higher mathematics, along with any understanding of economics and political systems, is all gone. A child can graduate from an American high school without having taken algebra, geometry, physics, botany, geology, biology, economics, American government – hell, half of them are unable to write a paragraph, and most will never read another book after graduation.

This provides the perfect fodder for the Illuminist "school to work" programs that are now beginning to appear in almost all high schools. There will be no more HS diplomas. They are to be replaced by school records appropriately constructed for future employers' needs; they will be required for employment. The student's needs are unimportant, because he is only a part of a huge beehive of workers to meet the demands of employers. Advancement beyond HS will be determined by the "System," not the parents or the student. This is what I call the educational insect mentality that has become so prevalent in education of the 21st century. Today education is not education; it is a method of social conditioning by the edu-crats that they deem appropriate to the future needs of society. Individuality is to be eliminated.

All this stands in the face of reality and what education is supposed to do. The job of education, before all else, is to teach the pupil to think. Modern education strenuously avoids teaching anyone to think on any topic. Thought leads to query and questions lead to opposition. Likewise ethics and morals, the foundation of Western civilization have both been eliminated, and replaced with moral relativism. Why do students rebel and even kill one another, that is a very simple question once you remove God, eliminate any moral input, and have no ethics: murder, and theft, are no longer crimes. If in addition you teach that society is a democracy, where the majority makes the rules in accordance with the norms of that day's society, opposition is moot because everything is simply a different shade of gray, and changes on a daily basis.

That education is gradually being centralized within the federal sphere is not in dispute. We have traveled from all-private education in the 1700s to the Germanization of centralized federal education. These actions were initiated at the turn of the 20th century, having been brought here from Germany. Bismarck, the very same man who came up with centralized state welfare in the medical field, introduced the socialist state education enterprise in Prussia in 1884. In the last 40 years, through their surrogates, the NEA and AFT[100], the programs of federalization of American education have accelerated rapidly. Every single year, regardless of the rhetoric by Republicans, the Department of Education grows. They rule over school districts nationally by controlling the purse strings. Either a district conforms to federal edicts or the money spigot is turned off. This is even more the case in higher education, where thousands of federal statutes must be obeyed, or no money for student loans. If loan funds are cut off the school will go bankrupt. The only college to my knowledge that will not accept any federal funds in the form of student loans or borrowing is Hillsdale in Michigan.

Part of this is about money; the more money dumped into education, the more teachers, professors and administrators earn. I really think we should examine some up-to-date information on:

1 Productivity: Let's look at a comparison of SAT scores and compare them in relationship to dollars spent. If we begin in 1960 with a value of 100 and make an annual comparison every year until 2000, a term of some 40 years, we come up with a decline all the way down to 26, or a 74% drop.

2 Student/Teacher Ratio: If we now make a comparison of the student to teacher ratios from 1960 to 2000 we find that the average classroom size went down from 30.7 in 1960 to 15.0 in 2000, in other words the size of classrooms is now less than half what it was 40 years ago.

3 Spending: The average cost per student in 1960 was $2,120 per year. That cost has risen to just under $7,000 for 2000. But what is really telling is that the reading ability of students has stagnated at the same level as it was 40 years ago. Yes, that's right, we more than tripled our tax contribution and got nothing for it.

On January 25, 2002, our president proudly announced that he was budgeting another billion dollars for education. He further stated that all of these funds would be used to improve reading and English skills of students. Another monumental waste of our taxes! While the Department of Education is given one billion, the federal bureaucracy will consume 400 million; the remaining 600 million will go to state education departments, who will undoubtedly waste another 150 million in administrative acrobatics. This will leave a meager 450 million to go to individual school districts: 90% of that will go to hiring more inadequate, unqualified teachers. The only way education in America can be fixed is to privatize all of it, and get state and federal bureaucrats, the AFT and the NEA, out of it.

A New Weapon; environmentalism as a tool for changing society.

This contentious issue again is being implemented through the environmental lobby and government edicts. The largest of the government actions of the immediate past is the Clinton act of the creation of a National Monument in the state of Utah larger than the state of Rhode Island and Providence Plantations. Actually Clinton killed two birds with one stone when he made the Grand Staircase Escalante National Monument via an illegal EO (Executive Order). First he fulfilled one of the "prime directives" of his masters, and incidentally closed the largest low-sulfur coal mining operation in North America, and thereby insured his friends and political financiers, the Rhiadi family of Malaysia, continued sales of their low-sulfur coal in America.

By creating this National Monument based on "historic" grounds that did not exist he committed the second crime. Mines were closed, villages were vacated, school districts evacuated, all for nothing. I do not know the total scope of Clinton's national parks and National Monuments directives, I really doubt that anyone does; however, I am reasonably well informed that the total area in all his acts exceeds the land mass of the state of Massachusetts. To their credit, the Senate reversed numbers of his destructive EO's after he left office.

Environmentalists, lest we forget, have wreaked havoc upon private as well as public lands. Among some of their brighter ideas has been the re-introduction of wolves and grizzly bears into public lands used by ranchers for generations. It does not take these predators very long to realize what easy pickings farm animals are. Instead of government or, better yet, environmentally active organizations paying for livestock losses, they fine and imprison farmers and ranchers for protecting their property.

In Southern California the goofy environmentalist whackos refused to allow firebreaks to be cut into pampas-type grass because of the "endangered" (who cares) kangaroo rat. This has resulted in the wanton destruction of millions of dollars in real estate due to fires that could easily have been prevented. In that same area, a Korean immigrant farmer had his farm confiscated, equipment auctioned off, and livelihood destroyed, when it was found out that he had inadvertently run over a kangaroo rat with his tractor while plowing a field. We already covered the spotted-owl fiasco.

We are indoctrinated *ad infinitum* about non-existent environmental problems concocted by a strident lobby, whose primary interest has nothing whatever to do with the environment and everything to do with raising money. The cause of my statement is that in all environmental organizations, which I have examined more than 70% of all the funds collected, go towards payroll – in some it is as high as 85%. No commercial enterprise, excepting an accounting, legal, or management-consulting business, could survive with such payroll allocations. The fact that American do-gooder organizations pay their executives outrageous salaries is typified by the over $450,000 paid the administrative head of the American Red Cross, a job held by Elizabeth Dole for many years. (It helps to be politically connected.)

In any event and in order:

Greenhouse Gases: more commonly called CO_2. Contrary to advertised percentages, America produces about 4.7% of the total industrial CO_2 worldwide. Just in America we are out-produced by termites, swamps, and in the 11 Western states by Yellowstone National Park, which all by itself produces 40 thousand tons per year. If we shut off every power plant and turned off every car, the resulting impact would be insignificant.

The Ozone Hole: has been a fact for thousands of year and has nothing at all to do with man. The ozone hole is a product of the earth's turning on its axis, thus creating an alternate six months' winter in the South and North Polar Regions. Ozone is a triad of oxygen atoms, the sources of which are lightning and solar radiation. Winter (darkness), no radiation, no ozone.

Chlorofluorocarbons: these, we have been told, destroy the ozone layer. Baloney! Freon, as it is more commonly called, is a very heavy gas that sinks to the ground immediately upon being released. Ozone is one of the lightest gasses traveling directly to the stratosphere upon being released. Furthermore ground bacteria destroy Freon. How can a gas that travels downward destroy a gas that rises?

Acid Rain: is the product of two distinct actions. First and foremost it is produced by rotting plant matter in swamps (wet-lands, for you soft-brained environmentalists). Secondly, by coal-burning power plants; this is undoubtedly the reason that all environmental active groups are opposed to nuclear energy generation, the only source, outside hydroelectric, that does not pollute.

All these issues are used to attack the ownership of private property, and the forced relocation of population. I am fascinated by the propaganda from Hollywood, as well as in the media, on these issues, where in every single case it is a Caucasian businessman who is the despoiler of the environment. Even a cursory examination will confirm that, worldwide as well as domestically, serious environmental catastrophes, with few exceptions, have been the result of government action. Let's face it; if you own a piece of property, you have a vested interest in taking care of it; if you don't the value is ruined. If a bureaucrat administers it he gains nothing and loses nothing, so why should he bother? Does anyone remember the Three Mile Island nuclear fiasco, which did not even hurt a single blade of grass? Or, on the other hand, government projects like Love Canal, Hanford, Chernobyl, and the scores of government-operated fiascos that caused huge environmental and human damage?

The Last New Weapons: fourth generation warfare to reduce population.

All of society is a fabric; the binding ties are family and community. There are two ways by which society can be destroyed; one is the introduction of an issue foreign to that society, which in Western nations of the world is legal and illegal immigration. I certainly hope that no one is stupid enough to dispute that this is taking place. The second is war. War removes males and, in the 21st century, females from society, thus disrupting not only family but also community. Terrorism is fourth-generation warfare; it differs greatly from conventional warfare because the enemy is not evident or identifiable. It is this factor that allows third-party participation; by that I mean that terrorism is not necessarily always the act of the assumed protagonist. Often governments anxious to increase their power over the indigenous population are more than just involved in acts of terrorism. This, as we have come to understand, was the case in the first Twin Tower bombing, in which the FBI, in a sting operation gone awry, was the supplier of the explosive as well as the detonators. The Oklahoma City federal office building bombing was also an operation in which our government was heavily involved. Complicity in numerous other heinous terrorist acts demonstrates the presence of the CIA, FBI, and BATF, and in a large number of cases the Israeli Mossad.

That terrorism is one of the Illuminist means of changing society is without question. That they are involved in terrorism is indisputable. The Zionist state is the only government in the entire world, which openly sponsors state terrorism against all opponents, domestically, as well as in foreign lands. Assassination, murder, kidnapping, home and business destruction, community envelopment, and attacks on mosques and churches are practiced daily. The hidden hand of the Mossad has been seen in acts of terror inflicted on all nations around the world. In the 9-11 occurrence, 68 Mossad agents were deported from the United States within days of the attack. Mossad people are always present when one of these attacks takes place.

What are glaringly obvious are the complicity of Israeli state security services in terrorism around the world, and the additional complicity of Communists and socialists; thus we have the instruments of social change as wanted by the Illuminist conspiracy. There are numerous other structures used by Illuminism in their attempts to bring about their New World Order; most of these utilize nice people who want to do good, like environmentalists, to reach their nefarious goal.

Illuminism is an amalgamation of
Communism, Socialism and Zionism.
This fact is indisputable!

UNASSOCIATED ALLIES

There are a number of issues that do not appear in Weishaupt's dicta. They are nevertheless relevant factors, and used by Illuminists.

Drugs:

I certainly hope that you, dear reader, are not one of those naïve people who suffer the notion that our government and the managers of it are not involved in the illicit drug industry right up to their proverbial eyeballs. Let's face the primary fact in the first paragraph; America's drug industry is the largest single industry in the country. It is larger than General Motors, Mobil oil, or any single corporation on earth. Anyone who believes that an enterprise of such magnitude is possible without the involvement of the government, politicians, courts, and banks must be comatose. I also don't want to hear any of the waffle about the "War on Drugs," which has proven equally as effective as our "War on Poverty." Consider that money transactions in this industry, most of which are carried out in cash, amount to over $600 billion per year, or $50 billion per month, or $961 million a week, or $137 million a day. The old British drug industry, which was the beginning of it all, amounts to another $520+ billion annually. With such a transaction rate, how is it that bankers and government agencies are unable to identify who the major drug traffickers are? I have just seen the enemy and it is our bankers! Without complicity of the banks, acquiescence of the media, and protection by the political system, we would have won this conflict years ago.

The Shah of Iran became fed up with the drug industry and its poisoning of his people. He made a moratorium: after a fixed date all drug dealers would be shot, on the spot; when caught all users would be forced into a rehabilitation clinic. Shortly the Iranian drug industry was eliminated, and not long thereafter the Shah was deposed.

Afghanistan was the second largest producer of opium: the Taliban was unhappy about this, and began active incursions and warfare against the producers. Not long thereafter we located an active terrorist organization in Afghanistan (with, to date, not one single item of real proof) and invaded Afghanistan. That nation has now attained the number one rank in poppy production, and is the world's largest exporter of heroin as of 2004. The war in Afghanistan was centered on only two issues; one was heroin production and the other was a pipeline that American contractors wanted to build but for which a French firm had a contract.

The Golden Triangle bordering Vietnam, Cambodia, and Thailand is the second largest production region, and we all know what has transpired there over the last two decades of the 20th century.

Kosovo gives us yet another example. It is a well-known fact that the CIA financed the Albanian Muslim KLA establishing bases inside (Christian Serb) Kosovo, where the Bundeswehr trained the KLA. Now it should not surprise you to learn that the KLA operates the largest drug distribution network in Europe. They are the drug couriers for Middle Eastern and Oriental producers. They further act as a destabilizing force against the Orthodox Christian Serbs and Roman Catholic Christian Croats, both of whom, God bless them, are opposed to the drug industry.

I should also point out the situation in South America, namely Columbia, and its neighbor Bolivia, in which a war of sorts has been raging for decades that also shows more than slight CIA as well as Special Forces activity. Now my detractors will tell you that we are the good guys fighting against the drug cartel, to which my only response is, why, after over 20 years of this foolishness, have we seen no results?

Mexico is a country that is best defined as a narco-republic. The last president's brother, acting as bagman for the Salinas crime family, had skimmed over $300 million from the drug industry to Swiss bank accounts. It was only through the offices of Swiss bankers that the money was repatriated to Mexico. Mexico to this date is one of the largest producers of marijuana, as well as the prime entry point for all other illicit drugs (cocaine) from South American producers.

To all of this I will say, and emphatically so: "there is a consortium in America that wants the *status quo* in drug sales and distribution." They want this status because it is a very profitable business. They want this business because people under the influence of drugs do not oppose the governing structure. They want this business because druggys' only interest is their next fix, not the loss of their liberties. There is so much bribery, payola, chicanery, and influence peddling in the drug industry that it touches every citizen in the Western world, whether they use drugs or not. To assume that the Illuminati are not involved in this industry would be foolish.

The Illuminists have gone the extra mile in the effort to increase drug dependency, as well as in support of drug legalization.

The Campaign for New Drug Policies that has been active not only in California and in Arizona expanded their efforts into Michigan in 2002. Funded by multi-billionaires George Soros, Peter Lewis, and John Sperling, it is their hope to expand their successful CA, and AZ, initiative not only to MI but also to FL, and OH. Their battle cry is, treatment not jail. To improve that situation we should begin by deporting Soros, who is not native-born.

Silly fiction about destroying agrarian production fields, as the War on Drugs has done in the past, is equally as stupid as trying to get a whore to become a secretary. In both cases the existing occupation is 1000 times more lucrative than honest work; thus the chance of change is wholly unrealistic. In both cases we have masquerading do-gooders pretending to offer a solution, in order to retain the moral high ground, while in fact cavorting in the sewers.

Language

Language is the most obvious feature tying the members of human groups into communities. Any sociologist will tell you that the very first requirement of any community must be its facility of communication. This very basic need is being assaulted from within. Very small but vocal groups of Hispanics, who refuse to assimilate into American society, are the supporters of it. The Illuminists give this cause money, influence, support, and anything else that it requires; yes, exactly the same group of foundations and multi-national corporations funds this effort. It serves the overall goal, the dismemberment of the United States, and the creation of a hemisphere-wide socio-political structure to be called FTAA. For 200 years foreigners, including myself, immigrated to what used to be the greatest republic in history. We, the immigrants, learned the customs and language, and assimilated as fast as we could. I came in 1952; I did not know one single word of English when we landed in NY. I did not have a German language aid: I simply learned. In a few short months I spoke English, in a few years I lost my accent. It is not difficult; all that is required is the desire to succeed.

What has changed? Hispanics, particularly the lower classes of Central Americans, and Northern South Americans, a large percentage of who are Indios, are at the bottom of the socio-economic ladder in the places from which they came. They are for the most part uneducated, some don't even speak Spanish, most are hostile to Caucasians because of the poor way they have always been treated by the ruling Spanish and Portuguese classes in their countries of origin. They distrust police, from experience and not without good cause. They are culturally, socially, linguistically, and economically very difficult to assimilate, because they, mostly through fear, band together in tightly-knit communities, continuing their foreign-to-America existence here. People will now say that this is no different from any of the groups of immigrants who came to America. They are dead wrong. Not only are they racially different from any other group of past immigrants, they are culturally different. The concept that America's Southwest must now become multi-lingual is very dangerous, in view of the fact that Hispanic birthrates, plus immigration, outpace the indigenous population by a substantial margin. This will result in the *Re-conquista* we hear about from Mexicans. I lived in Mexico for some time and love the people and the country, which, however, does not mean that I want to relinquish our great American Southwest to a horde of stampeding Indios, whose primary motive is to get away from the ruling narco-republics in which they previously resided.

Cultural Marxism

Political Correctness is the most insidious of all the methods used to divide us from each other. Although this is not a new propaganda tool, it was refined in the 1940s by an Illuminist think tank in the UK. The process is dictatorial and Marxist in nature; it denies freedom of expression, limits personal liberty, and utilizes mass hysteria to reach a pre-determined outcome. It is the ultimate Marxist tool for the destruction of republican values. Every single dictator in the 20th century used the process. The use of words that are designed to convey meaning far beyond verbal content is part and parcel of the process. Consider now the following words: gay, cop-killer, bullet, never again, holocaust, assault weapon, and homeless. How did these words evolve? Where did these words come from?

- Sodomite to homosexual to gay:
- military ammunition to jacketed bullet to cop-killer bullet:
- rifle to gun to semi-automatic to sub- machine gun to assault weapon:
- bum to hobo to homeless:
- Never again – a phony concoction to pretend that Jews are universally persecuted:
- Holocaust –a trademark used by Zionists to expand their embezzlement empire.

Now if you follow the progressions above you will note distinctly and different resulting factors, with intentioned consequences. Sodomite is a harsh word describing a behavior; from this we go to homosexual, a word that is neutral in conveyance of feeling, and then we progress to a word, gay, that in fact praises a perversion. The ultimate aim is to make this perversion seem not only natural but also beneficial. If we now examine rifle we see the reverse; rifle is in concept a useful tool to hunt, or protect, gun becomes somewhat more harsh, semi-automatic then denotes a rapidly firing device and is thus associated by the general public with a weapon of war – which it most certainly is not exclusively, semi-automatic guns were invented before 1900 and are used in hunting, skeet and trap shooting, match shooting, by police, and for target shooting. This brings us to assault weapon; the ambiance of this word denotes a product exclusively used in aggression. This is false. It denotes a material device, which has no opinion, no character, and no life. Assault weapon is a stupid term to use, because anything can be an assault weapon, from a hammer to a baseball bat.

So we see words utilized to influence actions. We see words specifically designed to alter the concept of a product or act. We see words used to change societal behavior. This is the inspired legacy of the Tavistock Institute, which has been the culprit behind much of the sickness inflicted on society.

Other factors of CM relate to forcing free people to express themselves in a pre-determined manner as postulated by its inventors. These falsifications cover the entire gamut of human intercourse; gender, race, religion, government, as well as education. In fact education, particularly higher education, is where these aberrations are most prevalent. Today they have infiltrated every facet of American life, and are just beginning to develop in Europe.

During a four-week stay in England I had ample opportunity to observe the BBC in action. What once was the premier radio and TV broadcast organization in the world has sunk to a level equal to, if not worse than, our own Talmudvision. They have a program comprised of young adults discussing race and politics; I have never heard such drivel in my life. The most common theme was that all cultures and all art from all places have equal value. That there was no difference between blacks, Caucasians and Orientals. That industrial development was fostered by blacks. That government must make laws to enforce racial and gender equality. And that there was no difference between males and females. I really wanted to ask the white male moron who made that statement when he was planning to deliver his next child.

Judicial Activism (JA)

JA is a process restricted to government, more exactly to the judicial, and law- enforcement branches of it. It is the insidious method by which the judicial branch of government, in violation of constitutional precepts, makes law. The primary way this is done is though precedents. Every time a judge adjudicates a verdict, that verdict is made part of the bulk of law upon which future decisions will be based. The person who in most jurisdictions decides what law is to be included in official records (precedents) is the state prosecutor; surely none thinks that he will list cases he has lost as part of the official record. Thus as time passes the bulk of filed precedents always favors the state.

The Supreme Court, (that body of judges, most of whom have not read their oath of office since the day they took it), uses the other method: most often these are the creation of new law based not on the Constitution, which they are supposed to interpret, but rather on personal opinion. Hallmarks of this have been school desegregation issues, infanticide, abortion, school bussing, and various housing issues. The matter before us is not whether you agree or disagree with any of the aforementioned decisions, but rather if the decisions were based on the Constitution? The Supreme Court is not permitted to make law, that prerogative rests solely with the legislative branch. Thus we must conclude that these issues that are totally absent from the Constitution were in fact concocted by judicially active judges and were their personal opinions.

JA is an ongoing Illuminist practice to change society into the beehive that I call insect mentality. It has proven very effective, particularly in the last 30 years. It has succeeded in changing most citizens' concept of legitimate law into a structure of social engineering; something the founders most certainly never meant it to be.

Gun control

I don't want to appear trite, but in my opinion gun control is the ability to hit what you are shooting at. Just simple facts that may have eluded your attention; county by county, all those with the highest degree of gun control have the highest gun-related crime rates, and conversely those states and counties with the least restrictive laws and carry-permit laws have the lowest crime rates. Some would believe this to be an American phenomenon, but they'd be wrong; so devastating to the gun-control lobby was the information presented by the Dutch ICVS[101] poll that the British government has refused to publish its results. This survey interviewed a total of 34,000 crime victims in 17 industrialized nations. You will not have heard of it also because it has been strenuously avoided by all media sources since it was published in March of 2001. The country that tops the violent crime list is Australia – the very same Australia that confiscated all guns three years ago and whose violent crime rate has skyrocketed ever since. England and Wales are next:

they also confiscated guns, to the point where the English Olympic team has to go to the Continent to practice. Then comes Scotland; all those mentioned to this point have violent crime rates about double those of America. Next in succession are; Finland, Northern Ireland, France, and Holland – America is eighth.

Let's be very clear about one thing; the first act of any planned despot in the entire history of the world has been the confiscation of any and all weapons of defense. The basis of the entire gun-control issue is one of the New World Order's comprehending the fact that you cannot dictate unpopular ideas to an armed public. It should also be pointed out that Switzerland has the very highest gun-ownership population, and, similar to Vermont, requires no carry permits for any citizen; it has one of the lowest crime rates in the world, substantially below the top ten and including Japan. Now you have probably seen billboards from Hand Gun Control Inc., which more aptly should be called Hand Gun Lies Inc., stating that every day 18 children are killed by guns. What they neglect to tell you is that 14 of those are drug-related gang killings by late teenagers, between 14 and 18 years of age. And of course no-one in the media tells you that pediatricians, drowning, falls, car accidents, all produce 100 times the number of childhood deaths. The Illuminist plan cannot be instituted until all the people are disarmed.

State Terrorism

The Zionist state has reached a new crescendo when it comes to violence. They are the only nation in the world, which practices state-sponsored terrorism worldwide. Recent actions by Israel, however, lead one to believe that they have now turned the edge and entered a new venue. In early spring of 2004 they used an American

HA 64 helicopter to murder a blind 67-year-old paraplegic in a wheelchair at the front of his mosque where he had just finished Morning Prayer. This abomination is an insult to all monotheists and clearly demonstrates Zionism's perversion of Judaism, and their disdain for all religion. Sheik Ahmed Yassin was the founder of Hamas, the Palestinian organization set up by Arabs to counter Israeli aggression and the occupation of their homeland for over 34 years. He had been in Israeli jails on numerous occasions, but rather than arresting him this time they decided to simply murder the elderly cleric. His stature, in a religious sense, was about the same as that of a Roman Catholic cardinal.

Sharon, the Zionist prime minister of the mini-empire, the man who has been indicted in various world courts for the murders ordered by him at the Shabra and Chatila refugee camps in the 80s, ordered this murder. By 1982 the Zionist state had already driven three million Arabs off their land, and killed 17,500 of them. Why are America and Britain in the loop of fourth-generation war worldwide by Islam? Simply because we not only support Israel with weapons, money, and technology, but because we actively support murder. We also act as a mercenary military by providing the military muscle and manpower for Israel. When the matter of Sheik Yassim's murder came before the UN, Jack Straw, the British foreign secretary and a Jew, called it "an illegal and criminal act." We were the only nation who did not condemn the act; in fact, we blocked the resolution using our veto in censure of Israel in the General Assembly. Now, in the second week of April 2004, when Sharon visited Washington, our president actually supported the present policy of his government. Not only is this act counter to logic, it will result in escalated mayhem throughout the Middle East. It is nothing more and nothing less than bribery of Jews in America to vote for the Republican Party. Jews in the past had supported the Democrats hands down, but with the advent of the neo-cons, who are all Zionists, that has changed.

The neo-cons produced various documents through their organization JINSA (Jewish Institute for National Affairs) among these was *A Clean Break* authored by David Wurmser, Richard Perle, and Douglas Feith, who also produced *Project for a New American Century*; both of these documents approve of murder as a means of Israeli foreign policy. One can only wonder and wait for religious American Jews to step up to the plate and tell these public servants where to go. I for one do not intend to hold my breath, when it comes to treason against our country I can only say: Pollard, Rosenberg, Fuchs, Pontecorvo, Gold, Greenglass, Bloch, Perle, Bronfman, David, the list is endless.

What exactly is the mini-empire's plan for the Middle East? First, there is the "Greater Israel" policy. This is simply the geographic expansion of Israel to include the West Bank, the Golan Heights, the Sinai Peninsula, Lebanon, Syria, and Iraq to the Euphrates River and to the Turkish border. The fact that over 40 million Arabs of Christian and Islamic heritage populate this region seems irrelevant to the Zionists. The first step in this process has been beginning the construction of a wall, totally on Palestinian land, and including 66 existing kibbutzim, which were in Palestine, now moved into Israel. This is the means used to claim a reduction of kibbutzim on Arab land. The second step is linking the entire kibbutz system in Palestine – linking them with roads containing barriers, which will make travel for Arabs in their own nation impossible. The next step is to allow the Palestinians neither a seawater port nor an airport within Palestine. The presently ongoing war in Iraq is another tenet of their policy of destabilizing any government, which might possibly be able to defend itself from Israeli aggression. We can therefore assume that Lebanon, Syria and Iran will be the next targets of American and British military actions, as both these nations' foreign policy and media are under the control of Illuminist/Zionists.

All

We must not forget the control of all our facets of information, which are uniformly in the control of the Illuminati. News, theater, cinema, radio, television, and print in any mainstream concept are all controlled. It is sheer folly to believe that any citizen can obtain factual news or information from any of these sources. A verification of that is the myriad of news sources found on the Internet, most of which usually demonstrate a completely different view of what is reported nationally. In the last week of January 2002, Washington saw an abortion protest of over 400,000 people; any major news outlet did not factually report it. One of the networks did mention it, but gave 30 lesbians protesting the demonstration more time than they gave the demonstration. My local paper in Tampa had something in Section 3. Omission is a primary tool of these people. Consider the escalating scope of protests against the World Economic Forums; Seattle 14,000, Quebec City 34,000, and Genoa over 100,000. Every time these one-worlders have a meeting there are between 10,000 and 100,000 times more protesters than participants. Never ever reported! The American media in particular displays a monolithic leftist leaning that can be seen as having been learned in the various schools of journalism in which they were educated, if you can call it education.

These institutions use every imaginable form of propaganda. The processes of omission, distortion, linkage, falsification, creation, and invention are all used. Linkage is the process whereby two unrelated factors are linked within a sentence or paragraph. Per example, the use of an individual's name with the word Nazi is popular. Or the constant referral to someone as right wing, or conservative, while never ever referring to anyone as a liberal or socialist. Consider that Bernie Sanders is a socialist Representative from VT; he is always called an independent, (I,) never ever a socialist. Invention is like in the Vietnam-era reportage of (evil) American soldiers burning down a village. A reporter who wanted some action shots asked a soldier to ignite a grass shack and shoot into it, for some news coverage. More than likely the journalist was too much of a coward to visit the front lines. I can honestly say that I have not heard one single unbiased news program in ten years. This is particularly interesting when we consider the slant that is applied by the media to all conservative or politically right causes or issues. Illuminism is clearly seated in the leftist camp, for numerous reasons. Almost all social upheaval after the Revolutionary War has emanated from the political left. Consider; Communism, Socialism, Nazism, and Fascism – all on the political left. Or must I point out to you that all of these similar systems had the name socialist in their motto. *Die Nazionalsozialistische Deutsche Arbeiter Partei* (The National Socialist German Workers Party) The Union of Socialist Soviet Republics, the Fabian (socialist) British Labor Party, and so on.

Is it not ironic to see our government warning police agencies to be on the lookout for right-wing agitators, when the only violent demonstrators, as recently as the Seattle and New York anti-New World Order demonstrators, were all Communists and socialists? It has in fact been suggested by no less than a score of different sources that these violent demonstrators are hirelings of various federal agencies. This would certainly not be the first time that government bureaucrats utilized paid agitators to create situations that allowed them to increase their prerogative power. In fact this was the exact way the French, Russian, Italian, and German socialists came to ultimate political power.

Once again, the way this plan is supposed to work is:

Republic
– to –
Democracy
– to –
Socialist Empire
– to –
Revolution
– to –
installation of the Illuminists as
the saviors of all mankind.

Sadly, reason dictates that we cannot
Be spectators in the coming civil war
Between the people and the Illuminati.

With the return from Babylon and the
Introduction of the Babylonian Talmud
The end of Hebrewism and the beginning
of Judaism was at hand.
–Rabbi Stephen S. Wise

THE BLUEPRINT

Originating in the 19th century, coming to light in the 20th century, its first four words expose all of its true content: Right lies in Might.

WHILE the origin of *The Protocols of the Learned Elders of Zion* will probably always remain obscure, their impact on the 20th and now 21st centuries is astounding. I do not intend to go over the thousands of contestations and acceptances of the *Protocols*, as this would make a book in itself. The fact is that they are here and they were written. Many men have had much to say about the *Protocols*, of all of these the soundest statement as to their originality or origin has been the statement made by many, "if they were in fact a forgery to malign Zionism, then they are indeed the most astounding forgery in recorded history, most of its ideas having been realized."

For those not familiar with the issue, it is the contention of Zionists that the *Protocols* were a forgery made by the Czar's secret police, intended to be used by the Czar to promote his pogroms[102] against the Jews. This, in my opinion, is a fantasy, concocted along with one of the other major premises of the *Protocols* in order to achieve a desired outcome. One can deny anything forever; on the other hand, if something is written and ninety percent of it has taken place subsequently, one is hard put to call the document a fiction.

In the Soviet empire, which was started by Zionists, possession of the *Protocols* by anyone was a capital offence, to be punished on the spot by the Zionist commissar who discovered the crime. Soviet Russia, from its inception in 1917 until take-over by Stalin, was totally Zionist in nature. The membership of the quasi-cabinet of the Supreme Soviet of 1917 was 24; all of them were Zionists. The leaders of all Communist parties in the world in 1917 were Zionists. Lenin, Trotsky (Lev Bronstein,) Zinoviev (Hirsh Apfelbaum,) Kamenov (Rosenfeld,) Sederdov (Herbert Aptheker[103]) were the ones in Russia. The Communist Central Committee of 1935 likewise consisted of 59 members, of whom 56 were Zionists. Primary Communist theoreticians and national leaders in the world at the turn of the 20th century were Bela Kun, Rosa Luxembourg, and Emma Goldman, all Zionists. In the realm of commissars, of a total of 384 in 1917 13 were Russians, 15 Orientals, 22 Americans, and the remaining 334 were non-Russian Zionists.

The significance of these facts is that communism as plagiarized by Marx, and origination in the 1770s' in Bavaria by Adam Weisshaupt are thoroughly Zionist, communist, and Illuminist in nature.

In order to help you understand one of the false premises of the Protocols we shall examine how the Illuminists orchestrated the French revolution, implemented the Russian revolution, and managed to start W.W. W.W. II and I. In the 1770's Weisshaupt was catapulted into the canon law chair by a Papal Bull, removing the Society of Jesus[104] (3) from that position. It is imperative to understand that canon law, which is religious law, was in the 17th and 18th centuries of great importance. So Weisshaupt took a very significant and prestigious office. At this time in history[105] there was considerable social upheaval, and there were two organizations, the Rosicrucian's and the Free

Masons, who were powerful instruments in the modernization taking place. Weishaupt joined the Rosicrucian order in an attempt to find out the means by which secret organizations were run and managed. The Rosicrucian's were loosely organized and thus did not meet with his interest. Next he joined the Free Masons and gradually rose in rank. Then he succeeded in overtaking numerous lodges in Bavaria with his Illuminist philosophy and organization. From there it spread to the French lodges and then the Italian ones. It was not until Dec 3rd, 1913 that the Grand Orient of France succeeded in purging the remnants of Illuminists from their ranks, and was allowed to rejoin the Grand Lodges and Grand Orients of Free and Accepted Masons. These included the Grand Lodge of England, 1717, The Grand Lodge of Ireland, 1730, The Grand Lodge of Scotland, 1736, 14 Foreign Grand Lodges, seven Colonial Grand Lodges, the 50 Grand Lodges of the United States, 12 Lodges of the West Indies, and 656 District Lodges around the world.

The importance of this is that the *Protocols* attempt linkage with the Masonic orders, claiming them to be at one with their Zionist plans. This is absolutely not the case. It is certain that Illuminism had captured the Masonic bodies of France, Germany and Italy, but as mentioned the French succeeded in purging the evil from their midst in 1913, while no Lodges in the English-speaking world were ever infiltrated. The German lodges were eliminated by the Nazis, who had bought into the Illuminist fable that they were at one with the Masonic bodies. This left only the Italian Lodges that may at this time be assumed still to be under Illuminist sway. In fact, all the inferences in the *Protocols* about their affiliations with Masonry are a classic attempt to create a scapegoat and divert culpability away from the Illuminists. Through the *Protocols*, a false impression that the Masonic movement has been responsible for the spread of Communism and Illuminist Zionism has been spread worldwide. This reached a crescendo in the early 20th century in America with the short appearance of an anti-Masonic political party. This proves the case that Illuminists use subterfuge relating to Masonry in an attempt to create a scapegoat for their unpopular actions.

In any plan for world conquest – and this is what we speak of here – the founders of it must create a scapegoat in order to preserve their longevity. Illuminism does that with the Freemasons.

The fact that Zionism, Communism and Illuminism are one and the same philosophically is demonstrable: the entire cadre of Communist progenitors, i.e. plagiarizers, is Zionists and the leadership of every emerging Communist movement in the entire 20th century was Zionist. Then there is the Israeli construct called kibbutz, an agrarian or industrial co-op that is totally Communist.

I can already hear the "Never Again," or "he's a Nazi," shouts. Let us examine Zionism, which is a socio-political movement totally unrelated to any religion. Zionists take pleasure in hiding their evil construct in the Jewish religion. Because Jews in general gain some considerable benefits from Zionism, in that they are paid some of the enormous *erpressungsgelder* monies that the Zionists have embezzled from Christians, they keep quiet. Allegiance appears to be with Mammon, rather than truth. Jews believe in the Torah[106] as the basis of their religion. Real Judaism had hereditary priests as the interpreters of Jewish law as written in the Torah. This all changed between 200 and 600 A.D. The Babha, or Babylonian Talmud, is the rabbinical[107] interpretation of the Mishmeh, which was an earlier explanation of Jewish law also put up by rabbis. Zionists succeeded in placing their interpretation of the law before the Torah. As the only interpreters of God's law, they were the arbiters of all. Thus we see that in a period of 600 years[108] the Zionists and their rabbinical replacement priests perverted the entire Jewish religion – not so very different from any number of contrary Christian faiths diverging from true Christianity. In any event, beginning in the 1890s with the first Zionist conclave, held in Basel, Switzerland, Zionism affiliated with Communism and thus with Illuminism. They are all one and the same. Zionism is totally secular, as for that matter is the great majority of reformed Judaism. One of the copies of the *Protocols* comes to us from that first Zionist conference in Basel, where a fake fire alarm caused the participants to leave the auditorium, and a thief stole a copy of the *Protocols* from the platform.

The means used to lure believing Jews away form their religion may be seen in:

> Babha Metsia. Fol. 33a:
> *Those who devote themselves to the reading of the bible exercise a certain virtue, but not very much; those who study the Mishmeh exercise virtue for they will be rewarded: those however, who take it upon themselves to study the Talmud's exercise the highest virtue.*

In other words forget the word of God and follow the words of rabbinical interpreters of Gods words, thus making man more important than God, or Secular Humanism.

Any doubt of the secular nature of reformed Judaism may be put to rest by examining the tenets of well-known Jews and what they believe. Per example, the "conscience of the Senate" Joe Lieberman believes in abortion on demand, as do almost all Reformed Jews. This is in direct contradiction to Judaic philosophy and teaching. Without them, America would not partake of the slaughter of over four million babies every year. Who are the principal opponents of "In God We Trust" on American coinage? Well, I'll give you a hint; they are not Christians. Who is behind the pornography business? Every one of the large pornography producers is a Zionist. Who are the principal feminists? Every one of them is a Zionist. Who are the people funding racial and societal discord? All of them are Zionists. Who founded the NAACP? A Zionist. Who founded the Communist Party in America? An abortionist Zionist who was the father of Armand Hammer, the famous Communist agent of Stalin and benefactor to the Gore family. We could go into treason to the republic, the Rosenberg's, and all the evil Zionists who came after them.

All this, then, explains wars of conquest on behalf of the Illuminist conspiracy. Their first success was the French revolution, in which we witness the means by which a society may be utterly destroyed. The Illuminist Masonic Lodges of the French Grand Orient included such celebrities as Rousseau, the Marquis de Sade, and all the luminaries of the Enlightenment. They devised a plan to undermine society, which has been used by the Illuminati ever since. These processes are generally unknown outside a select group of sociologists, and consist of perverting the social structure of the society. Marquis de Sade was the drummer in the French revolution, which introduced sexual perversion, pornography, and sex in general into the French society. This resulted in a rupture with the Church, and a general decline of ethics and morals, which had been the purview of the church heretofore. Once the cement of the societal fabric is ruptured through the elimination of morals, man replaces God. As the old saying goes, you can serve but one master. By eliminating God the new master becomes sex. Now you understand why all the pornographers in America are Zionists Illusionists.

A good case in point is the German-speaking world of the early 1930s. Communists had succeeded in infiltrating all labor movements in Germany, Austria, and Switzerland. They, under instruction by the Illuminati, instituted draconian civil service strikes, crippling entire nations. The Swiss dealt with this by drafting all civil servants into the military, and then ordering them back to work in uniform. Since you would be tried for insubordination, and possibly shot for disobeying an order, the Swiss strikes ended quickly. In Austria, however, the nation in which Hitler belonged, things went differently. The Communists staged marches through the capital, sometimes six hours long. Civil society ceased to exist. These actions caused Hitler to become a violent anti-Communist. In Germany the process of moral decline had already begun in the '20s and was in full bloom. Did you see the film *Cabaret*? It demonstrates the moral decay that was Berlin in the Weimar Republic of the '20s. Social and political turmoil continued in Germany throughout the entire life of the Weimar Republic. The great inflation, by which the Illuminist bankers had totally destroyed the German Mark, and the implementation of the Versailles treaty were the meat and potatoes of the Nazi movement. The Versailles treaty, completely orchestrated by the Illuminati, was the set-up for W.W. II. All one has to do is to read the treaty; the fact that it caused W.W. II is not in dispute by any historian, to my knowledge. All that's left is to see who dictated the terms of the treaty to tie all the loose ends neatly together.

As we see, all these wars were started for the advancement of Illuminism. They can be shown, when we examine history, to have been completely financed by Illuminist interests. Zionist bankers financed both sides of both world wars, the French and Russian revolutions, and are without any doubt responsible for Gulf War I and II. America's neo-cons[109] have taken over the foreign and domestic policies of the nation (which was a republic), not to the interest or gain of its citizens, but for the advancement of Illuminism. I have said it often and will continue to say it; if the U. S. State Department were a foreign government, Congress would have declared war on it long ago!

The State Department is run by the CFR[110] and has been since the FDR[111] administration. With about four or five exceptions, every cabinet member of every party of every president since the 1930s have been CFR members, as have been most of the Joint Chiefs of Staff of the military. The CFR is located in NYC, a city whose Jewish population exceeds by percentage that of any other city in the Diaspora, at 18.7% of total population. The city in which the American communist party was founded, and the City that contains the *Grand Kahal*[112] of the Jewish population of the United States.

The CFR in its structure has numerous "Study Committees." These committees are responsible for developing policy. All of the committees have within their steering structure, as principal managers, Illuminists. Because the CFR steering committees develop American foreign and domestic policy, the marching orders for the Departments of Interior and State, they control the dialogue, and as we all learned in high school, through the Hegelian Dialectic, he who controls the dialogue controls the actions as well. All the neocons are Zionists/Illuminists. What is much worse is that these neocons' allegiance is not to America or its people, but to a philosophy that is counter to our interests and will lead us into the feudalistic dictatorship of Illuminism well within this century.

What I desire to impart to you in this chapter is that Zionism has no real relationship to Judaism, except that most Zionists were members of the Jewish religion by birth. Just because you are born with a practicing Jewish mother does not make you an adherent of Jewish belief, contrary to what Israeli laws accept. I further want the reader to understand that Zionism is simply an alternate name for Communism, and that Communism was originated in concept and philosophy by Adam (Spartacus) Weisshaupt, the founder of Illuminism, and was plagiarized by Karl Marx in his *Das Komunistische Manifest* (*Arbeiter Der Welt vereinigt Euch*) in England. In simple terms, Communism, Zionism, and Illuminism are one and the same.

There is one viewpoint that has one common thread:

The Communist philosophy
is found
in all three.
The first hides itself under the guise of
being a religion, it is Zionism.
The second hides itself under the guise
of being a political philosophy,
it is Communism.
The third is a secret organization [The Order] that hides itself in concealment, it is
Illuminism.

Illuminists have only one goal:
World conquest.

The American affiliate to Illuminism is
The Order.

Not all Illuminists belong to any
of the organizations listed here,
But those listed within are thoroughly infiltrated
And controlled by them.

THE ILLUMINATI PLAN

History is replete with wars that pundits said would never take place.

IT now behooves us to examine what the ultimate plan of these people is, and what course they will take in the final days to implement it. First we must examine how they plan to get to the stage where they can take over. As I have indicated in the previous text, this thing began in 1776 and has continued ever since. Our clue as to how they plan to take over is very clearly apparent in their two previous attempts, in France and then in Russia. They plan a war, the war to end all wars, a war pitting citizen against citizen, state against state, rich against poor, black against white, Islam against Christianity, and when all are exhausted, and world population is down to one billion, they plan to take over.

Before we go further we must dispel some false information that stems from various places, primarily the *Protocols of the Learned Elders of Zion*. This relates to the myth that Masons are involved in this plan, and are somehow related to the Illuminists. The first cause of this was the take-over in the 1700s of numerous Masonic lodges in Germany, France and Italy by Illuminati. By 1913 these entire Masonic lodges in France and in Germany were purged of Illuminism; Hitler eliminated the remaining Masonic lodges in Germany by 1940. The Illuminists never infiltrated the Masonic Lodges of England and Scotland. Italy's Masonic orders remain to this day under Illuminist control. Adam Weisshaupt was indeed a Mason; however, only long enough to learn how they operated and how they functioned as a secret organization. Prior to that he had joined the Rosicrucian's but he quit that organization, when he had obtained the secrets of their order. This is the manner in which he obtained his knowledge of secret organizations and of the large-scale management of such. The perpetual possibility of exposure of the personal history of its members prevents their exposure of its secrets even if they are no longer active members.

The second cause is found in the *Protocols,* which recommends the Masonic orders as a scapegoat to be used by the Zionists in their planned world conquest. The *Protocols* are very emphatic in instructing that there must always be a scapegoat to blame, so that the people's vengeance can be deflected away from the actual organizers (the Zionists) of the acts. It is very interesting to note that there is considerable convergence between the original plans of Weishaupt and the Zionists' *Protocols.* Understanding that Zionism is a development of the late 19th century and is substantially pre-dated by Illuminism, we can assume that the Zionists, like Karl Marx, plagiarized their theories for world conquest from the Illuminati. Maxi's prediction of a proletarian dictatorship was simply an allowable propaganda tool for Illuminists. One must remember that the ultimate plan is for the revolution (any revolution) to ultimately fail at which point the Illuminists take over everything. The said revolutionary government is nothing but a precursor of Illuminists final takeover.

Both the French as well as the Russian revolutions were managed by outside sources, were very violent, and resulted in the deaths of millions of people. In Russia alone, the numbers exceeded 66 millions. In organizational and social character, these revolutions were very similar. Of course they are similar, they were managed by the very same organization! In these revolutions we see a clear, concise and well-executed plan. This plan can be shown to have several features that are identical. Let us examine the similarities of these two revolutions.

- The majority of organizers were ex-patriots who had lived outside the country for some time. Many, in fact, proved later to be foreign nationals.
- Jews represented a larger than normal portion of the revolutionaries.
- A large portion of the financing was from foreign sources, and in both cases by Jewish-owned banking houses.
- Both were extraordinarily violent.
- Both resulted in the establishment of a dictatorship.
- Both resulted in severe curtailment of personal liberty.
- Both demonstrated unparalleled expansionist momentum, both militarily and economically.
- Both, immediately after becoming established, liberated Jews and protected them above and beyond any other group, gender, or religion.
- Both attacked the primary religious institution of the nation in question, in France, Roman Catholicism, and in Russia, the Russian Orthodox Church.
- Both followed all the dicta of Adam Weishaupt's Illuminist plan to the letter.

It is important, particularly in the light of present efforts to equate the French and American revolutions, to understand clearly how different they were. The French revolution was an Illuminist plan to destroy the "old" order and replace it with their New World Order: in fact, that was the first actual use of the phrase. It utilized a system of sexual revolution, and general societal debasement, as its *modus operandum*. It engaged in a vulgar eleven-year orgy of murder by the state. For its first two years it appeared to operate in compete anarchy, an idea which the Illuminists fostered to hide their hand in events. The primary resulting French revolution lacked any moral character and was totally devoid of any ethical disposition. The American Revolution, on the other hand, was based on moral convictions, had an ethical purpose, was grounded in religious principles, and displayed no murderous intent upon any opposing member of the society – the Tories were merely bundled out into Canada. Financially there was also a great difference; while the French revolution, and later Bonaparte, were both financed by the Rothschild banking empire (Illuminists) the American Revolution had no financial backers, until late in the war. It goes without saying that the American Revolution was a rebellion against outside forces, (George III of England) while the French was an internal matter (like Charles I.)

What we can garnish from this, coupled with current history, is that we are being set up for an event very similar but worldwide. What the Illuminati were unable to do piecemeal, one nation after another, they will now try to do in one well-planned event. This event is to include Europe, the Middle East, Africa, North and South America, and Russia. It is intended to make W.W. II look like a picnic, while reducing world population by two-thirds. How China is planned to be involved remains a mystery; however, a five-year-old can figure out India and Pakistan's involvement.

To clarify further: the present war on terrorism will be gradually expanded, from Afghanistan to weaker nations like Lebanon, Jordan, then Iran, and Syria; this will destabilize the entire Middle East, and begin a war of attrition between Christian Europe and America, and the mainly Islamic Middle East. Due to alliances between Saudi Arabia and Pakistan, it will expand into the Indian sub-continent. It will cause the Zionists to begin throwing some of their vast nuclear arsenal at their neighbors, and in turn bring Armageddon to the Middle East. Conflict will be intensified, and when the proper climax has arrived the Illuminati will come on their white steeds to save what's left, and take over. I am not a soothsayer, so this is only supposition of what I consider the plan to be. I have studied this situation for over ten years, reviewed thousands of documents, books, manuscripts, and interviewed scores of people from every walk of life, so my conclusions are based on a sound knowledge and understanding of the topic.

To bring about that scenario many differing factors have been caused to come into play. The present world economic condition, which verges on a global financial meltdown, is surely part and parcel of it all. The continuing conflict on the Indian sub-continent plays into the game. The increasing hostility between the two Chinas is a factor. But most strongly, the continued Zionist expansionism and the incitement of the Palestinians is part of it – while Africa as a continent has gradually, since the elimination of Rhodesia and the Communist take-over of South Africa, deteriorated into oblivion. Depopulation by the AIDS epidemic in the southern half of Africa will see to the reduction of that region's population by 60% at minimum by 2016. The most populous nation on the African continent, Nigeria, is at the verge of civil war, while the rest is in tribal anarchy. In the Pacific Rim, Indonesia, as well as the Philippines, are in serious turmoil. A great deal of this trouble can be seen to be financed from the same sources as the French and Russian revolutions of so long ago. Again I say, that this is my opinion based on extensive research and may well take many years to be implemented, but facts are facts and I have nothing to gain by making foolish pronouncements.

We are, I am afraid, in a weakened position for such a war. Consider that there are now well over six million adherents of Islam in America, and even more in Europe. Africa is at least 40% Muslim; most of the rest is tribal prehistoric in religious persuasion. The second largest number of immigrants into America and Canada are Muslim: in Europe they are the largest percentage. Thus we will have a homegrown opposition, in this planned religious war, which will not be easy to deal with. In addition to that, all the military services of the Western nations are in the midst of being feminized, which weakens them and totally destroys *esprit du corps*.

While in previous Illuminist actions the primary force of opposition was foreign, it will not be foreign in the coming conflict. They have seen to the establishment of a large segment of the population that is internationalist. These One-Worlders have no allegiance to community, church, or even family. Their primary allegiance it to money and ideology. Thus we have within our communities some fools who follow this and some true believers who place the Illuminist philosophy before all else. It may be said that Americans as a group have not in the past hated foreigners; this is due to their common belief that American political and social systems are far superior to those of any foreign nation. This has been changing over the past twenty years, and Americans are becoming very intolerant of the huge mass of legal and illegal immigrants who are refus ing to assimilate. Total immigrant count, according to the 2004 census, is over 30 million, of which two thirds are illegal. To make matters worse, 350,000 have been ordered by federal courts to be deported because of felonies committed, but the INS, part of the new Homeland Security Agency, avows inability to find them. This points to a direction, namely a political elite, which is presumed to be on the payroll of third parties, it has corrupted America and the citizens are losing confidence in the system. This again is manifest in the disquieting manner in which Americans are feeling oppressed and are thus beginning to imitate their oppressors. So we see the rapid demoralizing collapse of morality and ethics as members of the society try to outdo one another in reaching the new paradigms, me first, if it feels good do it, Mammon is my god, and so on. (Shades of the French Revolution!)

An important factor in the development of the Illuminist plot is the human characteristic to imitate actions perceived to be successful. As money and materialism have become the leading value considerations of modern society, so has the society manifested a regard for material wealth as man's greatest achievement. Thus many in society imitate the actions of political as well as business leaders, whose actions are far from any consideration of worth (Clinton, Gore, Lieberman, the executives of Enron, George Soros, *et al.*)

It is apt to consider the actions of the media in this. In February of 2002 the startling news leaked out; scores of media pundits – you know, the ones who are on talk shows continuously, and write columns, the very same people who demonize my books – were on the payroll of Enron. Just to clarify that, these people accepted from $25,000 to $50,000 for writing speeches for Enron executives. I trust that this allows you to understand why news about Enron was held up for such a very long time – and, as a personal note, no one pays $25,000-plus for any written speech. This is really not much different from Bill and Hillary Clinton jointly being given retainers for writing books of $20 million. This is payola, plain and simple. Journalists, like anyone else, are subject to the same social and financial pressures as are we.

The Nazis used a process called *Gleichschaltung* extensively; it means to switch into the same channel, imitation of group action by the general public in order for the leaders of the action to attain control of the populace. The passionate involvement with a cause of any nature can provide sense and direction to a life empty of all but a burning desire for more and more material wealth. This circumstance has been provided to society by courtesy of the Illuminati's plan. Through it, many people find a home in compliance with this doctrine by dedicating themselves heart and soul to the masters of it. They thereby gain all their desires for more materialist assets, which never satisfy them because their newly developed nature always wants even more. From the moment they join it offers them boundless opportunity for more worthless junk, which it has by that time become their burning desire to have.

We can clearly see by this that the plan is complex, well thought-out, and has in the latter half of the 20th century become very widely accepted by the public. Adjunct to it has been the systematic destruction of Christian monotheism, which has for the last 2000 years represented the backbone of ethical and moral behavior in Western society. With actions by people like Madeleine Murray O'Hare, and the resulting Supreme Court rulings on the separation of church and state[113] abortion, infanticide[114], school bussing,[115] and so on, Christianity, has beaten a quick retreat. This is why I stated so emphatically that judicial activism was a major portion of the Illuminist plan.

Hate is another major portion of the plan. Hate of those who have more, hate of those of differing color, hate of a different gender, hate of and between religions – all these things have been instituted by the Illuminati for the purpose of distracting you from their goal and plan. Hate is the strongest emotion, and because it is easier to hate a perceived enemy with some good in him, than one purely evil, their plan works perfectly. As a general observation, by and large, we do not hate people whom we despise. Thus we are reduced by the Plan to chasing our own tail on a never-ending treadmill, while the Illuminati slowly and gradually take over the entire society.

Minorities are protected under the (constitutional) law from discrimination against them. (Criminal law) This, however, is a two-edged sword and has been well wielded. The first and honest edge is equality under the law; I do not believe that any of us disagree with that premise. The second edge is evil; it is the attempt at restitution for past-assumed wrongs. This is a weapon in the hands of the Zionists, who also encourage blacks in a like direction.

Restitution for what? Slavery? What utter rubbish; slavery was abolished in the early to middle 1800s, in fact well over 130 years ago. No one today can make any legitimate claim on that issue. Restitution for W.W. II and what happened to the Jews? Rubbish, the Jewish organizations that promulgate this fiction are nothing better than cheap extortionists, as is more than amply proven in Norman Finkelstein's *The Holocaust Industry.* And then finally we have Affirmative Action, racial quotas, and equality of intelligence, fiscal ability, strength, and so on. These concepts are not only wrong but also stupid. By its nature it has the faculty to reduce everything to the lowest common denominator. This is more than amply demonstrated in the deteriorating state of education in the entire Western world, as well as the virtual collapse of America's military. In both, standards have been lowered year after year; West Point, per example, no longer requires an engineering major to graduate, because too many females were unable to complete engineering courses successfully, and all physical standards have been repeatedly lowered to allow females to graduate. Being a member of a minority insulates the individual from the majority, thus stifling assimilation. Furthermore, a minority that retains its identity is vaccinated against the majority. These matters have become pronounced in the '80s and '90s. Any individual who opposes this axiom becomes the bearer of guilt for deserting his group. Things were different in the past, because immigrant groups were rapidly dispersed across the nation, and, except in large cities, tended not to congregate together in closed groups. Today the majority of immigrants are Hispanics and Orientals who congregate in closed groups, refuse to assimilate, and establish closed communities within the ones where they reside. This recipe for disaster has been used extensively to the detriment of the entire society.

Every society has their poor. Societies could not function without them – facing facts, someone has to do the dirty work. Most people in generational poverty are socially satisfied sitting smugly in their slums. They are surrounded by people of like status and thus feel un-assailed by the outside world. Illuminists have seen to an ingenious plan to keep them there: this plan is social welfare, Food Stamps, housing subsidies, and all the sundry social programs offered by the state. The War on Poverty, President Johnson's contribution, was a big step in that direction. No person will have the initiative for self-improvement if they are kept in circumstances, which, while demeaning, allow for sufficient food and material wealth to prevent any desire for advancing mobility. Especially, black Americans are maintained by the state in a position that is designed to keep them in the same circumstance perpetually. This Illuminist concept is one of the major tenets of their construct. Further, I state emphatically that the middle class is in the same boat – also kept in a confined grouping constructed through tax laws. These two social groups, the middle class and the poor, account for over 90% of the overall population, and both are totally controlled from without by this intricate Illuminist plan. They are overwhelmed by the immutability of the system, they are satisfied within it, and only through a calamity, war or revolution, will they ever seek to circumvent it. The Illuminati count on it!

To understand the Illuminist view, or more exactly why they participate in this anti-social activity, one must look deeply into the character of those who represent Illuminism. What we see is a group who embody two distinctly different classes of individuals. First, those who go along because it allows them to be part of a mass movement, which is able to grant them certain favors. Most movie stars, journalists and politicians would be in that class. These are not true believers, but rather opportunists. They can in no way be considered Illuminists, but rather individuals who seek to benefit by following the appointed method of their chosen leaders. In the majority of the cases they have no idea that there is a plan, that Illuminism is the guiding organization, or that they are supporters of a plan to destroy republican governance in favor of a feudalistic dictatorship of the "chosen." The real original Illuminist followers are those initiated through the numerous clubs, associations, and senior societies, which are the core of Illuminism. A large percentage of these are initiated through family connections. They are international in membership, and primary allegiance – after becoming a full-fledged member – is always to the secret organization first and foremost. The process of initiation, whereby the initiate provides the information that allows him to be blackmailed all the rest of his life, binds membership in all cases. So secret is membership that all (Bones) members violate their oath of office when elected or appointed to any position in government[116], by not revealing it.

On the PC—Cultural Marxist side, one of the flag carriers of Illuminism, we see a very active process, which can only be described as bizarre. Take the case of New Jersey; newly enacted state standards of education have removed George Washington, Thomas Jefferson, and Benjamin Franklin from the history books. Also removed are all references to the Federalist Papers, the Pilgrims, and the Mayflower. The word *war* has been replaced by *conflict*. All allusions to cruelty in the two World Wars have been removed, but slavery, the Holocaust, and Iraq are prominently featured as cruel behavior. Mr. Jay Doolan is the Cultural Marxist acting commissioner of NJ's Academic and Career Standards; how such a total nihilist attains a position within the state hierarchy of <u>education</u> can only be attributable to one group.

Then we have the much-touted Kwanzaa festival, another splendid effort to drive a wedge between races and religions. This festival is the invention of ex-convict and University of Southern California Professor Ron Karenga—well, that's what he calls himself now. Where else but in California would you hire an ex-con to teach and mould developing minds? The entire festival from its Swahili name[117] to its racist, Communist ideology is a construct by an individual who knows nothing about Africa or the predominantly tribal African culture. Rest assured, no one in Africa ever heard of this festival. The by far most interesting fact comes to us from England, where the Runnymede Trust (an Illuminist operation) is more than just active in destroying any remaining remnant of Anglo-Saxon and Celtic culture. Dr. Christopher Brand wrote a book called *The g Factor* that was published and then withdrawn in 1996 by its publisher, John Wiley & Sons, acting on the ludicrous concept that the information brought out by it was "repellent." Unfortunately, the truth is often difficult to accept. To make a complicated matter short, *The g Factor* is a book about general intelligence and its implications, relating among other matters to race. The book studies IQ based on racial characteristics internationally. Naturally, the resulting research turned out to be anything but the mantra of the Politically Correct. Not one single fact in the book has been disputed by anyone; not one single academician disagreed with any tenet set forth in the book. The book was withdrawn because the resulting research indicated that blacks on average had IQs 30% below whites, and Orientals had the highest IQs, on average 8% higher than Caucasians. We can clearly see the hands of the elites in all of CM; it is one of the primary tools used to keep us divided. In publishing, there has ceased to be any intellectual freedom whatever. No major publishing house will publish any book that contradicts the current CM mantra. I know this from the personal experiences of not only myself but also scores of friends who are not Politically Correct authors. Reviews of any written text that even approaches revisionist writing or opposition to Zionism, or exposing Illuminism, will never be reviewed in any main-stream paper, regardless of who wrote it.

Most people have no real understanding of how secret organizations operate. Prior to initiation, Illuminist candidates are referred to as Vandals. I want the reader to understand that the process of initiation is lengthy and complex, and only after a time of 12 months is the vandal allowed to participate in his initiation. Structurally, the simplest way to explain the further advancement within the organization is to equate it with military rank. Let's say that directly after initiation the new member is a private. He is now made aware that there is a pyramidal structure through which he may, if allowed or he chooses, advance. Advancement is based on what actions the individual has accomplished that advance the Illuminist agenda. Advancement is not possible by asking for it, only by striving and working for the cause may one be chosen for advancement. Anyone is able to do this regardless of occupation, and advancement in occupation is usually achieved through the offices of senior members, often not even known by the recipient of the promotion. Understand that the true known structure of the organization is not known by anyone outside it. Thus the Illuminati structure known is private-to-general. But after that a new and different organization, made up of generals and others, represents an entirely new and different realm, secret even from existing members. Beyond that there may be as many as three levels of higher rank, each insulated from the previous ones.

It looks like this:

Known Structure:

Level I Vandal

The Initiate

Level II Neophyte

The Private:

A new name is given.*

Level III Patriarchs

The Officer

Advanced Structure:

Level IV

Group of officers comprising a controlling leadership.

Secret Structures

Level V

Unknown by all lower members: comprised of select members of Level IV.

Secret Specialized Structures

Level VI, VII, etc.

Composed of only members of group V.

These specialized structures comprise officers in certain occupations considered by the organization to be of special benefit for the accomplishment of the prime agenda: judges, bankers, lawyers, journalists, corporate managers, actors, legislators, and the military. We speak herewith of only the very top of all these occupations.

This clearly demonstrates that lower members are not aware who really runs the organization, nor do they have any lucid understanding of what the actual goal of the organization is. Thus when one pundit or another says; "What are you talking about, I have been a member of the CFR for over a decade and am not aware of any plan!" he is not lying; if he has remained a minor player within the structure he has no idea what the actual plan is or even that there is one. One way this can be demonstrated is military rank. Every few years some colonel advances at a ridiculous rate, Alexander

Hague and Colin Powell are prime examples: both are CFR members, as colonels both advanced far beyond any reason, to four-star status, without any serious military experience that would warrant it, because they were chosen by the elites to carry out their agenda. Both have done exactly that, without any deviation. Powell has even lied and made himself look a fool at the UN at CFR instructions.

Only if you understand the evil intent of Illuminism can you oppose it. Hiding your head in the proverbial sand serves little purpose. Help me prevent these evil bastards from attaining their goal – give this book to a friend to read.

We have damn little to fear from terrorism but much to fear from our legislators and presidents, who abolish our freedoms, pretending to protect us.

ARE WE FREE OR ARE WE SLAVES?

THIS question is applicable to all of Western society; we will use America as the demonstrating sample. Americans, on average, when all costs are counted, pay 49.20% of their total income to government in taxes, fees, licenses, and permits. Of the amount paid in taxes, 22+% are consumed in interest payments to banking interests. The collection agency on behalf of the FRS is another government agency called the IRS. The IRS is a government agency. It is a collection agency that acts as a conduit for the private banking monopoly. Neither the IRS nor the FRS has ever been audited by anyone. All the original deposits to the FRS came from the United States Treasury but they have never acknowledged that they are operating on our money; they even charge us interest on the use of it. All the (fiat) money printed and circulated by the FRS has no value; it is not backed by anything. The FRS is not Federal, it is not a Reserve because it has none, and it is not a System, it is a private corporation. The FRS operates on what is called "Fractional Reserve Banking". This term is self-explanatory in that the word *fractional* means that only a fraction of the asset is in reserve. In other words, or to be precise, less than 10% of all funds deposited by any member bank is available at any time in reserve.

Our banking system is the greatest hoax ever conceived. It is a construct of the Jewish Babylonian captivity and has been in use by them for eons. If any individual or business operated in a similar manner they would be thrown in jail instantly. The most odious portion of the entire scam is the "National Debt." The national debt is created when government (the legislative branch of it) spends more than they collected in taxes. All Western governments spend more than they take in. Upon doing so they have a shortfall and are not able to meet their payroll obligations, or to pay bills in a timely manner. The legislature then goes to the FRS and asks for an advance. The FRS has no funds, but takes out the proverbial checkbook; kites a check in the amount wanted by government and has them sign a loan agreement. They immediately run over to the Bureau of Printing and Engraving and have them run off the required amount of paper (fiat money). This is called inflation, and is a fraud. They then go to the capital markets and sell "Treasury Notes," at the lowest interest for which they can sell them. Thus all our fiat currency is based not on an asset or deposit but on debt. People or governments or corporations who purchase these instruments are owed a debt, which is why they say our dollar is valued by debt. The banks take a healthy fee for facilitating the sale of the bonds.

Now there is only one principal question in freedom, namely, **can you say no?** Can you say no to the Congress spending more than they project to collect in taxes? NO, you cannot. Can you say no, I do not want to pay the bankers 22+% of my taxes? NO, you cannot. Can you say no, I paid for my own education; I don't want to pay for your children's? Can you say no, I paid for my land and do not want to pay government a tax on something they had no part in acquiring? Can you say no, I do not want to purchase a driver's license or license plates; I have already funded the construction of roads, bridges and tunnels through confiscatory fuel taxes of over $1.00 per gallon. The fact of the matter is that you have NO choice whatsoever. You are a slave to government, and the more you own the more you are enslaved. The bankers in turn own the government, so in fact you are a slave to the Illuminati because you can't say NO.

Slavery is a very old institution, and about 12 years before the War of Northern Aggression Baron Rothschild made a very revealing statement. He was at the time the richest banker in the world and the owner of the Bank of England. Rothschild said, "We disapprove of slavery and the cost of the upkeep and maintenance of slaves. We prefer our English model in which we control the issuance of currency, and control of money, it allows us to control labor without the cost of maintaining it." Rothschild above all understood that if you control currency, its issuance and its value, you control it all.

Under *Pax Romana*, in the old Roman Empire, the rule for slaves was that your work ratio was regulated to 50% for yourself and 50% for your master. In medieval Europe the ratio was about the same. Can you honestly tell me that we are any better off under a system that forces us against our will to pay over half of our disposable income to government? What the hell is the difference between serfs in 15th century Europe or first century Rome and us today? We have no more power to say NO than did they, and we pay over half of our productivity to others who in turn provide us nothing.

Our "progressive," actually regressive, federal income taxes are based on a law purposely written in such a manner that it cannot be understood. The feature of paying higher taxes as you earn more is based on the known fact that inflation will cause all incomes to rise; thus taxes will rise at a even higher rate of enhancement, whereby government takes in more of your earnings. The law was written and structured so as to allow the inventors of it to escape paying any of it. Illuminists pay virtually no taxes. Illuminists' income is structured so that they control the asset and so that the asset pays their bills without their having direct contact. This is accomplished through trusts, and scores of legal documents making tax payment unnecessary. The Illuminists hold assets through third-party corporations, foundations, think tanks and such; these hold stocks the income of which is not taxable. When they live in a palatial home, it is owned by a trust, which is in turn owned by a foundation that pays no taxes. Foundations – in which substantial portions of Illuminist holdings reside – must contribute 10% of their earnings to some charitable cause. They get to keep 90%; how would you like to pay only 10% in taxes? Furthermore in every case the 10% is directed at causes favoring Illuminist plans, and in many cases payment is made to organizations that the Illuminists set up for that exact reason. The congressional Reese commission proved all that. WE ARE SLAVES!

As I write this we are entering a presidential election campaign; both of the candidates of the Republocrat parties are Bonesmen. Both are habitual liars, and have not told the truth on any issue that they have addressed. Can we say, stop it, we want some real choice? NO, we cannot. Both parties support NAFTA, the agreement that is debilitating America, can we say no, we don't want this agreement? NO, we cannot. Both parties support the new electronic voting systems that are being instituted in most state, and are known, due to the lack of a paper trail, to be unreliable. Can we say NO, we want honest voting? We cannot. Both parties continue to place millions of Americans in prisons – large percentages of them for political crimes. Can we say, stop it? NO, we cannot. Both parties have told us that they must continue the wars on terror, poverty, drugs, gambling; can we say, stop it, is a waste of money, and is stupid to boot? NO, we cannot. We are not given any real choice in the choosing of any of our leaders from the House of Representatives to the Senate to the Presidency. Can we say, NO, we don't want these bums, we want a real choice? NO, we cannot. WE ARE SLAVES!

Our leaders have instituted a new set of laws they call the USA Patriot Act. This law violates just about the entire Bill of Rights. The law is unconstitutional and has not been approved by any state. In fact, as of April 2004 four states have disavowed the law, and over 800 communities have voided it. Does the U.S. government pay any attention to this? NO, they do not; they enforce the law against the will of the people. NAFTA is opposed by over 80% of the population; at the time of its passing opposition was 87%. Are we able to have the illegally enacted agreement voided? NO, we cannot. WE ARE SLAVES!

Under the FDR administration our government instituted a mandatory pension scheme, actually a Ponzi scheme that they called Social Security. Congress removed themselves from SS and instituted their own system. Then they set up two programs that they call Medicare and Medicaid: they immediately removed themselves and instituted their own plan. They collect SS taxes from citizens for about 35 years but pay no interest on the funds retained by them. They collect an equal amount of tax from the employer but do not reflect those monies in statements reported to the taxpayers. Then they took the money in the Trust Fund and placed it in the General Fund, leaving behind a worthless IOU. Can we say this is corrupt, it is a sham, it is a Ponzi scheme, and we want what we paid for? NO, we cannot. WE ARE SLAVES!

Through the national debt that is owed to the bankers we have placed our children, our grandchildren and ourselves in hock to the Illuminists who run this crooked sham. Christian America has been enslaved by a bunch of grubby disgusting parasites that live like kings. They, with our acquiescence, have enslaved us our children and our grandchildren for generations. There is a solution, unless you like your status as a slave.

We must abolish the FRS. We must take back, with 100 years of compounded interest, all the moneys these swindlers and Gonif's obtained from the US Treasury in 1913. We must reinstate Congressional COINAGE money based on hard assets. We must eliminate the national debt by paying it off. We must pass a constitutional amendment forbidding Congress to spend more money than they collect in taxes. We must destroy the banking monopoly totally. We must reduce the size and scope of government to services necessary, not services desired. We must eliminate such departments of government as the Department of Education, the Department of Energy, HHW, HUD, and all the other agencies that waste 40% of the monies collected by government. We must localize all government functions. We must get out of the UN. We must cancel NAFTA, WTO, GATT, and all the treaties that serve to benefit others rather than the citizens who pay for them. We must scrap the entire tax structure, replacing it with a 5% flat tax and a 5% national sales tax; government will have to live on that income. We must freeze all government hiring and slim down government employment through attrition. We must fire every member of the State Department and start over with that agency. We must withdraw our military from all foreign postings and place them on our borders. We must privatize Social Security. We must become the self-reliant population that we were 200 years ago. We must do all these things now, not tomorrow but today – unless you like your status as a slave in perpetuity!

WE MUST HAVE THE PERSONAL ABILITY TO SAY NO!

BIBLIOGRAPHY

*Highly recommended

+ Excellent Book

- Tragedy and Hope*

  Prof. Carroll Quigley.
- The Anglo American Establishment
  Prof. Carroll Quigley.
- The World Order
  Eustace Mullins.
- Whatever Happened to America?
- Jon Christian Ryter.
- The Satori and the New Mandarins
  Dr. A. H. Krieg.
- 4th July 2016: The Last Independence Day
- Dr. A. H. Krieg.
- Our Political Systems*
- Dr. A. H. Krieg.
- The Secret Side of History

Dee Zahner.

- Toward a New World Order
  Donald McAlvany.
- The Road to Serfdom*
- Dr. F. A. Hayek.
- Trilateralism
  Holly Sklar.
- Plagiarism and the Culture War
  Theodore Pappas.
- The Birth Dearth
  Ben Wattenberg.
- The Decline of the West*
  Oswald Spengler.
- The Soldier and the State
  Samuel Huntington.
- Libido Dominandi*
  Dr. E. Michael Jones.
- Monsters from the ID
  Dr. E. Michael Jones.
- The Holocaust Industry,

  N. G. Finkelstein.
- The g Factor

  C. Brand. (Published by Wiley and withdrawn)
- Why do we Americans Submit to this?

  Dr. Susan Huck.

- The Nightmare of Camelot: An Exposé of the Free Trade Trojan HorseGus Stelzer.
- The State against Religion
  Gus Stelzer.
- The South Was Right
  Kennedy Bros.
- Politicide
  Baruch Kimmerling.
- The World Conquerors
  Louis Marschalko.
- The Bell Curve
  Herrnsten and Murray
- Race, Evolution, and Behavior*
  Rushton
- Jewish Supremacism*
  David Duke
- The South under Siege[+]
  Frank Conner
- Gold Wars
  Ferdinand Lip
- The World Conquerors
  Louis Marschalko
- Heinrich Mueller Gestapo Chief, Volumes 1-4
  Gregory Douglas
- Foundations their Power and Influence

Rene' Wormser

- Silent Warfare

  Arra Healy Shulsky

- Conspiracy against God and Man

  Rev. Clarence Kelly

- The True Believer
- Eric Hoffer
- The Holocaust Dogma

  Ben Weintraub

- Global Bondage

  Cliff Kincaid

END NOTES

[1] Guardians of the City (Aramaic.)

[2] Only marriage between Jews is considered legal in Israel. Only Jews are allowed to purchase land in most of Israel. All Israeli citizens must carry an ID card which lists their religion–remember the dreaded *J* stamp of the Nazis (same thing but reversed.)

[3] Neo-Con: New Conservative movement of the Clinton and Bush administrations, 1992-2004

[4] Over 70 UN resolutions!

[5] A kibbutz is a communist agrarian or industrial village.

* NEA, AFT – National Education Association, American Federation of Teachers are both American teachers' labor unions.

[6] Clinton implemented NAFTA by executive order. A treaty – and that is what NAFTA is – is law. First: Article 1, Section 1, of the Constitution prohibits the executive from making law. Second: The words *executive order* do not appear in the Constitution, and are thus beyond the scope of the executive to implement.

[7] USDC: United States Department of Commerce.

[8] FTAA: Free Trade Area of the Americas.

[9] In the Mexican presidential election all five political parties were allowed in the debates; the consequences were that the PRI lost the Mexican presidency for the first time in 70 years, a lesson not lost on the Republocrats.

* See, there is a God!

[10] Details on Bones may be found in Chapter 6 (The Order) page 191 *The Satori and The New Mandarins*: Krieg, 1998; Hallberg Pub.

[11] The Internal Revenue code is authorized in the U.S. Constitution's XVIth amendment. The XVIth was never ratified by the states, and furthermore is actually the XVth because the original XIIIth was removed during the War of Northern Aggression. As the XVIth was not ratified it is illegal.

[12] ANC: African National Congress

[13] CPSA: Communist Party of South Africa

[14] Karl Marx's father was a Russian Lawyer. When the Czar instituted laws that prohibited Jews from practicing law he converted to Russian Orthodox Christianity. Marx's grandfather was a noted Talmudic scholar.

[15] The *Journals* of M.Waldman, who was a Viennese journalist

[16] *The Protocols*, 24 in total, set out an elaborate plan for Zionism to attain world governance. Zionists and Jews claim they are forgeries, others point to the fact that virtually all of the Protocols have come, or are coming, to fruition.

[17] The numbers come from Kremlin statistics issued in 1998.

[18] EC: European Community

[19] EU: European Union

[20] In June of 2001 George W. Bush, the American president, in Sweden on a trip to the EU, promised the assembled heads of state that FTAA would be implemented by 2005.

[21] RIIA: Royal Institute of International Affairs (UK)

[22] TC: Trilateral Commission/Bilderbergers –secret world N.W.O. organization.

[23] NATO: North Atlantic Treaty Organization

[24] The Club of Rome, TC, Bilderbergers, Tavistock Institute, RIIA, and CFR have all made the "one billion sustainable world population" a centerpiece of their announced plans.

* "A thousand points of light," Bush Sr. in speech – the point of light refers to 1000 Illuminists.

[25] RFID: Radio Frequency Identification Device. These have been extensively tested in the UK. They are passive electronic signal broadcast chips, which can be powered up by a magnetic pulse. (Almost all quick-pass road tolls use them.)

[26] CCTV: These are Closed Circuit Television Cameras, which continuously scan urban areas: London has over 2000 such cameras.

[27] FDA: Food and Drug Administration [American]

* The Balkans.

[28] EO: Presidential Executive Orders (Illegal, not constitutional: see "necessary and proper" clause.)

[29] FEMA: Federal Emergency Management Agency.

[30] NSAP: Nazional Sozialistische Arbeiter Partei (National Socialist Workers Party.)

[31] WPA was a FDR-imposed system to put people back to work; it was copied from the Nazis.

[32] NGO: Non-Governmental Organization.

[33] In this instance I consider only the part of Germany that was previously West Germany.

[34] Presently, members of Congress and their staffs, along with the executive and part of the judiciary, have taxpayer-funded plans costing them a mere $300 per year for total coverage. This is less than 5% of the actual cost.

[35] RN: Registered Nurse, same as SRN in the UK.

[36] FRS, ECB: Federal Reserve System, European Central Bank.

* These funds all go to the Illuminist banking cartel.

[37] BIS: Bank of International Settlements, Basel, Switzerland.

[38] IMF: International Monetary Fund (UN, NY)

[39] CFR: Council on Foreign Relations. Note that Z.B. was one of the founders of the TC (Trilateral Commission.) Bilderbergers are the Euro/American secret banking association.

[40] NRA: National Rifle Association.

[41] Green Party candidate.

* Breaking wind through the mouth.

[42] NAFTA: North American Free Trade Area.

[43] FTAA: Free Trade Area of the Americas

[44] EU: European Union.

[45] GATT: General Agreement on Trade and Tariffs.

[46] WTO: World Trade Organization.

[47] EC: European Community.

[48] EU: European Union.

[49] IMF: International Monetary Fund.

[50] BIS: Bank of International Settlements.

[51] The economy of Indonesia, which has a population of over 100 million, now has about 50 million people living on less than $1 per day.

[52] Job losses to Mexico are 3 million direct as a result of plants moving to Mexico and 4 million as a result of American plant construction in Mexico. There are $2 billion annually by American manufacturers and new plant and an additional $1 billion construction by European and Asian manufacturers whose entire production is sold in America. All these plants would have been built in America if there had been no NAFTA. The last year reported by the USDL was 1996: by that time over 1500 plants had moved from America to Mexico.

[53] The Benin of Africa was the only black culture to attain

Bronze-Age development.

[54] Melanin is the substance responsible for skin pigmentation.

[55] INS: Immigration and Naturalization Service.

[56] PC: Politically correct.

[57] U.S. PATRIOT Act

[58] Ron Horiuchi, FBI sniper at Ruby Ridge.

[59] Violation of the Posse Comitatus Act.

[60] Sasol is the German W.W. II technology that was exploited by the South Africans, during the embargo against them by the UN, with seven coal-to-oil production facilities.

[61] The *Beck* decision is the requirement, by federal precedent, to advise employees what their union dues are being used for, and of their right to force the union to return to the employee any funds used for political purposes.

[62] OBE: Outcome Based Education has failed miserably everywhere it has been tried, Sweden, Germany, Chicago; it is now used to introduce Goals 2000 into local education.

[63] RFID (radio-frequency identification) technology consists of a card on which detailed information is stored, and which can be accessed by an electronic pulse that then transfers it to the sending party, who can access it on his computer. It is currently used in E-Z pass for tolls on highways.

[64] CODED in school means that the child is "entitled" by mandate to special expensive services, including tutors, one-on-one teaching, special classes, and so forth.

[65] All dyslectic children are coded. This is much more common with males. It presents special problems in reading, and often results in transposing of numbers and similar problems.

[66] Social Promotion in public education is the process of advancing a failing student to the next grade without his having attained the academic accreditation for advancement.

[67] Head Start is a baby-sitting service provided by taxpayers in a vain effort to take minority children with low or failing qualifications and to bring them up to parity when they enter first grade. It has completely failed from its first inception, for two reasons; first, you cannot increase IQ, and second, teachers of low IQ are incapable of elevating educational capability.

[68] Sabbatical and tenure are academic terms and exist nowhere outside education. Tenure is granted by an educational establishment after a set number of years of employment, and protects anyone tenured from being dismissed.

[69] TEAM is the process of dividing students into five-member groups to solve problems or work on assignments. Obviously it is counter-productive, in that the smartest kid winds up doing the work for the entire group.

[70] Mainstreaming is the process of incorporating disabled, handicapped, as well as social malcontents, troublemakers, and even paraplegics into regular classes.

[71] Gaia is the earth goddess who, we are told, is present in everything. Several UN meetings have seen prayers and services to Gaia.

[72] The Benin.

[73] Bush Gardens in Tampa, FL. The American Black Muslim movement.

[74] Ritalin is a mind-altering drug, which, if administered to a boy, disqualifies him from military service.

[75] Almost totally funded by the federal government.

[76] FRS: Federal Reserve System; not federal, not a reserve, and most certainly not a system. The FRS is a private banking monopoly granted by legislative fiat.

[77] PRC: Peoples' Republic of [Communist] China.

[78] MFNS: Most Favored Nation Status: lowest prevailing duty rates.

[79] J.P. Morgan, Goldman Sachs, Morgan Stanley, Rothschild, the US Treasury, etc.

[80] CPI: Consumer Price Index.

[81] Maquiladoro trade numbers are falsely reported, in that a product sent to Mexico for assembly is counted as an export, but when the assembled product is returned it is not counted at all.

[82] The 49.20% number includes all taxes, local state, federal, property, as well as licenses, fees, permits, and secondary taxes collected.

[83] It is imperative to understand that there is a huge difference between the way reactors were and are built in the

West as opposed to the old Soviet system. Soviet rectors do not, for the most part, have a containment vessel. This is why they had that costly failure at Chernobyl.

[84] NGOs: Non-Governmental Organizations, e.g. multinational corporations.

[85] By law, State must comply with FIR within ten days.

[86] United States, Canada, Mexico.

[87] IDF: Israeli Defense Force.

[88] CFR: Council on Foreign Relations, TC: Trilateral Commission, Bilderbergers: European secret organization, Bones: American branch of Illuminism.

[89] Hallberg refused to pay the royalties of $1.00 per book, or to re-pay a $3,000 personal loan.

[90] POD: Print On Demand. This process will in the future be how all books are published. The entire work, including binding and printing, is stored in a computer and printed as orders come up. In my experience, delivery time from Lightning Source, a subsidiary of Ingram, is faster than from stocked inventory.

[91] The Nixon tapes.

[92] Rapture is a convoluted scriptural concept in which born-again Christians are immediately taken to heaven, while the rest of humanity is transported to hell or gets to fight in the losing side in the battle of Armageddon.

[93] Kibbutz: a communal farm or industrial co-operative.

[94] Words of Theodore Herzel, (1860 Hungarian Jew) President of the first Zionist conclave at Basel, Switzerland, in 1886.

[95] Diaspora is the Jewish community scattered around the world.

[96] The word rabbi simply means lawyer, i.e. the interpreter of the Talmud (Jewish law) as expressed in the Mishmeh.

[97] Kahal is the word for a community within the Diaspora.

[98] CFR: Council on Foreign Relations, located on 68th St. in NYC.

* First five books of the Old Testament.

† Jewish law.

‡ The interpretation of the Mishmeh.

[99] Fiat: paper money, valuable only in one or another jurisdiction.

[100] AFT: American Federation of Teachers, NEA: National Education Association, the two largest labor unions in education.

[101] ICVS: International Crime Victims Survey.

[102] The pogroms were instituted by the Czar at the instance of the Russian people to stop the taking over of various professions in the Russian empire by Jews.

[103] Encyclopedia Judaica.

[104] Roman Catholic order, the Jesuits.

[105] The Enlightenment.

[106] First five books of the Old Testament.

[107] A rabbi is a Jewish lawyer who explains the Talmud.

[108] During the Babylonian captivity.

109 Neo-Cons: New Conservatives are in fact all Zionists or, to be correct, Illuminati.

110 CFR: Council on Foreign Relations, located on 68th St. in NYC.

111 FDR: Franklin Delano Roosevelt, elected president in 1932, '36, '40 and '44.

112 Headquarters of the Jewish community of a nation.

113 The entire issue of separation of church and state is contrived. It does not appear anywhere in the constitution. The only place it is found is in a letter by Thomas Jefferson, from which it is taken wholly out of context. What Jefferson meant in this letter, which by the way has no legal implication, was a state run and managed by religion – that is, theocracy – something no one ever proposed.

114 The tolerance of abortion and infanticide (the murder of children past the third trimester who are killed at the time of birth) was an invention of the Supreme Court.

115 School bussing to attain racial balance was also provoked by the Supreme Court. Blacks as well as whites dislike it. It has resulted in the expenditure of huge amounts of money for busses, fuel, drivers, and maintenance, diverting it from useful education.

116 Bones, The Order of Death, 322, (or Scroll & Key) have never indicated membership on government application or release forms.

117 Kwanzaa (Swahili): no slaves came from any region in Africa where Swahili is spoken. Slaves came from Ghana, Kenya, Tanzania, and parts of West Africa.

* A. Weishaupt's name was Spartacus.

* Dr. Jones's book is outstanding in recording the beginnings of Illuminism. It is a consummate work on the sexual revolution, its introduction and its debilitating results.

INDEX

AN AID FOR ABBREVIATIONS:

ADA	Americans with disabilities Act
AFT	American Federation of Teachers (Union)
AIPAC	American Israeli Political Action committee
AP	Associated Press
BATF	Bureau of Alcohol Tobacco and Firearms
BBC	British Broadcast Network
BIS	Bank of International Settlements
Basel Switz.	
CBM	Continental Ballistic Missile
CFR	Council on Foreign Relations
NYC	
CPI	Consumer Product Index
CPSA/RSA	Communist Party of South Africa
CPUSA	Communist Party of the United States
EC/EU	European Union
ECB	European Central Bank
EO	Executive Order
EPA	Dep. of Environmental Protection
FBI	Federal Bureau of Investigations
FCC	Federal Communications commission
FDA	Food and Drug Association
FDR	Franklin Delano Roosevelt
FECA	Federal Finance Campaign Act
FEMA	Federal Emergency Management Association
FRS	Federal Reserve System
FTAA	Free Trade Area of the Americas
GATT	General Agreement on Trade and Tariffs
HUD	Dep. of Housing and Urban Development

HUD Dep. of Housing and Urban Development (Fed)
ICBM Intercontinental Ballistic Missile
IDF Israeli Defense Force
IMF International monitory Fund
IMF International Monetary Fund
IRS Internal Revenue Service
JDL Jewish Defense League
KKK Klux Klux Klan
LBJ Lyndon Baines Johnson
MFNS Most Favorite Nations Status
N W O New World Order
NAFTA North American Free Trade Agreement
(Clinton EO)
NATO North Atlantic Treaty Organization
NEA National Education Association (Union)
NGO Non Governmental Organization
NRA National Rifle Association
NSAP Nazi National Socialist Workers Party
OBE Outcome Based Education
OSHA Occupational Safety and Health Act
PBS Public Broadcast Service
PNAC The Project for a New Century funded from Jerusalem
PNAL Project for a New American Century New Jerusalem Foundation
POD Print on Demand
RFID Radio Frequency Identification Device
RIIA Royal Institute on International Affairs London
RSA Republic of South Africa

SE	Special Education	
TC	Trilateral Commission	NYC, Paris, Tokyo,
London		
UPI	United Press International	
USDC	United States Department of Commerce	
USDJ	United States Department of	
USSR	Union of Soviet Socialist Republics	
VA	Veterans Administration	
WDM	Weapons of Mass Destruction	
WO	World Bank	
WTO	World Trade Association	

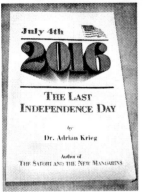

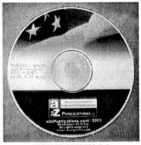

Visit Our Web Site at: www.a2zPublications.com

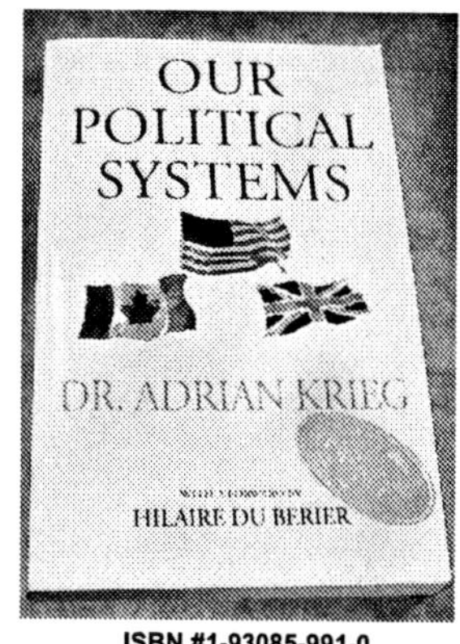

ISBN #1-93085-991-0
268 pages – $19.95

Examine the two party political systems as they exist in American, England, and Canada.

- How the two party system operates;
- What the public thinks of it;
- How in operated in the past and how it works now;
- How it's financed;
- How elections, debates, and candidacy is manipulated;
- How the Judiciary and Executive interrelates with the system and how to fix it;
- The US Constitution and the Bill of Rights: A lucid explanation of it and how the system has violated and altered our basic legal scheme.

PLEASE EXPEDITE MY ORDER

Our Political Systems $19.95ea x Qty. ______ = $ Total ________

Name ______________________________

Address ______________________________

City ____________________ State ____ Zip ______

Send check or money order to:
a2z Publications
23207 Night Heron Way • Bradenton, FL 34202

VALE

ISBN # 0-9748502-3-3
pages – $

PLEASE EXPEDITE MY ORDER

VALE $19.95ea x Qty. ______ = $ Total ________

Name ______________________________

Address ______________________________

City ____________________ State ____ Zip ______

Send check or money order to:
a2z Publications
23207 Night Heron Way • Bradenton, FL 34202

PLEASE EXPEDITE MY ORDER

VALE $19.95ea x Qty. ______ = $ Total ________

Name ______________________________

Address ______________________________

City ____________________ State ____ Zip ______

Send check or money order to:
a2z Publications
23207 Night Heron Way • Bradenton, FL 34202

Visit Our Web Site at: www.a2zPublications.com

Printed in the United States
34572LVS00006B/16-33

9 780974 850238